IDENTIFYING THE
HIERARCHY
OF SATAN

A HANDBOOK FOR WRESTLING TO WIN!

Matt & Chantal,
May the desires
of your heart be
met in His unlimited
supply! Rev 21:6

Jay
You have been a
blessing to many
families!

IDENTIFYING THE HIERARCHY OF SATAN

A HANDBOOK FOR WRESTLING TO WIN!

JOY A. SCHNEIDER

WATER OF LIFE UNLIMITED

Copyright © 2002 by Joy A. Schneider
All rights reserved
Printed in the United States of America

Revised Second Printing 2010

International Standard Book Number: 978-0-9710460-0-9

This book or parts thereof may not be reproduced in any form without prior written permission of the publisher.

For information contact:

 Water of Life Unlimited
P.O. Box 348
Fort Collins, CO 80522-0348
(970) 482-8699
E-mail address: joy.wolu@gmail.com
Website: www.wateroflifeunlimited.com

Editor: Melanie Hemry
Cover Design: Vision Communications
Layout Design and Pagination: Norm Kitten, A Key 2 Design

Unless otherwise noted, all Scripture quotations are from the King James Version of the Bible.

Scripture quotations marked (AMP) are taken from The Amplified Bible. Old Testament copyright ©1965, 1987 by The Zondervan Corporation. The Amplified New Testament copyright ©1954, 1958, 1987 by The Lockman Foundation. Used by permission.

Scriptures quotations marked (NIV) are taken from the HOLY BIBLE, NEW INTERNATIONAL VERSION NIV. Copyright ©1973, 1978, 1984 by International Bible Society. Used by permission of Zondervan Publishing House. All rights reserved.

Scripture references marked TLB are taken from the Living Bible, copyright © 1971 by Tyndale House Publishers, Wheaton, Illinois. Used by permission.

DEDICATION

This book is dedicated to the Holy Spirit as He uses it as a tool in His hands to glorify and exalt Jesus Christ and Our Heavenly Father; to the precious prayer warriors who have carried the battle to the spirit realm and stood in the gap with their faith and prayers, and to those who are stepping into the call of the Lord for the end-time events before us.

ACKNOWLEDGEMENTS

In memory and honor of my husband Ken, who stands in the presence of His Lord and Savior, having seen a glimpse of His greatness, stepped upward into His embrace. To my wonderful daughters, Kristie and Angie who encouraged me to begin writing many years ago, and have been a constant source of encouragement, joy and friendship.

My heartfelt appreciation goes to the precious souls who critiqued the manuscript and gave of their gifting towards its completion: My wonderful sons-in-law, Kyle Alons and Blair Greimann; my precious mother-in-law, Helen Waag; my ever-so-busy sister-in-law, JoAnn Sloan; the Director of Preparing the Way Ministries and long-time friend and prayer warrior, Deborah Kellogg; mighty prayer warrior and Intercessory Prayer Pastor, Diane Blanco of Resurrection Fellowship; evangelists and pastors, Pastors Becky and Lynn Wickstrom of Wickstrom International Kids Krusades, Inc.; Clarice Alons for her English and grammar expertise; and to my very special long-time friends, Nanci LeDoux, Lee Herzfeld, and Althea Prull.

My sincerest appreciation goes to my sister, Jeanette Willox, the Preparing the Way prayer partners, and the other many family members and friends who helped contribute to the completion of this book through their encouragement, prayers, words of direction and excited expectation.

Special thanks goes to those at Vision Communications for their graphics creativity and counsel, and to Melanie Hemry for seeking the heart of God as she edited the manuscript, and to Norm Kitten for his pagination work and gifting. I am thankful for the many friendships which sprang from working together on this project.

Only eternity will reveal the value of the time and caring contribution each of you made. *"For God is not unrighteous to forget your work and labour of love, which ye have shewed toward his name, and that ye have ministered to the saints, and do minister"* (Hebrews 6:10).

CONTENTS

Chapter 6

INTRODUCTION

The purpose of this book is to help you gain a better understanding of the spiritual warfare that goes on in your life every day. You will learn about your life in Christ and how you can overcome the enemy. You overcome by commands of authority grounded in who you are in Christ and who Christ is in you. Many people are ignorant about who their enemy really is and don't know how to effectively appropriate what Christ has done to ensure their victory. An understanding of the difference between fallen angels and demons is vital for effective spiritual warfare. Light will be shed upon this topic which has been kept in darkness for too long.

This is not a book of do's and don'ts, but one with the intent to encourage and cheer you onward. It is intended to be a tool in the hands of the Holy Spirit for His use in equipping you to fight the fight of faith. Just as God put a rod in the hand of Moses as a tool to deliver His people out of oppression and bondage, this book can be a tool for the Lord to provide deliverance for God's people today. When you know how to use the "weapons" God has given you, you can more accurately discern your enemy and become skillful soldiers. There is confidence that comes with experience—having knowledge and applying it in wisdom.

As we mature in spiritual things we learn, *"Thou therefore endure hardness, as a good soldier of Jesus Christ. No man* (or woman) *that warreth entangleth himself with the affairs of this life; that he may please him who hath chosen him to be a soldier...Consider what I say; and the Lord give thee understanding in all things"* (II Timothy 2:3,4,7, *explanation and emphasis added).*

It is important not to place your confidence in the "weapons" but in the person of Jesus Christ, who is the embodiment of our weaponry. The Holy Spirit is the Spirit of Jesus in you carrying out the will of the Father. This book is intended to expose satan, showing how his influences can affect our lives. Satan has many tactics that he has used successfully, but he is limited to variations of the same old tricks.

Becoming a Christian means you are enrolled in an army, a fight of faith. Spiritual warfare is not for the faint-hearted. Be aware—being a Christian is not for the faint-hearted. You may have come to Christ when you were in a faint-hearted condition, but He lifts you up and causes you to become strong. You might say, "But I don't want to have to deal with satan and this spiritual warfare business." Be sure, satan is dealing in spiritual matters against each and every person. His kingdom is actively involved in the business of evil—to kill, steal and destroy in any way he can.

When Christ came into your heart, you left your citizenship in the kingdom of darkness and were transferred into the kingdom of light. Since evil workers of darkness hate the light *(John 3:19-21)*, satan's efforts to keep our souls from living in the kingdom of light is the battleground we live in day after day. The battle is before you. To what measure you pursue your victory in Christ is an individual decision. Making the decision to allow the Holy Spirit to teach and train you opens the door to all the resources of God's heavenly kingdom. Jesus has won the victory and has given us His weapons of warfare.

Whether you take up your weapons, or just let them lie, is up to you. If you are one who has been "slam-dunked" or suffered devastation in some way in your skirmishes with satan's kingdom, take heart. You will see your enemy with new eyes and will also see that the weapons of your warfare are readily available to you. Don't be surprised if in the course of your stumbling around in the dark, the Holy Spirit has you bump into weapons and resources that flood your darkness with His light. May the Holy Spirit enlighten your understanding, strengthen your soul and fill you with joy for the path He has set before you.

Before we begin, let's lift each of our hearts to the counsel of the Holy Spirit.

Heavenly Father, I come to You in the mighty Name of Jesus Christ of Nazareth. I acknowledge that I cannot come to You by my own deeds of righteousness. I believe the Blood shed by Jesus has cleansed me from sin and made me righteous before you in His death, burial and resurrection. I believe Jesus came that I might have abundant life. I believe Jesus came to destroy all the works of satan. I believe Jesus has given me power and authority to carry out Your will on the earth. I now declare that satan's efforts are bound from hindering, masking, hiding, distracting or harassing me as I seek truth. I declare that satan's assignment against my reading of this book is cancelled and his strategies are set to confusion. I declare that as I read this book I shall receive revelation and understanding from the Holy Spirit. I shall receive strength and courage to take a stand against the methods and tactics of satan's works and plans—for myself and those I pray for. I loose and untie every evil tentacle of the enemy against God's destiny for me and declare that I am free to live and move and have my being in Jesus Christ the Lord.

Holy Spirit, as the Spirit of Truth and the Spirit of Grace, I invite You to have Your way in my life. I ask You to bring answers to questions, counsel from the throne of the Most High God, and impart what is on the Father's heart for me, His beloved child.

I boldly come to the throne of grace to receive mercy and grace to help me in my times of need, so that I might know and receive the things freely given to me of God.

In Jesus' precious Name. Amen.

CHAPTER 1

THEN CAME THE RAIN

The warm spring sun kissed the Rocky Mountains in the background and dried the white paint on the quaint old barn almost as fast as my husband and I painted. When the final strokes were applied, we climbed down from the scaffolding for the last time and stood back to survey our handiwork. The barn, like the land where we live in Colorado, was a legacy from my husband's family. He'd spent his childhood jumping from the hayloft and playing in the barn's shadow. Now, after five weeks of scraping, priming and painting, it glistened as white as the snow that clung to the mountain peaks.

Stumbling back to the house, we were almost too exhausted to care. It was time to catch up on other matters. Still weary, the following day I slipped outside and stood in the shade of the Russian Olive trees, almost weeping at the sight of my vegetable garden. For five long weeks it had been neglected. Now I couldn't even see my seedlings. Ironweeds—three feet tall—tauntingly gripped the ground. Kicking the hard, dry dirt with the toe of my shoe, I tried to remember the last time it had rained.

I leaned down and tugged at the weeds. I may as well have tried to pull an olive tree up by its roots. The weeds had taken over and weren't going to give up without a fight. I didn't have any fight left.

I guess I'll just plow it under, I thought as I crawled into bed that night. There would be no fresh cucumbers, corn, squash, tomatoes or peppers on the table this summer. There would be none canned to replenish my pantry. I fell into a troubled sleep and didn't hear the first rumblings of thunder as rain clouds gathered over the mountains. I slept through the slow, gentle rain that ran in rivulets down the freshly painted barn.

The next day, the sky cleared and I walked outside to drink in the smell of rain-drenched earth. Wandering back to my garden, I knelt and tugged at an ironweed—it pulled up easily!

Excited, I grabbed weed after weed tossing them aside like so much stubble. There, green and budding with life, were my seedlings. The Lord spoke to me at that moment, "Do you notice how easily those weeds came up when the soil was moist? That's exactly what happens when the Holy Spirit rains on your heart. He softens the soil where the enemy has planted evil. The Holy Spirit moistens the heart making it possible to uproot the 'weeds' so that you can bear fruit in your life."

That summer and fall my table was laden with platters of delicious food from our bountiful harvest, and my pantry bulged with plenty. The true bounty I received still graces the table of my heart as I remember that the Holy Spirit will work powerfully and gently to remove the weeds in my heart that keep me from bearing godly fruit.

Like me, many of you have experienced the "plantings" of the enemy in your life. But God knows what He has planted in your heart. He will send the soft rain of the Spirit to moisten those hard, painful places in your life and bring His plan to fruition.

THE PARABLE OF THE SOWER

In one of His parables, Jesus used the example of planting seeds in a field—perhaps not too unlike my garden *(Mark 4:3-20; Matthew 13:18-23)*. Some of the seeds fell on the way where people walked—a place hard and dry. Fowls of the air devoured the seed. Other seed fell in stony places, but it was hard, dry and stones kept the seedlings from putting down roots. Still other seeds fell in soil that had thorns and briers in it. When the good little seeds sprang up to grow, so did the thorns and briers. In the midst of wrestling for a foothold in the soil, the competition between the good seed and the thorns—the thorns edged out and choked the good seed. But the seed that fell in good soil—my, my, those seeds sprouted, grew up and became strong. Before long there was corn in the ears, cucumbers peering through the leaves and wheat plants reaching skyward. They were experiencing what they were purposed to do—bear fruit, or produce a desired result.

JESUS SOWS THE WORD

If we look more closely at this parable *(Matthew 13:37)*, we find that the Lord Jesus is the Sower, and He is sowing the Word of God—seeds of life with the purpose and inherent ability to bring forth godly fruitfulness. I have always been puzzled by the seed falling on the wayside or into the stony ground, or even falling among a bunch of thorns for that matter. Doesn't a good farmer plant seed in soil that is plowed and prepared to receive the seed? Wouldn't sowing seed in hardened, dry or rocky ground where growth is unlikely be illogical? One thing is for sure: The circumstances have an impact on whether the seeds ever become fruitful. Jesus was clear when he explained the hindrances that hampered the harvest—much less an abundant harvest. He informs the listeners that the fowls of the air were agents of satan sent to steal the seed, or the Word. He explained stony, hard places kept the Word from putting down roots. Tribulation, persecution or offense because of the Word soon caused the seedlings to dry up.

Then there are the seeds that had thorns and briers as neighbors in the field. Those thorns and briers of worldly cares and the lure and lust of other things crowded out the life of the Word in the seedlings, and eventually the life in them suffocated.

Can we make the connection that the various types of soil represent the hearts of humankind? Are we to presume that there are hearts that fall into one or more of the types described in the parable of the Sower? Can we find within us spiritual soil which causes us to have hard hearts, stony hearts, thorny hearts or good hearts? Actually, all of humankind is on equal ground—so to speak. All of our hearts have been affected by Adam's fall. The heart is desperately wicked *(Jeremiah 17:9)*. There is nothing good in it— nothing that makes it true, godly or righteous. Even though we are created in the image of God—the heart became separated from God because of sin.

THE HEART TRANSPLANT

That is the dilemma that required a sacrifice—a holy sacrifice. The holy sacrifice would bring the ability to have a heart transplant—a heart exchange. Jesus took His sinless heart and exchanged it for my wicked, sinful heart. He gave me (and you, if you want one) a new heart. He gives us a promise in Ezekiel 36, *"Then will I sprinkle clean water upon you, and ye shall be clean: from your filthiness, and from all your idols, will I cleanse you. A new heart also will I give you, and a new spirit will I put within you: and I will take away the stony heart out of your flesh, and I will give you an heart of flesh* (life). *And I will put my spirit within you, and cause you to walk in my statutes, and ye shall keep my judgments, and do them"* (*verses 25-27*, emphasis and explanation added).

But what about the four descriptions we read about in the parable of the Sower? Perhaps they are "heart conditions," ones which give us a picture of how the enemy devours, steals, chokes and invades our lives to keep us from experiencing the richness of the harvest we know down deep within us is our destiny. Is God rooting for us (excuse the pun)? Of course, He is! It is HIS desire that is inherent within the purpose and plan woven within our innermost being.

There are, however, many "weeds" that spring up to oppose our desired harvest. Have you ever wondered where those pesky weeds come from? You don't plant them, you don't water them, you don't nurture them, and yet they grow like—weeds?

We read that Adam's punishment was that he would die (spiritually) when he rebelled against God but also, *"cursed is the ground for your sake; in sorrow shalt thou eat of it all the days of thy life; Thorns also and thistles shall it bring forth to thee; and thou shalt eat the herb of the field; In the sweat of thy face shalt thou eat bread..."* *(Genesis 3:17-19).* Perhaps that is an explanation of why weeds, thorns and briers spring up without welcome in the earthly sense, but it also brings to light why the "weeds, thorns, briers, and stones" of our hearts and of our souls spring up to trouble us in the spiritual sense.

THE POWER OF A SEED

Was Jesus negligent or unskillful when He sprinkled seed on the various types of spiritual soil? No! What Jesus knew was the power that was in the seed. The earth contains many types of soil, all of which produce many different varieties of harvest. Every soil has the potential for a beneficial yield.

I have a greeting card with a picture of a street with a manhole cover in it. The hardness of the concrete appears obvious, but there is a crack in it. Growing in the crack is a lovely flower. There is beauty and life in the midst of what appears to be a precarious and unacceptable place to grow. I've seen beautiful little flowers grow similarly in the cracks of sidewalks. Haven't you?

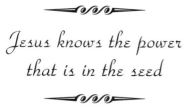

Jesus knows the power that is in the seed

My husband and I used to hike quite a bit. One of our hiking trips took us to the top of a mountain in the Rocky Mountains of

Colorado. The wind blew cold and swift even though it was summertime. Trees were not able to survive in the rocky soil and harsh weather conditions that faced the mountaintop. As we reached the summit, we were surrounded by thousands of fragile little flowers of varying shades of pink, yellow, violet and white. A flowery blanket covered the whole area like a coat of many colors. Oh, the power of the seed.

THE MUSTARD SEED

Our Heavenly Father declared that the Seed of the woman would crush the head of the serpent and utterly destroy him, *"...it shall bruise thy head" (Genesis 3:15)*. Jesus is the Seed that accomplished that prophetic promise. Oh, the power of the Seed.

The Lord used the illustration of a mustard seed as He taught faith, *"If ye had faith as a grain of mustard seed, ye might say unto this sycamine tree, Be thou plucked up by the root, and be thou planted in the sea; and it should obey you" (Luke 17:6)*. The Lord testified about the power of the seed—the faith that is IN the seed—the faith that IS the seed. Jesus was crucified that we can live and that we would be able to live by faith, *"I am crucified with Christ: nevertheless I live; yet not I, but Christ liveth in me: and the life which I now live in the flesh I live by the faith of the Son of God, who loved me, and gave himself for me" (Galatians 2:20)*. Oh, the power of the Seed.

WHO IS THE TROUBLER?

Jesus explained who was responsible for the fowls of the air coming to devour, *"...where the word is sown; but when they have heard, Satan cometh immediately, and taketh away the word that was sown in their hearts" (Mark 4:15)*. We must understand that satan cannot be everywhere at the same time. He must use those under his authority to perform such thievery. He also has under his domination those who do the evil work of affliction and persecution. They apply pressure in an attempt to make us fall away from our walk in Christ *(Mark 4:17)*. There are still other agents of the enemy that work through the lure and lust of power, pleasure, prestige, reputation and money to cause our lives to become unfruitful in godly endeavors. It is the WHO of evil tactics and pressures that we propose to identify in the following pages.

WEEDS OF TRIBULATION

All of us would like for our lives to be garden paradises free from all harm, oppression and evil. That is what our Lord designed and desired for us as well. That is what He provided and presented to Adam. But, because of Adam's fall, we face tribulations, persecutions, rejection and buffeting from satan's evil kingdom. Jesus often taught His followers that they would be faced with such things, but He repeatedly gave them (and us) consolation, encouragement and direction about overcoming the problems we encounter. *"These things I have spoken unto you, that in me ye might have peace. In the world ye shall have tribulation: but be of good cheer; I have overcome the world"* (John 16:33, emphasis added).

Oppression equals op-position—trying to make you lose your position

Jesus said we would endure tribulation and persecution, and be misrepresented and rejected for His sake. *"Blessed are they which are persecuted for righteousness' sake...Blessed are ye, when men shall revile you, and persecute you, and shall say all manner of evil against you falsely, for my sake. Rejoice..."* (Matthew 5:10-12). He let us know that He is not going to remove us from the battle but that He will provide us with the ability, the grace, the faith and the power to overcome. *"I pray not that thou shouldest take them out of the world, but that thou shouldest keep them from the evil"* (John 17:15). And if we are at a desperate point, He even gives us a door of escape if it becomes necessary *(I Corinthians 10:13)*.

PRIOR DEALINGS WITH EVIL

Prior to Jesus' coming to earth, we find reference to people dealing with satan and his companions. David, while he was a shepherd, was called upon to play music for King Saul in order to drive away the evil spirits that were oppressing the king. The evil spirits would not stay where the anointed music of the Lord was played. Even today many receive consolation and reprieve by singing songs (Psalms) written by that same David.

It is interesting to note people in Jesus' day were aware of devils as "personalities" and understood those personalities caused oppressive and tormenting manifestations. Jesus did not go around trying to explain to or convince people there were such things as devils—they were well aware that such beings existed and were responsible for tragic events. *"And, behold, a woman of Canaan came out of the same coasts, and cried unto him, saying, Have mercy on me, O Lord, thou son of David; my daughter is grievously vexed with a devil"* (*Matthew 15:22*, also see *Mark 9:17-27*).

Even the Pharisees were acquainted with efforts to try to dispel or overcome evil spirits or devils. When they accused Jesus of trying to cast out devils through the prince of devils, Beelzebub, Jesus questioned by whom *they* cast out devils.

"But when the Pharisees heard it, they said, This fellow doth not cast out devils, but by Beelzebub the prince of the devils. And Jesus knew their thoughts, and said unto them, Every kingdom divided against itself is brought to desolation; and every city or house divided against itself shall not stand: And if Satan cast out Satan, he is divided against himself; how shall then his kingdom stand? And if I by Beelzebub cast out devils, by whom do your children cast them out? therefore they shall be your judges. But if I cast out devils by the Spirit of God, then the kingdom of God is come unto you" (*Matthew 12:24-28, emphasis added*).

THEN CAME JESUS

When Jesus came, He demonstrated a far greater way of dealing with the evil personalities that afflict lives. He walked in total and absolute authority over satan and his evil kingdom. *"And they were all amazed, insomuch that they questioned among themselves, saying, What thing is this? what new doctrine is this? for with authority commanded he even the unclean spirits, and they do obey him"* (*Mark 1:27*).

Jesus revealed the personality of satan, the works of satan and his evil tactics. Not only did Jesus reveal the enemy, He explained His purpose in coming was to show us, *"The thief cometh not, but for to steal, and to kill, and to destroy: I am come that they might have life, and that they might have it more abundantly"* (*John 10:10*).

Time after time Jesus gave not only His disciples but also others who followed Him power to cast out devils, heal the sick and to preach. *"Then he called his twelve disciples together, and gave them power and authority over all devils, and to cure diseases. And he sent them to preach the kingdom of God, and to heal the sick"* (*Luke 9:1,2*).

"After these things the Lord appointed other seventy also, and sent them two and two...And the seventy returned again with joy, saying, Lord even

the devils are subject unto us through thy name, And he said unto them, I beheld Satan as lightning fall from heaven. Behold, I give unto you power to tread on serpents and scorpions, and over all the power of the enemy..." *(Luke 10:1,17-20).*

Jesus not only commissioned the twelve, the seventy and those who followed him along the shores of Galilee, but all those who know Him as their Lord and Savior.

"And Jesus came and spake unto them, saying, All power is given unto me in heaven and in earth. Go ye therefore, and teach all nations, baptizing them in the name of the Father, and of the Son, and of the Holy Spirit: Teaching them to observe all things whatsoever I have commanded you: and, lo, I am with you always, even unto the end of the world. Amen" *(Matthew 28:18-20).*

The Gospel of Mark gets a little more specific. *"And he said unto them, Go ye into all the world, and preach the gospel to every creature. He that believeth and is baptized shall be saved; but he that believeth not shall be damned. And these signs shall follow them that believe; In my name shall they cast out devils; they shall speak with new tongues; They shall take up serpents; and if they drink any deadly thing, it shall not hurt them; they shall lay hands on the sick, and they shall recover"* *(Mark 16:15-18).*

THE PARABLE OF THE TARES

In Matthew 13:24-30, we find Jesus telling another parable immediately following the parable of the Sower. It is the parable of the wheat and tares. Jesus tells of an enemy sneaking into the wheat field while men slept (under cover of darkness) to plant tares. Tares looked very much like wheat, but at maturity its "fruit" was black and poisonous. Time passed and eventually the farmer realized that something undesirable had been planted in his field. Jesus' recommendation was not to destroy the whole field, but at the harvest to sort out what was good from that which was to be cast aside and burned.

Satan has not been removed from the earth but a day is coming when he and his followers will be cast into the lake of fire. Satan continues to sow his poisonous seed. However, Jesus defeated satan through His death, burial and resurrection. Believers who have Jesus Christ as their Lord and Savior are anointed, appointed, equipped and commissioned to go into all the world to preach the gospel, baptize, cast out devils, heal the sick and do all that the Heavenly Father in Christ Jesus by the Holy Spirit directs.

WATCH FOR THE RAIN

We live in an awesome time. Rain is on the horizon. *"Then shall we know, if we follow on to know the Lord: his going forth is prepared as the morning; and he shall come unto us as the rain, as the latter and former rain unto the earth"* (Hosea 6:3).

Sure, we have had rains of the Spirit, but nothing like what is in the heart of God. He is waiting for precious fruit, and He has had long patience for what He is about to do. The earth has had a time of the enemy sowing numerous things that are dark and poisonous. Our Husbandman is bringing the rain, and the Holy Spirit will assist believers in uprooting the plantings of the enemy.

"Be patient therefore, brethren, unto the coming of the Lord. Behold, the husbandman waiteth for the precious fruit of the earth, and hath long patience for it until he receive the early and latter rain" (James 5:7).

Our Lord is preparing us to go into the harvest in a way far greater, more powerful and more abundant than what we have experienced thus far.

WHAT ABOUT NOW?

The soil of our lives has many things planted in it. We are created in the image and likeness of God, and we are intricately and wonderfully made (Psalm 139:15). There are abilities woven into our framework of body, soul and spirit so embodied by the design of God that they are fearsome intimidation to satan. Things like the ability to choose between right and wrong. Like the power of our words. Like the ability of the body to heal itself from scrapes, wounds and other trauma. Like the yearning within to worship, and so much more.

Many things also have footing in our lives things that are rooted in error and evil. Satan has had many years to develop his strategies, but not being the creative sort, he has been confined to using the same tactics over and over. He is, however, ever endeavoring to dress up his works in modern attire. Whatever devious plan he used on the people hundreds and thousands of years before, he uses on people today. That is why the Bible is so wonderful. It gives us examples of how satan and his workings have been thwarted before and brings us inspiration and confidence in the faithfulness of our Lord. That is also the power of true witnesses who testify and give us instruction and illustrations of our victory in our Lord Jesus.

Whatever is good in God, satan desires a counterfeit for his kingdom. But whatever satan's plan may be, every effort, every activity, every success he has had or ever will have, has been conquered by Jesus Christ. Jesus has provided the victory, and we can receive it if we will believe.

THE BATTLE OF UNBELIEF

Unbelief is a sneaky thing. We can have weeds of unbelief growing in our lives, and like the tares of Matthew 13, they can be there a long time without us being aware of any poison until its evil hinders or impacts us. At times, the dirty work of unbelief reaps great defeat. We have the lesson of the Israelites coming out of the bondage of Egypt. Even though they didn't want the bondage they had been in, they did not want to leave the gods of Egypt. Though they'd been witness to mighty miracles, even to the parting of the Red Sea, they questioned the continuing presence of God. When Moses was delayed on Mount Sinai, they became impatient and demanded a golden calf be fashioned for them to worship *(Exodus 32:4)*. Their hearts were focused upon their fears and selfish desires.

As they approached Canaan, the land of milk and honey God promised them, they camped in the wilderness of Paran *(Numbers 12-16)*. The Lord told Moses to choose men of authority (rulers) to search out the land. One man from each of the twelve tribes was chosen to be a part of the reconnaissance group.

What they found stunned ten of the twelve men. They saw giants in the land—along with abundant fruitfulness—but the stature of these "giants" grew so perilously in their minds they saw themselves as mere grasshoppers by comparison. But two others, Joshua and Caleb, saw those same giants and confidently declared, *"...Let us go up at once, and possess it; for we are well able to overcome it." (Numbers 13:30)*. Ten men persuaded the waiting Israelites that the giants were too much to deal with, and they turned back. God had ordained they would be victorious. It had been decided and prepared in God's divine purpose, *"...although the works were finished from the foundation of the world" (Hebrews 4:3)*.

The victory was "in the bag," —the fight had been finalized before it began. The problem was—there was no fight. Why? What was the reason for this retreat?

"Wherefore, (as the Holy Ghost saith, To day if ye will hear his voice, Harden not your hearts, as in the provocation, in the day of temptation in the wilderness: When your fathers tempted me, proved me, and saw my works forty years. Wherefore I was grieved with that generation, and said, They do always err in their heart; and they have not known my ways. So I sware in my wrath, They shall not enter into my rest.)...So we see that they could not enter in because of unbelief" (Hebrews 3:7-11,19).

They did not obey God's voice. They hardened their hearts. They erred in their hearts, and they did not know His ways. God was going to fight for them, defeat their enemy and give them the land—but unbelief led them to the wilderness.

Unbelief was not just a problem for the Israelites traipsing around the wilderness.

PREACHING MIXED WITH FAITH

The Apostle Paul, by the inspiration of the Holy Spirit, is tackling this matter of unbelief in Hebrews 3 and 4. *"For unto us was the gospel preached, as well as unto them: but the word preached did not profit them, not being mixed with faith in them that heard it...Seeing therefore it remaineth that some enter therein, and they to whom it was first preached entered not in because of unbelief"* (Hebrews 4:2,6).

They didn't enter into the rest of God or the promises of God, because they did not hear, comprehend, understand or receive the good news that was declared to them. The gospel was preached, but they did not mix faith with what had been preached.

On many occasions Jesus confronted this matter of unbelief, even with those who knew him best. Mary Magdalene was the first person that Jesus appeared to after His resurrection. Jesus told her to go tell his disciples that he was raised from the dead. Where were the disciples? *"And she went and told them that had been with him, as they mourned and wept. And they, when they had heard that he was alive, and had been seen of her, believed not"* (Mark 16:10,11). They were mourning and crying and refusing to consider the validity of her news. Why do you suppose Jesus appeared to Mary Magdalene first? Because she was looking for him and was ready to accept His resurrection, *"...tell me where thou hast laid him... Jesus saith unto her,*

Mary. She turned herself, and saith unto him, Rabboni, which is to say, Master" (John 20:15,16). The disciples however, didn't believe it even though eyewitnesses were testifying to His resurrection.

Jesus scolded them for their unbelief, *"Afterward he appeared unto the eleven as they sat at meat, and upbraided them with their unbelief and hardness of heart, because they believed not them which had seen him after he was risen" (Mark 16:14).* Who were *them* that told the disciples Jesus was alive? Of course, it was Mary Magdalene, but also two men on the road to Emmaus who Jesus walked with and explained scriptures *(Luke 24:13-35).* After Jesus revealed who He was to them, they excitedly scurried to Jerusalem to tell the disciples the wonderful news of Jesus' resurrection *(Luke 24:33).*

This goes to show unbelief can get to any of us. But what happens next reveals the heart of our wonderful Lord. Almost in the same breath that He scolded them, He commissioned them to, *"...Go, ye into all the world, and preach the gospel to every creature..." (Mark 16:15).* Jesus does not desire to leave us wallowing in unbelief. He is endeavoring to equip and send us forth to achieve and overcome.

WE HAVE AN ADVOCATE

You might think it a shame and a disappointment to have the Lord expose unbelief in your life. But this is not necessarily the case if you are looking for what is hindering breakthrough and victory. When the Lord revealed to me unbelief was a major stumbling block in my perception of a certain matter, I was relieved. However, when the list of what could be wrong—hardness of heart, err of heart, not knowing God's ways and not mixing faith with the gospel, it had the nudging of something like a giant trying to swell up in my mind. I cried to the Lord, *"Shew me thy ways, O Lord, teach me thy paths. Lead me in thy truth, and teach me: for thou art the God of my salvation; on thee do I wait all the day" (Psalm 25:4,5).*

The Holy Spirit came to the rescue. Just as the Lord promised back in my garden, when the weed of unbelief was identified, the Holy Spirit brought forth the necessary information for uprooting and removal of that deceitful strategy. I discovered in Hebrews 3 and 4 that the Apostle Paul taught in some detail about the dilemma of unbelief. His lesson on unbelief is sandwiched between the beginning of Hebrews 3 and the end of Hebrews 4. He counsels us to consider (observe fully) Jesus Christ, the Apostle and High Priest of our profession (our terms of surrender to our life in Him)—and Jesus our Great High Priest.

"Wherefore, holy brethren, partakers of the heavenly calling, consider the Apostle and High Priest of our profession, Christ Jesus" (Hebrews 3:1).

"Seeing then that we have a great high priest, that is passed into the heavens, Jesus the Son of God, let us hold fast our profession. For we have not an high priest which cannot be touched with the feeling of our infirmities; but was in all points tempted like as we are, yet without sin. Let us therefore come boldly unto the throne of grace, that we may obtain mercy, and find grace to help in time of need" (Hebrews 4:14-16, emphasis added).

Because Christ Jesus is our Great High Priest, we can be assured of acceptance before our Heavenly Father. Jesus can *identify* with us, because He suffered the same things that we experience—yet He did not sin. Because He did, we can come boldly unto the throne of grace to obtain mercy (for our sin, failings, backsliding, hardness of heart and our unbelief) and find grace to help when we need it. We can come with confidence—even boldly—recognizing that our sin requires a penalty, and we are in need of mercy bestowed upon a truly repentant heart. Jesus will compassionately assist us with counsel and direction.

> *When God wants to remove a stumbling block, He will expose it, remove it and replace it with solid truth*

The high priest had the responsibility of receiving gifts and sacrifices and offering them unto God. *"But into the second* (veil) *went the high priest alone once every year, not without blood, which he offered for himself, and for the errors of the people"* (Hebrews 9:7, explanation added).

Jesus entered the holy place in the heavenly temple of God with His own Blood, *"But Christ being come an high priest of good things to come, by a greater and more perfect tabernacle, not made with hands, that is to say, not of this building; Neither by the blood of goats and calves, but by his own blood he entered in once into the holy place, having obtained eternal redemption for us"* (Hebrews 9:11,12, emphasis added).

This is the good news preached to us—that Jesus has made the way for us. He has suffered the penalty for all our sin and offered

His holy Blood as the sacrifice for our sin. He defeated the enemy and won the victory. We can come boldly to the throne of grace and receive whatever we need to achieve godly success. When we come to the throne of grace, we can be assured, even rejoice, that God's grace will accomplish what is needed to make our lives complete in Jesus.

GRACE—GOD'S ABUNDANT SUPPLY

Weeds of unbelief are trying to put down roots where there are areas of fear, lack of love, rejection, offense, legalism, performance and bitterness (to name a few). Roots of unbelief cause us to miss the blessings of God and bring us sorrow. *"Looking diligently lest any man fail of the grace of God; lest any root of bitterness springing up trouble you, and thereby many be defiled"* (Hebrews 12:15,17).

Jesus, as our Great High Priest, makes lavish portions of grace available to us as we confront and uproot unbelief. *"For if by one man's offense death reigned by one; much more they which receive abundance of grace and of the gift of righteousness shall reign in life by one, Jesus Christ...But where sin abounded, grace did much more abound* (Romans 5:17,20). Jesus lives in the hearts of believers by the Holy Spirit. The Holy Spirit manifests the victory of Jesus within us and causes us to have fruitful lives.

"What fruit had ye then in those things whereof ye are now ashamed? For the end of those things is death. But now being made free from sin, and become servants of God, ye have your fruit unto holiness, and the end everlasting life" (Romans 6:21,22).

SO WHAT ABOUT SPIRITUAL WARFARE?

The bottom line of successful spiritual warfare is the knowledge, wisdom and understanding of what Jesus has done to establish our victory. He is solidly involved in bringing us godly success within each of our lives. As we begin to learn about satan, his fallen-angel strategists, his demon pawns, and the tactics and strategies of his dark kingdom, we can be assured that the kingdom of our Heavenly Father is mobilized to assist and direct us in our quest to be triumphant.

CHAPTER 2

FINDING THE BATTLE FRONTS

I was raised to know about Jesus. I prayed, went to Sunday school and church occasionally and tried to live as good as I knew how. I tried to do all the "dos" and strived to not do all the "don'ts" of what I had been taught. I grew up, got married and had two beautiful little girls. Even though I was making my best effort at being a Christian, I did not know Jesus in a personal way. Through the course of several events, the witness of a friend and the testimony of a rodeo clown, I asked Jesus into my heart at 26 years of age. I asked Him to be my Lord and Savior and to fill me with His Holy Spirit. I was flooded with an all-encompassing love, and I knew I was born-again.

In the beginning weeks as a new believer, even though I was profoundly experiencing the love of God, I also became acutely aware of a dreadful hate directed towards me. I knew enough about good and evil to know that satan was the one directing the hate. Immediately, the Lord began to teach me about warfare between the kingdoms of good and evil. I read many books and gained much knowledge from wonderful men and women of God. I learned a lot about healing, miracles, casting out of demons and prayer, and I experienced the glorious goodness of God. Those who received Jesus during the Charismatic Movement most likely learned many of the same things.

I learned of the divisions of the enemy the Apostle Paul describes in Ephesians 6 where he lists principalities, powers, rulers of darkness of this world and spiritual wickedness in high places. I learned about the authority that is given to believers in Jesus Christ. I prayed many prayers for others, and myself, including casting out demons. I learned about my authority in Jesus. I was to discover that battling entities of satan's kingdom was more than casting out demons. There were other entities to be dealt with.

I had been taught, like many people, that when the angels rebelled with satan, they became known as demons—the demons which have oppressed humankind throughout the ages. We will learn that when a person confronts demons, the person has not dealt with the real strength of satan's hierarchy. I have come to the certainty that demons and fallen angels are not one and the same.

Let's look at a scripture which describes events of the end times, *"And there was war in heaven: Michael and his angels fought against the dragon; and the dragon fought and his angels, And the great dragon was cast out, that old serpent, called the Devil, and Satan, which deceiveth the whole world: he was cast out into the earth, and his angels were cast out with him"* *(Revelation 12:8,9, emphasis added)*. If satan's angels became the demons we know are (and have been) oppressing people on the earth, then will they somehow change back into being angels and return to heaven during the last days to war against the archangel Michael and God's holy angels? No, this scripture indicates satan and his angels will be *cast into the earth* during the last days. Satan and his fallen angels are yet in the heavenly realm doing evil business. They are in the second heaven working as strategists (which we will discuss later). This scripture does not indicate that demons will be cast down to earth—but only the devil and his angels. Why? Because demons are *already* on the earth carrying out satan's assignments.

Let's also look at the matter of demons. We do not find the term "demon" or "demons" when we read through scripture (King James Version). We find them referred to as "spirits" or "devils." The Greek word for devil is *daimon*, pronounced "dah-ee-mown," meaning a supernatural spirit of a bad nature. Quite possibly, the pronunciation of the Greek word for devil has become our accepted word of "demon." The Greek word for angel is *aggelos*, pronounced "ang-el-os" and is defined as one who brings tidings or is a messenger. Incidentally, the same word for angel is used both for God's holy angel or satan's fallen angel. Satan uses his messengers to propagate his evil kingdom. God sends forth His holy angels on behalf of the heirs of salvation *(Hebrews 1:14)*.

Consider what the Apostle Paul wrote in Galatians chapter one, *"...but there be some that trouble you, and would pervert the gospel of Christ. But though we, or an angel from heaven, preach any other gospel unto you than that which we have preached unto you, let him be accursed"* *(v. 7-8)*. Paul knows that the holy angels of God will not bring the message of *another* gospel, because they are observing born-again believers to understand the manifold wisdom of God *(Ephesians 3:10)*.

Paul is indicating there are *angels from heaven* who would bring a perversion to the gospel that he preached. The warning Paul gave was warranted, because there are religions today that are perversions of the gospel that were spawned through fallen-angel visitations. (I recommend reading a book by Terry Law, *The Truth About Angels* if you want to know more about angels.) The unholy angels are not resident on the earth, but have their habitation in the heavenly sphere.

Devils or demons, however, are in the earthly sphere and are carrying out assignments given them from fallen-angel superiors.

DEMONS—OFFSPRING OF FALLEN ANGELS?

There is a train of thought that some people have as their understanding of the origin of demons. It is the teaching that demons are the offspring of the union between fallen angels and the daughters of men spoken of in Genesis 6:4, *"There were giants in the earth in those days; and also after that, when the sons of God* (fallen angels) *came in unto the daughters of men, and they bare children to them, the same became mighty men* (giants) *which were of old, men of renown" (explanation added)*. This perversion to the human race became so rampant upon the earth that God brought judgment upon the earth through the flood. There was one man who found grace in the eyes of God, *"But Noah found grace in the eyes of the Lord. These are the generations of Noah: Noah was a just man and perfect in his generations, and Noah walked with God" (Genesis 6:8,9)*. Noah and his family were *perfect in their generations*, meaning they had a pure bloodline. The rest of the world's people that existed at the time were destroyed in the flood.

From my understanding, such belief indicates that demons are the offspring of fallen angels that perished in Noah's flood. It is an interesting thought. We might also consider that they are reserved under judgment for their sin. *"For if God spared not the angels that sinned, but cast them down to hell, and delivered them into chains of darkness, to be reserved unto judgment; And spared not the old world, but saved Noah the eighth person, a preacher of righteousness, bringing in the flood upon the world of the ungodly..." (II Peter 2:4,5, emphasis addad)*. The word spared in this scripture means "to treat leniently." God did not give leniency to the angels or to the old world, but says he has reserved the angels in chains until judgment. Neither were those that sinned with those angels given leniency. Why is God's judgment so severe? Because satan had instigated a plan to pervert the human race. It was his attempt to prevent God's promise of the Messiah, the Seed of the woman from crushing his head *(Genesis 3:15)*.

Jude 6 also gives an account of what judgment was upon the angels who left heaven to mate with the daughters of men, *"And the angels which kept not their first estate, but left their own habitation, he hath reserved in everlasting chains under darkness unto the judgment of the great day."* What would be their own habitation? I believe it is the heavenly sphere where satan and his angels currently have their habitation and will be cast to the earth at the last days.

DOING BATTLE ON ALL FRONTS

As we will read in following chapters, what you believe will have a profound bearing on how you deal with demonic and satanic opposition. What happens when a believer is ignorant of who demons are and who fallen angels are? When we cast out a <u>demon or demons</u>, we have accomplished one level of warfare. We, however, have gained the attention of and mobilized <u>fallen-angel</u> intelligence forces. Although we have aptly evicted the demons, we have attacked satan's territory. Satanic or fallen-angel forces will seek to restore their influence. If we are ignorant of this, we will not understand that we are going to be attacked from behind, in our blind spots or in any area of weakness, sin or error we have in our lives.

In the following chapters, we will be identifying and explaining the fallen-angel divisions of principalities, powers or authorities, rulers of darkness of this world, and spiritual wickedness in high places. If we are ignorant of the realms and the differences between demons and fallen angels, lack of knowledge of the way they operate will cause us to falter as evil strategists set themselves against us. Casting out demons is only one front. There are other fronts that need attention and skillful action. Fallen angels are the foe with which to reckon.

Military-oriented thinkers understand the need to maintain pro-tection and defenses on all fronts. They recognize their own weak areas and provide appropriate support or protection where needed. They also send out intelligence gathering patrols to gain knowledge of the weaknesses and penetration points of their enemy. The Lord has provided weaponry for assault, defense and knowledge into the plans and tactics of our enemy, satan. In the following pages we will look at some identifying characteristics of our spiritual opponents.

FALLEN ANGELS? DEMONS?

The fallen angel's function and operation differs from that of a demon. Demonic activity is related to demons and the way they operate. *Satanic* activity is related to fallen-angel strategists, the operations and activities of satan as their chief.

Demonic activity is subordinate to satanic activity in that demonic activity carries out *satanic* strategy. Demons take orders from their satanic superiors and do the actual application of satanic strategies. So to say something is demonic means it is merely demons at work. To say something is satanic is to say there are assignments and strategies at work. We cannot get caught up in trying to determine whether something is to be "termed" demonic or satanic, but we do need to recognize just who is the highest one in control of the situation in order to appropriate the weapon the Lord has provided for us.

Satan fights for his ground even though many times he holds it illegally. We must know and gain confidence and experience in who we are in Christ and who Christ is in us. If we endeavor to walk as Jesus walked and do the things that Jesus did, we will be treading upon territory satan thinks is his. We have an enemy who does not fight fair. He lies, condemns, steals and every evil way fills his being. There is NO TRUTH in him.

HOW DO THEY WORK?

Fallen angels and demons are both spirit beings. When one-third of the angels fell, they retained their spirit bodies but now exist in a fallen state without the glorious bodies they once had when they were in the Lord's presence and kingdom. They, as we read in Revelation 12:9, exist in the heavenly sphere.

Demons have no spirit body. Even though they have a spirit form, they do not have a spirit body in the same way that angels do. Demons' spiritual existence is such that they are insistently seeking a body, whether human or animal, to attach to or indwell in order to have connection or expression on earth. Demons have a limited sphere of operational power, area of responsibility or authority. In the army of the kingdom of darkness, they are the lowest in rank and power. They are the ones assigned and delegated to do the "dirty work." Demons carry out the detailed assignments against human beings in the earthly sphere. Demons cannot function or fully express their character unless they are attached to, or have some connection with a human being. They so desire a "host" they will crowd together and seek to be joined to a person. We find this occurring in the Gospel of Mark where 4,000-6,000 demons inhabited the madman at Gadara. Some are so intent on staying with a living being, they will even enter animals, as in the case when Jesus cast the demons out of the man from Gadara and the demons asked to be cast into swine *(Luke 8:33)*.

Angels do not indwell human beings. They have their own spirit body and must work from an outward approach when they deal with people. Fallen angels assault people through the mind, intellect, will and bodily oppression. They are strategists and are active in seeing that evil plans and strategies are carried out. They are rulers over demons (who are the ones who carry out orders).

Again, demons are the peons in satan's kingdom. They are not strategists, they have limited authority and do the bidding of fallen angels who *are* the strategists and command authority. Whenever believers cast out demons, they have only dealt with the lowest rank of satan's fighting force.

How do believers confront fallen-angel personalities? By greater power—far greater. Jesus said He has given all power unto His followers. Jesus is all in all. He has won the victory and given authority and every provision to enforce what He has already won.

When we cast out demons, we are not really dealing with satan's strong-arm forces. That's why we sometimes experience oppression and other bombardments. Wherever a demon or demons have been cast out, satan realizes he has lost ground, and he does not like to lose any advantage. Therefore, believers who know and walk in their place and position in Christ are a threat to satan's purpose and territorial reign.

Satan is afraid of any believer who begins to gain confidence and faith in Christ's Name and authority. *Satan* knows a believer in Christ has power over his own power and authority. When *believers* know and walk in the knowledge of their power over satan, in Christ Jesus, then satan's kingdom will suffer. Therefore, satan makes every effort to deter us from realizing our power, position and authority over him.

WHERE ARE THEY?

It helps to get a mental picture of where our enemy is. Demons can inhabit the earthly sphere. They live on the earth and interrelate with any human being that will tolerate them. They also live under the earth. Their headquarters is hell or Hades. Jesus descended into hell after His death on the cross. It is there that He burst open hell's gates and led out those righteous souls imprisoned there. Demons witnessed the victory of Jesus.

Principalities, powers, rulers of darkness and spiritual wickedness in high places do their strategic planning, not on earth or in the belly of the earth, but in the second heaven. There, the headquarters of the *satanic* kingdom operates as a tyrannical system of strategists set against God, God's people and every human being.

Until the time Jesus came, saints who died were taken to a place called Abraham's Bosom, also referred to by Jesus as paradise. These saints were not intermingled with the wicked but held apart in a separate place. Luke 16:19-26 tells of a wicked rich man who was in the torment of Hades. He looked over to a place that apparently had refreshing water. He recognized a beggar, named Lazarus, who sat at the gate of his house while they were alive on earth. Undoubtedly he had passed by the poor man many times. Now, as the rich man was anguishing in his eternal destination, he pleaded with Lazarus to dip his finger into water and come to try and quench the awful dryness of his tongue. But it could not happen, because there was a great gulf between them. Travel from one place to the other was not possible.

When Jesus died, he descended into the belly of the earth, and in victory lead the souls that had been held captive out of their holding place in paradise. For a short time, Jesus allowed the saints to walk the streets of Jerusalem, *"And the graves were opened; and many bodies of the saints which slept arose, And came out of the graves after his resurrection, and went into the holy city, and appeared unto many"* (Matthew 27:52, 53). Jesus then triumphantly led them through the heavens—the first heaven and the second heaven, where he stripped satan's power and dominion from him and made an open show of defeat and shame before the whole spiritual realm. We read in Ephesians chapter four, *"Wherefore he saith, When he ascended up on high, he led captivity captive..." (verse 8)* and *"And having spoiled principalities and powers, he made a shew of them openly, triumphing over them in it" (Colossians 2:15).* Jesus displayed His triumph as He stripped satan of his credentials of power before the heavenly kingdoms. He brought His beloved saints into the heavenly kingdom of eternal life in the third heaven and into the presence of their Holy God.

When Jesus ascended into heaven, He sat down at the right hand of the Father—far above all principality and power. Jesus, before His death and resurrection, foretold that there would be a day when believers would see heaven opened and God's angels would ascend and descend upon the Son of Man. *"And he saith unto him, Verily, verily, I say unto you, Hereafter, ye shall see heaven open, and the angels of God ascending and descending upon the Son of Man"* (John 1:51).

Jesus said the day would come when, in Him, holy angels would ascend and descend *freely* from the throne of Father God to humankind. Through Jesus' resurrection, we are afforded the awesome privilege of walking in that reality every day. Holy angels can now freely travel through the heavens bringing godly provision and protection to those who pray.

ADAM COMES ON THE SCENE

Adam was the first creature who was made something other than just a spirit or a spirit with a spiritual body as the angels were. He was a spirit being, but he was given a physical body that was made out of the dust of the earth. When God breathed into him, he became a living soul with flesh and blood. The life is in the blood, and when God breathed into Adam, that breath was the physical manifestation of life-giving substance. God robed His spirit being (Adam) in a body that would physically occupy the earth. He gave him command to have dominion over it.

As we revisit Genesis 1-3, the reasons behind satan's hatred of humankind will help us understand why we are involved in daily warfare.

CHAPTER 3

UNDERSTANDING THE PERSONALITY AND MOTIVATION OF SATAN

S atan came as a serpent to entice Eve. When we see why he came to her and the fervency of his desire to deceive her, we will better understand the enemy who still works today with a hate that must be taken seriously.

THE BEGINNING—REVISITED

God created a perfect heaven and earth. God created Lucifer, filling him with beauty and wisdom. He gave him authority and rule over the earth. Lucifer ruled earth and its inhabitants. He was the Anointed Cherub *(Ezekiel 28:14)*, supremely wise *(Ezekiel 28:12)*; beautiful beyond description *(Ezekiel 28:11,17)*, and music emanated from him *(Ezekiel 28:13)*.

The earth was a prosperous and bountiful habitation. Lucifer walked up and down the earth and ruled the kingdom of this earth *(Ezekiel 28)*.

Lucifer traveled to the mountain of God from his earthly throne. A throne depicts a kingdom and subjects. Lucifer was a faithful archangel for a time because Ezekiel describes, *"Thou wast perfect in thy ways from the day thou wast created until iniquity was found in thee."* Lucifer ruled earth in perfection until a despicable plan took root. He became jealous of the Godhead and was lifted up in pride. In that pride, he sought to overthrow God.

TRAFFIC ON THE EARTH

At the moment of Lucifer's decision to rebel, all of his beauty, wisdom, anointing and music became perverted. His once holy abilities became deceptive and manipulative power directed toward his kingdom and subjects. The vastness of his riches, resources and kingdom of inhabitants bolstered his confidence in his quest to overthrow God *(Ezekiel 28:4,16)*. He trafficked *(verse 18)* up and down the earth, gaining converts to his hideous plan by choice and command. Eventually, they, too, joined his rebellion against God.

Believers generally accept that Lucifer deceived one-third of the angels, and they fell with him when he was cast out of heaven. Is it possible angels ruled on earth in territories and regions during a time before Adam? Ezekiel describes a time when there was traffic, commerce and activity over the earth during satan's reign. Is it possible there were beings on earth ruled by angels, ones that existed on earth and traveled back and forth over the earth as described in Ezekiel 28? Satan, one-third of the angels, as well as the earth's residents, gathered to mount their attack against the Trinity of heaven.

A FAST FALL FROM HEAVEN

Lucifer and his host attempted to invade and overthrow the God of heaven. Instead, he and all with him were cast down. Jesus related to his disciples, *"...I beheld Satan as lightning fall from heaven" (Luke 10:18).* It was a fast fall from heaven. Lucifer's judgment was set, and his kingdom was removed from God's presence and glory.

The earth then became a mass of matter that became *"without form, and void; and darkness was upon the face of the deep" (Genesis 1:2).* Without the light of God's kingdom to enlighten it, the earth became a kingdom of darkness, emptiness and chaos.

IN THE BEGINNING

As I grew up, I heard the creation story. When the science books at my small country school told of how many hundreds of thousands of years old the earth "supposedly" was, I reasoned that science and the Bible were simply at odds with each other. I thought if anyone believed the earth existed for hundreds of thousands, even billions of years, they would be in danger of anti-Christian belief. After all, "In the beginning..." and "Let there be light" of Genesis 1 were separated by only one scripture. Therefore, I concluded they must have happened at the same time. I would reason that the carbon dating of fossils and dinosaurs was a miscalculation of atheistic scientists. I believed then and still do believe that the Bible is the true, infallible, inherent, and inspired word of God. I was persuaded in my young mind that the earth was five or six thousand years old, and some day science and scientists would figure that out if they wanted the truth. I even heard explanations taught that dinosaurs don't exist today because they just couldn't fit in Noah's ark. What do you think happened to them?

PRE-ADAMIC PEOPLE

As I was studying one day, I came upon a commentary explaining the pre-Adamite people. The more I studied the Word, the more I could grasp the concept that carbon-dating science and the Bible were not in conflict, but that science would actually support biblical data.

To think the earth could be billions of years old and have supported a kingdom of beings in ages past became a distinct possibility. If indeed Lucifer did once have a kingdom on this earth, could it have existed during the time between Genesis 1:1 and 1:2? How long did Lucifer rule earth? Could this have been the time span when the earth was full of commerce, riches and inhabitants described in Ezekiel 28? Could that be the era described taking place over the hundreds of thousands of years that scientists feel they document?

When Lucifer was cast out of heaven, he, together with his kingdom, became separated from God. Could it be that without the light of God's glory and presence, the earth became the chaotic mass of matter described in Genesis 1:2? Without light and God, the earth was nothing more than a lifeless void of dirt and ice. Could this be what scientists describe as "the Ice Age?" Scientists contend the Ice Age lasted about 2.5 million years and ended about 10,000 years ago. It is interesting to listen to documentaries about the ice age and "prehistoric" events in light of an understanding of the possibility of Lucifer's reign on earth and the earth's subsequent turmoil because of his rebellion.

After satan was expelled from heaven, his once glorious existence and influence was replaced by darkness, exile and cold emptiness. Satan lost claim to the earth when he was deposed, a kingdom without a habitation. He was set to NOTHING. All his fallen angels and earthly inhabitants were dispelled as beings without a home. They were not destroyed but were cast away from God's presence.

THE EARTH IS RESTORED

The Father, Word (Jesus' name according to John 1:1) and Holy Spirit determined to again bring forth life upon the earth. The Father sent the Holy Spirit to move upon the face of the "waters." The earth was set in order and chaos was dispelled *(Genesis 1:2)*.

God said, " LET there be light..." The "let" of that verse means to permit or allow. God was no longer withholding His light from the earth. Magnificent light burst forth in mighty splendor to bathe the earth once again in God's presence and glory.

Each day God pronounced restoration of the earth. The earth bloomed with foliage, forest and fruitful trees. The waters teemed with fish and whales. Birds chirped and sang. A myriad of animals filled the land. Prolific beauty and fruitfulness accented the tranquility of earth's life and living things. All things were set in order. The earth had been delivered out of its chaos and emptiness. God had yet another restoration to accomplish.

IN GOD'S IMAGE

As the Father, Word and Holy Spirit set forth their plan, they made a distinction about a new type of creation. They, the Trinity, Elohim, had chosen to create a totally new species of being—not like angels, not like the beings that were created before. Their new creature would be beautifully unique. It would receive the responsibility of dominion over all the earth. God said, "This species will be made *in our image and likeness.*" Man was created in God's OWN image, a quality so spectacular and wonderful the holy angels of heaven must have been amazed at this marvelous specimen. God took from the earth the dust of the ground, made man, and breathed His OWN life into man's nostrils. His breath of life caused man to become a LIVING SOUL. God named him Adam.

Elohim brought forth this man with God's image and human life pulsating in him. Dominion over all the earth was bestowed on him. God desired another social system. God put Adam to sleep, took a rib and made of it a woman.

God blessed them and commanded them to be fruitful, multiply and REPLENISH the earth. God did not say "plenish," meaning fill, but REplenish, or to fill again. God's desire was to fill the earth again. This time humankind would have the wonderful purpose of *fellowship* with Him. Adam and Eve walked in God's presence and enjoyed relationship with the Father, the Word, and the Holy Spirit.

EVIL OBSERVERS

WATCHING in his miserable fallen state was the dethroned evicted ruler of the earth—satan. As the earth became restored in beauty and splendor, all of those who fell with satan also watched.

What is this "being?" Who is this creature called "Adam" and this creature called "Woman?" They had something he had desired with an insatiable passion. They were "like" God.

As satan watched Adam exercise his dominion over all of God's creation, the pride that caused satan's fall was only exceeded by jealousy and hate for the creatures who ruled the earth *he* once controlled.

Satan (his deposed title) sought a plan to regain control of the earth once again. He watched and studied these human creatures. The wisdom he once had as a holy angel had been turned to evil deception, manipulation and lies. He would watch for any avenue of overthrow. He would have this Adam creature turn over his dominion to himself—so God would not be able to deny him the rule of the earth he seethed with jealousy to possess.

Satan saw an opportunity to make his re-entrance into earth's domain. *What was it God told Adam? Do not eat of the tree of the Knowledge of Good and Evil?* Perhaps, satan reasoned, *If Adam eats of this tree then he, TOO, shall know evil. God has commanded him to not eat from it and if he does, then he will die.* Satan knew, by experience, that rebelling against God brought severe consequences. Adam, too, would be deposed if he disobeyed. Satan focused his deception (which caused his inhabitants and one-third of the angels to fall) on Adam and Eve.

MEANWHILE BACK IN THE GARDEN

Adam maintained his daily activities of earthly life and fellowship with God—beautiful fellowship, walking and talking with God. Adam, as the original man, embodied God's dynamic and powerful breath of life.

God gave only one restriction—do not eat of one tree. Adam was able to maintain dominion over all the earth and fellowship with God through one simple task—obedience!

Adam was given dominion over the earth—he was not given ownership of the earth—for the Bible states the earth is the Lord's and all its fullness *(Psalm 24:1)*. When Adam was deceived by satan, he was deceived into letting satan again enter the earthly kingdom realm. All God created and restored in the earth was good. The dominion God commanded Adam to walk in included protecting the earth from evil spiritual intrusion. He was to subdue it *(Gen. 1:28)*.

God placed Adam and Eve on earth with a free will and the power to choose. Adam was able to maintain his position and exercise dominion for a span of time. There are many who look at Adam's fall and lament at his failure and the resulting fall of humankind. God knew the capability and strategies of satan. Satan had already deceived one-third of the angels and the race of beings known as the pre-Adamite people (the race of beings who populated the earth during satan's rule of the earth).

Satan has always been the master of deception, *"...He was a murderer from the beginning, and abode not in the truth, because there is no truth in him. When he speaketh a lie, he speaketh of his own; for he is a liar, and the father of it" (John 8:44).* Satan worked his strategy of trickery to deceive Eve into disobedience. We don't know how long satan continued to persist in trying various plans, seeking the one area of weakness where his destructive plan of defeat could work. Eventually, satan devised his plan and gained legal entrance back into the earth and its dominion. He had been successful in causing the "death" of the God-image man he so vehemently hated.

Satan is the master of deception

DEATH—A NEW PHENOMENON

Death was something that did not exist before Adam. What neither satan nor Adam could comprehend was what death <u>really meant</u>. Satan and his fallen-angel host experienced a form of spiritual displacement when they rebelled against God and were cast down. However, as satan entered into the earth's restored domain, he entered into a whole new dimension—one that established time and death. When the measurements of day and night were established within the restored earth, the dawn of the new dimension came forth—*time*. When God gave command not to eat of the Tree of the Knowledge of Good and Evil under penalty of death, He also brought forth the dimension called *death*.

The new dimension would have a judgment and an end. Within it, Father God ordained a time of judgment for satan and his followers. Their final destination would be the lake of fire *(Revelation 20:10)*.

God is all wise, sovereign and just. He knew satan would continue his hate and rebellion. I believe the Godhead allowed satan's access to the Garden of Eden. Even though Father God commanded Adam to have dominion over the earth and to subdue or protect it, His omnipotent, omniscient love and grace would undergird Adam and Eve's existence. If they fell—which they eventually did, the Lord had a plan for satan's ultimate destruction.

The Bible tells us of satan's destiny

THE MESSIAH IS PROMISED

Immediately after Adam's fall, God promised the woman her seed would one day overcome the serpent who caused their fall. The Seed of the woman would crush the serpent's (satan's) head and seal his doom *(Genesis 3:15)*. God provided a way for man to be saved. Man was made in God's own image, and in that capacity He also made a way for satan's end. The Bible reveals Christ was crucified from the foundation of the world *(Revelation 13:8)*. The Heavenly Father would send His Son, if Man were to fail. In the sacrifice Jesus, the Lamb of God, would be the saving of humankind and the final destruction of God's enemy.

SATAN REGAINS DOMINION

Satan took up residency again, in spirit form, over planet earth. He went about the business of trying to destroy every one of those "God-image creatures" called humanity or human beings. They reminded him of the God Who threw him out of heaven. He was made a shame before the nations of the earth as the earth was stripped from him and left in chaos. Every time he saw a human being, he feared their occupation of the earth's domain. He hated every one of these "human beings" with indescribable fury.

God had established a decree: The Seed of the woman would crush the serpent's (satan's) head. Any one of *them* was a threat to his control and power. *Any one of them could be the one who would crush his head and take his kingdom—again.* He set out to destroy them all.

UNVEILING THE HEAVENLIES

What happened to the fallen angels and the inhabitants that resided on the earth during Lucifer's reign? Where did they go when the earth was again restored and replenished?

The Bible speaks of three heavens. Paul tells us in II Corinthians, *"I knew a man in Christ above fourteen years ago, (whether in the body, I cannot tell: God knoweth;) such an one caught up to the third heaven... How that he was caught up into paradise, and heard unspeakable words, which it is not lawful for a man to utter"* (II Corinthians 12:2, 4).

We can see a portion of the first heaven with our natural eyes as we gaze into the heavens and take in the beauty of the sky, clouds and atmosphere of wind, rain and sunshine. The local weatherman gives us satellite pictures of first heaven activities in the atmospheric realm.

According to the description given by Paul, the third heaven is the residence of God. It is where His throne is and where Jesus went when He ascended to heaven and was seated *far above* all principality and power and might *(Ephesians 1:20-22)*.

SECOND HEAVEN

What about the second heaven? In the story of Daniel, we gain some knowledge of a hindering force separating humankind from God's blessings and provision. Daniel prayed, fasted and sought an answer from God. When the angelic messenger bearing Daniel's answer arrived, he explained the Prince of Persia had resisted him for 21 days *(Daniel 10:11-13)*. He needed to call upon Michael, the archangel, to come help him. What stood between Daniel and God's throne? There was an area of resistance between earth and God's throne (in the third heaven) which had in it those who wish to keep God's answers, blessings and impartation from reaching God's people and human beings in general.

The Prince of Persia was a satanic angel who ruled over the area where Daniel lived. In order for Daniel to receive his answer from God, a battle waged between angelic beings—God's angel verses satan's fallen angel. When God's angel finally brought the answer to Daniel, he told Daniel of the battle.

The second heaven comprises a realm of strategists who are fallen angel beings. The most important activities carried out in the second heaven are strategy planning and strategy implementation. Satan is not relegated to the hell located in the belly of the earth, as depicted by some. He is actively overseeing the workings of his subordinates within the second heaven. He desires to set up his kingdom in the earth and rule as he did before. He resides in the second heaven, developing and delegating strategies to kill, steal and destroy humankind.

Evil strategists in the second heaven are engaged in a myriad of plans and schemes. They are against, first of all, Israel and the promises given to Abraham, Isaac and Jacob, because satan fears the fulfilling of the promise of Messiah's return—which will be on the Mount of Olives. Additionally, they focus upon the Body of Christ who hinder, halt or interfere with their activities in the earth. And of course, the rest of the human race, who are hated for being images of God creations in the earth.

On-fire believers are satan's biggest threat. Those who set out to thwart the devil's kingdom and take it by force have his respect and his attention. They also attract his bitter hatred and contempt. Even meager efforts by any believer sets off alarm in satan's command post. His soldiers of doom are dispatched to halt any defiance against his kingdom.

> *God's power is the only foundation for warfare. No other will succeed.*

When we set out to challenge satan, we must not be equipped with the weapons of man's warfare, but be strong in the Lord and power of His might.

THIRD HEAVEN

God's throne, according to Paul, is located in the third heaven *(II Corinthians 12:2)*. Jesus is seated at the right hand of the Heavenly Father. Paul also described *where* Jesus is seated...*far above* all principality and power and might. In Christ Jesus, Christian believers are seated together with Him in heavenly places, in the third heaven *(Ephesians 1:20)*. Believers, then, by faith and revelation by the Spirit of God, are in a position to look down on satan's kingdom below them in the second heaven. Believers who do so will uncover satan's strategies and pray effective prayers to prevent or frustrate satan's plans.

- ◆ Third heaven—God's throne, holy angels, saints of God
- ◆ Second heaven—Satan and his fallen angels (principalities, powers, rulers of darkness and spiritual wickedness in high places)
- ◆ First heaven—Earth's atmosphere

When Jesus became man, submitted to dying on the cross, and rose from the dead, He did so that we could exercise His overcoming power and overturn the strategies of the enemy.

TAKING CAPTIVITY CAPTIVE

Jesus' Blood blotted out the ordinances (strategies and judgments) against humankind and nailed them to the cross, and as we have read, He made an open show of his enemies and triumphed over them *(Colossians 2:14,15)*. Jesus routed hell and freed the saints being held there. He took them captive and led them down the streets of Jerusalem on their way to the third heaven *(Matthew 27:52,53)*.

When He ascended into heaven, Jesus sat down at the right hand of the Father. Paul's letter to the Hebrews states that Jesus is ever making intercession *(Hebrews 7:25)*. The Godhead is continually producing doors of escape or preparing pathways of success for God's people. The Heavenly Trinity is fully aware of satan's schemes and observe his every move. They, by the Holy Spirit, freely reveal satan's schemes to any of us who press in to find answers.

Jesus made a way for us to be victorious over satan. Humankind could not have authority over satan while in sin. Therefore, Jesus came to earth as a man to take humankind's punishment. God purposed victory for every one of us even before Adam's fall, because Christ was slain from the foundation of the world *(Revelation 13:8)*. In His death, Jesus destroyed the enemy's power and stripped him of his exalted standing. Father God was faithful in sending Jesus. He was not unfaithful or unjust to leave us unequipped to do battle against the deceiver who had caused the fall of angels and the human race alike.

Throughout the Bible we see numerous examples of victories of faith over satan's devices. Jesus Christ provided a new and living covenant, the glory of which is greater than the old. How much more shall God's people be victorious since Calvary and satan's subsequent defeat!

SECOND HEAVEN BATTLES

Most of us have experienced times when the heavens seemed like they stood hard against our prayers. Most assuredly, there were fallen-angel strategists wrestling against the faith that was petitioning heaven. The second-heaven hosts battle against answers to prayers and try to project that *they* have the greater power in the heavens.

When we ask Jesus into our hearts, each of us becomes a new creation in Christ *(II Corinthians 5:17)*. We also learn that, by faith, we transcend the second heaven and take our place at the right hand of the Father IN JESUS CHRIST, *"And hath raised us up together, and made us sit together in heavenly places in Christ Jesus" (Ephesians 2:6)*. We gain confidence and boldness against the enemy as we understand more fully how, *"Ye are of God, little children, and have overcome them: because greater is he that is in you, than he that is in the world," (I John 4:4)*. The assurance of our position and rights in the spirit realm in Jesus Christ cannot be emphasized enough.

Try to get a picture of an area located in the second heaven that has in it the four divisions of fallen-angel strategists hard at work devising plans against God's people. Seated far above them is Jesus at the right hand of the Father, watching their every move, knowing their every thought and tactic. Jesus hears the prayer or request of His beloved believer. Jesus' interceding request to the

Father comes back as abundant grace as He freely imparts His mind, knowledge and instruction to defeat satan's plan *(John 16: 13-16)*.

We can freely access the throne and receive the answer. However, we often get caught up in many distractions, worries and pursuits which keep us from availing ourselves of *God's strategies.* Strategists in the second heaven realm inspire those very distractions!

Strategists in the second heaven inspire distractions!

Fallen angels may become directly involved in a strategy in which they are in charge, but they do not have ongoing personal contact with individuals. They delegate demons to carry out personal attacks, harassment and information gathering maneuvers.

HOLY ANGELS

God's holy angels are capable and powerful beings. The Father's holy angels continue to carry out the wishes of the Father. We have discussed how Jesus, in the first chapter of John, gave us a picture of angels ascending and descending upon Him, the Son of Man. A host of holy angels are in the presence of the Father and Son in the third heaven. Our Heavenly Father dispatches holy ministering spirits on our behalf because we are redeemed by the Blood of Jesus Christ and have become heirs of salvation *(Hebrews 1:14 and 2:1).* Holy angels are ascending and descending THROUGH THE SECOND HEAVEN TO THE THRONE AND BACK fulfilling God's desire upon His people and bearing with them the impartation of God. God's holy angels continue to ascend and descend upon our prayers.

PREPARING FOR BATTLE

The bottom line of our stand in spiritual warfare is WE MUST BE STRONG IN THE LORD AND THE POWER OF HIS MIGHT. The power of HIS might! We have no basis for battle in anything but what Jesus has already done for us to overcome the wiles (methods) and power of the enemy. We are empowered to enforce what Jesus Christ has already completed at Calvary and established through His resurrection.

SPIRITUAL AND NATURAL

The spiritual is more real than the natural, even though it does not seem so to the natural eye. Natural events and circumstances are temporal, whereas spiritual realities are eternal. Most people realize there is a spirit realm. But what they do not realize is that they are involved in a wrestling match in the midst of all the spiritual activity that is unseen to the natural eye.

Believers are instructed not to be ignorant of satan's devices *(II Corinthians 2:11)*. Many have experienced the fierce intimidation of the enemy. We need to understand we are set on a course of spiritual wrestling for our stand in Christ. We are swiftly learning more of the wrestling and warfare call of the Lord for today. Wrestling, godly wrestling, has rules that give believers the upper hand in overcoming the wiles or methods of the enemy.

CHAPTER 4

WRESTLING RULES

*F*or we wrestle <u>not against</u> flesh and blood, but <u>against</u> principalities, <u>against</u> powers, <u>against</u> the rulers of the darkness of this world, <u>against</u> spiritual wickedness in high places *(Ephesians 6:12, emphasis added)*.

The Apostle Paul issues a command in God's word that instructs believers not to wrestle, or contend, with flesh and blood. "Flesh and blood" clearly identifies that we are not to wrestle with other human beings. The rest of the verse, however, <u>compels</u> us to wrestle *against* principalities, powers, rulers of the darkness of this world and spiritual wickedness in high places. Try to get a picture in your mind of a genuine wrestling match (not the phony theatrical kind) but a high school wrestling match, a world class wrestling competition or perhaps an arm wrestling contest.

> *Spiritual wrestling is the mechanics of pressure and resistance to pressure*

The thing that stands out immediately is that wrestling involves the strategies and mechanics of pressure and resistance to pressure. The definition of wrestling is "to vibrate, to throw down more or less violently, to strike, thrust, to struggle." Wrestlers contend by applying pressure, trying to throw down, wear down, press down and wear out their opponent. The wrestler who is able to apply the most consistent and increasing pressure, as well as maintain strength against the opponent's pressure, is the one who succeeds. Each will move quickly in order to obtain a better hold or position, while keeping the pressure on.

THE VIOLENT TAKE IT BY FORCE

This is a simple illustration of the principle of wrestling which is done in the spiritual realm—pressure and resistance to pressure. Pressures come as a natural part of daily living. However, people who engage in spiritual warfare must realize that much of the pressures that buffet their lives are orchestrated in the heavenly realm. Believers have been commissioned to battle, *"...the kingdom of heaven suffereth violence, and the violent take it by force"* (Matthew 11:12). The second heaven kingdom is a kingdom that is violent against humankind. Satan's hatred is intense. His kingdom is violent against believer and unbeliever alike. His handiwork can be seen in the mutilation and destruction of people in wars, murders and tortures of all kinds against every creed and tongue.

We are called to wage war against the enemy of the spiritual realm. When Jesus stated the violent must take the kingdom by force, he was describing a pressure verses pressure situation. Forms of spiritual battle come into play. Satan's battle is against flesh and blood people. The *believer's* battle is not directed toward flesh and blood but against spiritual personalities set out to kill, steal and destroy *(John 10:10)*.

SEEING THE UNSEEN

How do you wrestle what is unseen with the natural eye? Spiritual warfare is a <u>faith-based warfare</u> because the opposing forces involved are unseen by the natural eye. Spiritual warfare, therefore, can only be carried out by what is learned and understood about spiritual realities. The Bible is the book that is the inspired Word of God. The Bible unmasks satan and his plan and yet reveals the glory and power of God and His plan. The Holy Spirit of God enables seekers to see and understand the truths written there.

The Word of God equips us to see spiritual strategies and discern the enemy's pressures and tactics

Understanding spiritual warfare is not spooky or so spiritual as to be beyond comprehension. *"But the wisdom that is from above is first pure, then peaceable, gentle, and easy to be intreated, full of mercy and good fruits, without partiality, and without hypocrisy"* (James 3:17). Many people shudder when the subject of spiritual warfare arises because they are unaware of facts and information regarding spiritual things. What is unseen to them becomes a source of fear. The Word of God takes what is unseen by the natural and causes it to be seen by the heart and the mind. By reading the Word of God you gain the ability to see what is unseen and receive spiritual eyes and understanding.

Radio waves are unseen to the physical eye, but they are there. The right equipment enables us to see radio waves that cannot be seen without it. Likewise, the Word of God equips believers to *see* what is unseen to the natural eye. Without the equipping of the Word of God to see spiritual strategies, we cannot discern what pressures and tactics are being implemented against us and our loved ones.

WORKS OF THE FLESH AND THE FALLEN NATURE

Some may ask, "But what about the flesh? Isn't a lot of our warfare just the battle of the flesh verses the spirit which Paul talked about in Romans 7?" Yes, the fallen nature which humankind received because of Adam's failure has produced a disposition toward sin. However, believers have been given a new nature and the ability— in Christ, to overcome. Believers in Jesus Christ do not have an excuse to sin. They are directed to crucify the flesh *(Romans 6:6,11)* and not give place to the enemy *(Ephesians 4:27)*.

Satan, as god of this world, is not happy about those who have been snatched from his kingdom. He is aware of humankind's fallen nature tendencies and works diligently to take advantage of any weakness there. Yes, human beings may have an inclination toward living life in fleshly attitudes and weaknesses, but God has given us all that is necessary to overcome the flesh and the works of the flesh. Our victory is in Christ Jesus and in Him are the abilities to overcome. *"There is therefore now no condemnation to them which are in Christ Jesus, who walk not after the flesh, but after the Spirit"* *(Romans 8:1)*. We can determine and make every effort not to let the fleshly nature rule our lives. When the Lord says not to give place to the devil, our flesh is one of the "places" we are to protect from the enemy's influence and control. If you read Ephesians 4:20-32, it clearly indicates that the devil will take advantage of the flesh if he is allowed to, *"Neither give place to the devil"* *(Ephesians 4:27)*.

WHAT ABOUT TESTINGS?

There are times when the problems we face, or afflictions we suffer, are testings from the Lord to purge and purify. However, correction from God does not injure and wound us. A loving father or mother does not injure and wound his child in order to teach them. Discipline may include a stinging swat to the derriere, but you do not break an arm in order to teach the child not to steal. The enemy has often brought doctrines that blame God for injurious things happening to us. The Lord said to me, "How can you trust someone who you are afraid may injure you?" The answer is, of course, "You can't." The Lord wants us to discern the difference between testing from God and oppression from satan. It makes all the difference in how you respond to the afflictions that occur in our lives.

When God tests a person, He wants to reveal what is buried deep within. You really don't know what you know—and don't know—until you are tested. In Deuteronomy 8:2,3, I believe the people of God were afflicted so that THEY would know what was within them.

ABRAHAM AND ISAAC

It may seem like a contradiction, but let's look at Abraham during his testing. Abraham was directed by God to sacrifice Isaac *(Genesis 22:1-18)*. This test would be required of only one man for the purpose of establishing an eternal covenant.

Even though it has been taught that Abraham profoundly anguished about sacrificing his son—I personally do not believe Abraham ended up anguishing over Isaac in the way it has generally been depicted. Romans 4:21 states that Abraham was FULLY persuaded that God would do as He promised. We also read his faith was even to the point that he believed God would raise his son from the dead if He needed to, *"By faith Abraham, when he was tried, offered up Isaac: and he that had received the promises offered up his only begotten son, Of whom it was said, That in Isaac shall thy seed be called: Accounting that God was able to raise him up, even from the dead; from whence also he received him in a figure" (Hebrews 11:17-19).* I believe Abraham was willing and had such confidence in God that even if the angel had not stopped him, he would have seen Isaac brought back to life. Abraham's faith was established before he ever left home. God had given him revelation of prophetic dimension. He believed God's love in the surrender of his son. This was the kind of man God could choose to make covenant with—a covenant through which God could send of His Son—the Messiah. All the nations of the earth would be blessed, for it is through the lineage of Abraham

that the promised Messiah would come. Was Abraham's faith
tested? Certainly, because faith without works is dead *(James 2:26)*.
When God told Abraham what to do—most likely in his place of
prayer—Abraham trusted the Lord.

THE LORD WILL PROVIDE

God did not say, "Okay, *I* believe that *you* believe so I am going
to make an eternal covenant with you through which my Son will
become flesh and dwell among men. He will become the sacrifice
of sin of all the ages by dying a painful shameful death at the hands
of wicked men." Faith requires works—works instituted by the
direction of God. Abraham loaded the donkey with firewood for
the fire. Abraham did not take a "just in case" sacrifice along—even
Isaac asked about the animal which would be sacrificed. Abraham
made a profound statement, "the Lord will provide himself a
lamb" which was prophetic of the Messiah, Jesus Christ, the Lamb
of God. Abraham raised his knife, fully persuaded that if Isaac's
life was taken, his son would live again *(Genesis 22:5)*. Father God
instructed the angel to speak His message to his friend Abraham,
*"...for now I know that thou fearest God, seeing thou hast not withheld
thy son, thine only son from me."* Isaac was not harmed.

Did Father God *really* just find out that Abraham would be
faithful to obey His direction? God is all knowing. He knew
Abraham's every thought and innermost motive. I believe the
"now" was: You have now fulfilled all the requirements and testing
required to become my covenant man through which my beloved
Son, my only begotten Son, may come in the flesh.

FOLLOWING ABRAHAM'S FAITH

Abraham also was profoundly established in a truth—the covenant
would continue for all generations. He would teach it and declare
it to Isaac, who in turn was to teach it to Jacob and Jacob to his
sons from generation to generation.

How do you and I arrive at faith that follows after us? II Peter
1:5-9 says to add to faith, virtue; add to virtue, knowledge; add
to knowledge, temperance; add to temperance, patience; add to
patience, godliness; add to godliness, brotherly kindness; and add
to brotherly kindness, love. The fleshy attitudes and behaviors we

have in our lives are being rooted out. All of these directives are not to undermine and destroy the person but to build strength and character. In the midst of becoming mature in godly things we will have opportunity for them to be refined, *"Knowing this, that the trying of your faith worketh patience. But let patience have her perfect work, that ye may be perfect and entire, wanting nothing"* (*James 1:3, 4*).

How can we tell if we are in a test from God or whether we are wrestling against satan's forces? Ask Him! Ask the Holy Spirit to reveal what is going on! He will reveal to us when our faith is under assault and when we are being refined and polished for the Master's use. Jesus is the Purifier and the Refiner (*Malachi 3:2, 3*). The same love that became the sacrificial Lamb also exquisitely shapes our hearts and lives for holy service.

SPIRITUAL WRESTLING

Much of our spiritual wrestling is experienced in the mind and the senses. One of the greatest senses we will wrestle against is the sense or emotion of fear. Fear is intended to cripple and paralyze. Additionally, fear is intended to stop any forward progress. Fear produces confusion. Satan makes use of numerous demons in his various maneuvers because of the effectiveness of their task. Demons of fear are assigned along with other demons to work in conjunction with one another to paralyze or immobilize their target and create a lack of resistance to other demonic activity.

Fear is a spirit, a demon spirit, and should be dealt with as such (*II Timothy 1:7, Mark 16*). Demons of fear can be very subtle or very "in your face." They often roar to instill fear. The same principle is used in battle charges or athletic games, where opponents yell and roar in order to intimidate their foe. We cast out demons in the Name of Jesus Christ. The roar of a demon cowers when the Lion of the Tribe of Judah in us roars back! (You will read more about demon characteristics in Chapter 10).

Demons of fear can take up residence and stay with their target for as long as they are tolerated. They pour lies into our minds then watch for the effect through our words. We need to realize that the words we speak help inform demons of their success or failure. We often discuss fear we feel and lament of the torment we experience. Demons hear those words and relish in their achievement. *Demons know what we think by what we say.* They also read our actions, facial expressions and attitudes. They gleefully watch our reactions when they see they have pressed the right buttons to get their desired result.

However, we begin to thwart the enemy when we recognize that God has not given us a spirit of fear, but of power, and of love, and of a sound mind. *(II Timothy 1:7)*. Fear is the opposite of power, love and soundness of mind. Whenever we feel powerless or hopeless, feel unloved and abused, or confused and unstable, we are being harassed and assaulted by demons of fear. Pressure from fear must be met with pressure of fearlessness that comes from confidence in the love and power of God within us. Fear is an assault against the love and faithfulness of the Lord toward his beloved. Demons of fear tremble when confronted by boldness of the Lord in us.

You may be surprised to know demonic informers have spent years gathering statistical data on you in order to predict your reactions and responses. That's why we need to get beyond the patterns we have set in the past and break the repetitious ways we've handled pressure, responded to trials or simply given up.

BEWARE OF METHODS

The "wiles" of the devil spoken of in Ephesians 6 can be defined as "methods." Beware of entering into methods where satan can anticipate your actions and reactions. If he can figure out your course, he can easily set up snares and ambushes. The Lord gives His people daily bread which can be interpreted as daily courses of action and direction. We must seek His direction to avoid demonic pitfalls.

Think of the President for a moment. When he travels, his route is a highly guarded secret. Why? Because anticipated paths give time for assaults to be planned and carried out. Likewise, Christians are ambassadors for God Almighty whom the enemy would love to assault. Seeking the Lord and being aware of his counsel is powerful protection. Obedience is also an integral part of the Lord's protection. As we grow in obedience, we become skillful in avoiding the snares and traps set before us by the enemy.

David was a wise man of war who sought the Lord's counsel each time he went into battle. For instance, David did not rush into battle with the Philistines in the Valley of Rephaim without consulting God. I Chronicles 14:10 tells us, *"And David enquired of God, saying, Shall I go up against the Philistines? And wilt thou deliver them into mine hand? And the Lord said unto him, Go up; for I will deliver them into thine hand."*

Some time later the Philistines arrayed themselves against God's people again. David did not presume to attack without asking God. This time God said, *"...Go not up after them; turn away from them, and come upon them over against the mulberry trees. And it shall be, when thou shalt hear a sound of going in the tops of the mulberry trees, that then thou shalt go out to battle: for God is gone forth before thee to smite the host of the Philistines. David therefore did as God commanded him..."* (I Chronicles 14:14-16).

David faced the *same enemy* in the *same valley* with the *same outward circumstances,* but the Lord gave him a *different* strategy. The Lord gave him the victory in both battles, but the Lord of God's army led each assault in a different way.

We can take a valuable lesson from David, a man skilled in the ways of battle. He did not depend upon past successes to determine the counsel of the Lord for future battles. He knew the Lord had the wisdom to know the enemy's maneuvers and would give him the strategy to overcome.

BECOMING MATURE

To be effective in spiritual warfare, we must continually mature in the Lord. Hebrews 5:14 explains, *"But strong meat belongeth to them that are of full age, even those who by reason of use have their senses exercised to discern both good and evil."* Mature believers are no longer dependent on others to feed them, stroke them and keep them from whining. They are able to handle the solid matters of life and living.

Believers who regularly and consciously exercise their senses in sorting out what is good and what is evil will train their eyes, ears, feelings and emotions to discern between the two. God has given us our senses as an avenue for direction. Many times the "gut feeling" is counsel from God in the situation. Our body is the temple of the Holy Spirit, and as His temple, the Holy Spirit takes His place to exercise Jesus' authority in this world. We have the mind of Christ and the personal habitation of the Holy Spirit within. We are enabled by God to do battle against the evil host set against humankind.

WRESTLING REQUIRES COMMITMENT

We should not wade into spiritual warfare if we are wavering in our decision to wrestle. *"But let him ask in faith, nothing wavering. For he that wavereth is like a wave of the sea driven with the wind and tossed. For let not that man think that he shall receive any thing of the Lord. A double minded man is unstable in all his ways"* (James 1: 6-8). God is not sitting on His throne withholding good things from us until we someday, somehow get into un-wavering faith. No, the writer of James is telling readers there is opposition to receiving what God wants to give.

Just as in wrestling, wavering causes us to relax, lose resistance and ultimately weaken under the pressure applied by evil forces. Satan attempts to toss God's people around and keep them from standing strong. If you don't know what to do, simply ask God. *"If any of you lack wisdom, let him ask of God, that giveth to all men liberally, and upbraideth not; and it shall be given him"* (James 1:5).

Faith is on the first line of defense against what satan desires to keep from God's people

Wavering is satan's strategy. God says, "Don't waver, I'll give you what you need, just ask me. Don't let anyone or anything keep you from receiving!"

WRESTLING REQUIRES A DECISION

To become unwavering requires a decision. Once the wrestling has begun, pressure is inevitable. That is what wrestling is—pressure verses pressure. As hard as it seems at times, we must understand that the battle between the kingdom of satan and the kingdom of God is not free of pressure. We can't wait until we are in the heat of battle to decide if we can handle the pressure. Satanic pressure is designed to make us quit. Our mind, emotions and senses will feel the full frontal attack.

A decision to meet whatever pressure that may come with the power of the Lord means that we have already won the battle!

WRESTLING REQUIRES ENDURANCE

Our strategy against the enemy is not only to apply pressure, but to resist as well. That means we need endurance to wrestle. What will help you endure when you're tired and want to quit? The secret lies in knowing that satan, the father of lies, has built his whole case against you on the unstable foundation of lies. That means simply you will win if you endure. Jesus was able to endure the cross for the joy that was set before him. We are able to endure incalculable obstacles and discouragement when we have an assurance of the final outcome.

—⌀⌀⌀—

The decision to endure eliminates the decision of when to give up

—⌀⌀⌀—

Endurance means, "to remain firm under suffering or misfortune, to continue in the same state, to bear with patience." Hebrews 10: 35, 36 beautifully reveals this double fisted approach to warfare regarding decision and endurance, *"Cast not away therefore your confidence, which hath great recompence of reward. For ye have need of patience, that, after ye have done the will of God, ye might receive the promise."*

WRESTLING REQUIRES TIME

Walking out the wrestling pressures of our lives often takes time. Some victories come more quickly than others, but many times our confrontations can be long. In each area that becomes a battlefront, God is able to sustain and equip His beloved children.

It is interesting to note that one of the definitions of wrestling is "to vibrate." It is intriguing to think what might be learned about this definition. A wrestling match can become so intense that the wrestlers begin to shake. The straining muscles almost vibrate when victory is imminent. Our souls can come under similar shaking and vibrating from the intensity of spiritual battle. It may seem as though satan's power is increasing when in fact, he is about to collapse. Satan and his cohorts do not have long term enduring power when they are resisted in the Name of Jesus and the power of the Holy Spirit abiding within us. God is good and His mercy *endures* forever. His mercy enables us to endure, *"...as we have received mercy, we faint not"* *(II Corinthians 4:1)*. Call on His mercy in those times of straining, vibrating pressure. Receive mercy and strength to not just make it, but take the victory by force. The violent (against satan's schemes and pressures) have conquest promised. Satan's desire for believers is breakdown. God's desire for each one of us is breakthrough.

Satan tries to get our eyes on the <u>short-term effect</u> rather than on the <u>long-term power of God</u>. Satan has short-term ability and thrust. God has eternal purposes for everything. Therefore, He works out eternal plans and purposes even in the midst of satan's evil workings in this world.

<u>SATANIC PRESSURE</u>

Satan applies pressure through accusations, harassment, oppression, discouragement, doubt, by challenging a person's worth, reputation and convictions, only to name a few. Great numbers of demons are assigned to gather information. They gather facts and keep copious records which they give to satanic superiors who examine them in order to develop strategies. Satan's purpose in gathering information from demon informants is to become aware of the areas where evil strategies may work against the person. The informants also keep records of how long a person can last under various pressure situations. How long did it take for someone to fall under similar circumstances? When God gives *His* input and strategy into the problem, He will reveal to us how to not fall into the same scenario, and will provide what is needed to bring lasting strength, faith and confidence.

Where we consistently try and fail, chances are our resistance record is well known to evil planners. In those instances, press in hard against the enemy's pressure and misinformation to hear what God's strategy is and get His direction. It builds confidence in us as we see the old patterns loose their hindering ability. That is why it is good to testify—to tell others of victories in our lives. It reinforces our confidence in God and it turns resistance against satan. Don't keep God's works to yourself!

FINANCIAL WAR ZONE

If finances are the area that causes the greatest discouragement, then satan will apply pressure on the person through breakdowns, impulsive buying, debt, fear of lack, stinginess, and a poverty mindset. Strategists check their records to see what has caused the person to stumble in the past and develop similar plans for the next attack. Believers who know their own weaknesses will overcome as they seek the Lord for wisdom and strength. The Lord knows we have weaknesses and He does not condemn us for having them. He has, instead, given Himself so weakness does not rule. *"...My grace is sufficient for thee: for my strength is made perfect in weakness. Most gladly therefore will I rather glory in my infirmities, that the power of Christ may rest upon me"* (II Corinthians 12: 9).

Finances are an area that everyone will, in one way or another, come under spiritual attack. Every person is either trying to gain money or trying not to lose money. Behind all the effort is the financial emphasis of the two warring kingdoms. *"No servant can serve two masters: for either he will hate the one, and love the other; or else he will hold to the one, and despise the other. Ye cannot serve God and mammon* (money)*"* (Luke 16:13, explanation added).

We are warned about financial pressures, *"For the love of money is the root of all evil: which while some coveted after, they have erred from the faith, and pierced themselves through with many sorrows"* (I Timothy 6:10). If the love of money is the <u>root of all evil</u>, then money must play a major part in the workings of satan's evil kingdom. The Lord says we cannot serve two masters, God and money, so money holds powerful implications to the person who stands on the battlefield of financial bombardments.

GOD'S STRATEGY FOR FINANCIAL BLESSINGS

The Lord's answer to financial blessings involves giving, *"Give, and it shall be given unto you..."* (Luke 6:38). Tithes, offerings and giving as directed by the Holy Spirit are *not a passive activity* in the kingdom of God. If the love of money is a root of *all* evil, it must require much attention and asserted pressure applications from satan's kingdom—the pressures that come with making the decision to tithe and give have the full attention of fallen-angel strategists. They promote a lengthy portfolio of excuses and reasons for not tithing or giving.

Their success blocks the flow of provision and protection from heaven.

Tithes and offerings to the Lord apply pressure to evil strategists. They must stand aside as God marches His provision into the hands of those who trust Him for their needs and desires. Those who tithe and give offerings can be encouraged their obedience has levied a blow to the enemy. Expectation of godly blessing gives the giver added strength and endurance during the wrestling pressures from the kingdom of mammon.

Money pressure comes in many forms. People can be tempted to cheat on the job or in a place of trust. Taking money from someone in your household without his or her knowledge or permission, not telling the waitress she forgot to add the cost of coffee to the bill, or perhaps buying a dress and taking it back (really intending only to wear it once), are subtle ways we are tricked into mishandling money. Money pressures, large and small, are under the watchful eye of both kingdoms. A door is but a small opening into a larger room. A small act of obedience or disobedience is a door into a larger room of blessing or sorrow.

We can learn to experience the faithfulness of our loving Heavenly Father. He gave His most precious gift of all, Jesus Christ, His Son. As we continue to grow deeper in our personal relationship with the Lord, we will gain an unshakable confidence in the character and loving kindness of God.

TIME PRESSURES

Time restrictions and deadlines are another favorite tactical tool of the enemy. Time pressures draw people into areas where they might not normally go. Time pressures cause people to spend money they cannot afford. Time pressures seek to draw people out of God's sphere of protection. In rushing to meet deadlines, racing to get somewhere, or making hasty decisions, they become vulnerable to traps set up by the enemy. Applying pressure to satan's kingdom isn't difficult when you refuse to let time pressures stop you from seeking God and waiting on Him. You cannot be led by the Spirit and driven by pressure. God has an answer to time and deadlines pressures, *"Be careful* (anxious or filled with panic) *for nothing; but in every thing by prayer and supplication with thanksgiving let your requests be made known unto God"* (Philippians 4:6, explanation added).

We must understand fallen angels are limited in number and cannot be everywhere at one time; *they* are under time restraints. They will apply pressure to try to put us into *their* time frame. When we are able to resist the temptation and pressure of time, then we free ourselves from potential damage.

—◦◦◦—

The Word of God will always apply pressure to satan's pressure. Consistently and fervently applied, it will undo any pressure satan or his cohorts can instigate.

—◦◦◦—

DECISIONS

Decision-making is an area for great pressure because of the positive or negative consequences of the decision. Fear, doubt and indecision fueled by ignorance create a wrestling in the mind because decisions can ensnare or set free. You apply pressure in the spirit realm by engraving scriptures like Proverbs 3:5,6; Psalm 119: 105, 133; and Jeremiah 33:3 upon your heart and mind as you make decisions.

PRESSURES HAVE MANY FACES

Pressure comes in many ways. It can come through circumstances, and it can come through people. Most people are not aware of the evil influences that are affecting their actions and conversations. It is by the Spirit of the Lord that we can discern how satan's evil kingdom is working against us.

Do not be mistaken—pressure will be applied against anyone who holds influence in your life. People such as family members, acquaintances and co-workers are targeted to bring pressure against the one who spiritual strategists want to overcome. (We will read more about pressure from those in authority in Chapter 11).

The Lord comforted his disciples, *"...In the world ye shall have tribulation: but be of good cheer; I have overcome the world"* (John 16:33).

The Lord has a plan for overcoming tribulation. Ask Him for the step-by-step instructions.

We must also be objective to discern if evil is working through ourselves. One day I pondered a plan to get my husband to do something I wanted him to do. The Lord interrupted my mental conversation.

"Quit your manipulating!" He ordered as I lifted the stack of plates into the cupboard. I didn't think I was doing anything wrong. My mental reasoning excused my motive, but God looked upon the heart.

"Me?" I dumbfoundedly replied. I was shocked by His correction— unaware I needed it.

You cannot get God's results with satan's tactics

"You cannot get God's results with satan's tactics," He added. "Wow! What a concept!" I thought. Isn't that like God to amaze us in the midst of correcting us?

He showed me how my thought processes were leading me into manipulation regarding the situation, and to carry out those thoughts would not be godly, but evil. I needed to repent and let go of my desire for control in the situation. Repentance applies great pressure on evil and, in this case, shut the door of manipulation inspired by evil influence. "Solutions" that do not line up with God's character or teaching should be discerned and rejected.

ANNOYANCES ARE NOT LITTLE

Pressure can come from small annoyances that have the "dripping faucet" effect, where the annoyance itself consumes our emotional and mental patience. For instance, evil strategists make use of parroting demon spirits that do nothing more than sit on a person's shoulder (so to speak) and whisper, repeating over and over a particular phrase. The repetition is intended to wear down the person's resistance and mentally deprive the person of power. One such parroting spirit chants, "I can't take any more, I can't take any more, I can't take any more." Although the demon has little power, if left alone to carry on the continual "dripping" of mental poison into the mind, it can produce an effect that will defeat or destroy. (This will be discussed more in Chapter 10).

Keep in mind the fallen angel is not the one who is applying direct pressure but a demon that has nothing to do BUT sit there and at certain opportunities whisper its deadly message. Its only strengths are its words and its hiding place.

Pressure against this type of activity is done first of all by RECOGNIZING that the *words are not godly words and the intent is not a godly intent.* Dealing with the demon is simple. Mark 16 says that in the Name of Jesus believers cast out demons. They must depart. *However, the fallen angel who assigned the demon must also be dealt with.* If it is not dealt with, then sooner or later, the situation will replay itself. The strategist will try to work again even if the parroting demon is removed. Therefore, confronting and wrestling against the *strategists* is where the pressure applied will set you free, because the root of the assault is dealt with. This may involve investigating your own thought processes and evaluating what pathway is being granted. Is it what the Lord would want? Is the end result of the suggestions coming to your mind what *you* want?

The Lord will help you find the answers to your innermost desires and needs. *"Behold, thou desirest truth in the inward parts: and in the hidden part thou shalt make me to know wisdom"* (Psalm 51:6). The Lord desires us to be free and He will help us to know wisdom. What a promise! How can He do that? *"...If ye continue in my word... And ye shall know the truth, and the truth shall make you free"* (John 8:31, 32). The Word of God and the counsel of the Holy Spirit will give divine wisdom and understanding to those who seek answers.

RUN, BABY, RUN

Examples of other forms of pressure are found in the story of Samson and Delilah (Judges 16). Samson placed himself in a pressure situation when he entered an area where he compromised his call from God and his faith—he rested in the lap of his enemy. While Delilah was entertaining him, his fleshly desires and appetites caused him to be blinded to the intent of his enemy. Three times Delilah pressed him for the secret to his strength. She emotionally pressed and pressed him by inquiring, *"...Tell me, I pray thee, wherein thy great strength lieth, and wherewith thou mightest be bound to afflict thee" (Judges 16:6)*. She accused him of lying to her, not loving her and mocking her, when her intent was to discover his secret and cause his destruction.

Finally, *"And it came to pass, when she pressed him daily with her words, and urged him, so that his soul was vexed unto death; That he told her all his heart..." (Judges 16:16,17)*. His ears were deaf to the deceit of her words. He was spiritually blind to his temptress's intent, and he ended up physically blinded as they put out his eyes as part of their torment to him, and then threw him into prison. Samson's best reaction to Delilah's pressure would have been to leave. *"Depart from evil, and do good: seek peace, and pursue it" (Psalm 34:14)*.

Sometimes the Holy Spirit will bear witness within us to follow peace. He might instruct us to leave a situation of impending conflict, confrontation or strife. Sometimes the Lord's answer to pressure is to leave—leave the room, leave the premises, leave the situation, maybe leave the relationship which is seducing you into destructive areas. Where evil may be luring you into its grasp, God says, "Depart from evil."

Satan applies pressure with the intent of getting us to speak unadvisedly with our lips—to say things, to make commitments, to reveal something, to pass judgment. Basically, satan's desire is to ensnare people by the words of their own

The pressure of the moment will pass!

tongues, just as happened to Samson in revealing his secret. The same thing happened to King Herod when he promised anything to the damsel who danced before him. He was caught in his words when the damsel requested the head of John the Baptist.

Much pressure comes at us regarding the words of our mouth. Sometimes the answer to satan's harassing is *not to answer*. The pressure of the moment will pass.

If an answer is to be given, the Lord will give it to you. Consider the counsel of the Holy Spirit when impressed to answer. The Bible tells us, *"Settle it therefore in your hearts, not to meditate before what ye shall answer: For I will give you a mouth and wisdom, which all your adversaries shall not be able to gainsay* (refute) *nor resist" (Luke 21:14,15 explanation added)*.

WRESTLING REQUIRES
DISCIPLINE OF THE TONGUE

We must understand effective wrestling means we become disciplined in our words. Like we read earlier, there are demons listening to our words and passing on details of our lives to evil strategists. Knowing this, it sheds a whole new light on the power of our words. Scriptures admonish us to guard our words, for words bring protection or defeat, *"For by thy words thou shalt be justified, and by thy words thou shalt be condemned"* (Matthew 12:37) and *"Death and life are in the power of the tongue..."* (Proverbs 18:21). The Book of Proverbs has many nuggets that tell us of the dangers of ill-spoken words such as, *"A fool's mouth is his destruction, and his lips are the snare of his soul"* (Proverbs 18:7). James warns us that our tongues, though a little member of our bodies, can kindle great fires, change courses of lives and defile the body *(James 3:3-10)*.

Your ability to wrestle effectively will greatly depend on the use and control of the words you speak. Words contain the ability to shape life or promote death; therefore, our words are powerful weapons in the spirit realm. Why? Because the power of heaven or the power of hell are released by them.

WORDS REVEAL THE HEART

We can become wise about what we speak, *"...The heart of the wise teacheth his mouth, and addeth learning to his lips"* (Proverbs 16:23). You will be able to see what is in your heart by what comes out of your mouth in times of pressure, *"...out of the abundance of the heart the mouth speaketh"* (Matthew 12:34). Sometimes pressure situations bring out strength and wisdom we did not know was in us. There are also times when besetting sins and spiritual weaknesses come to light. Now, don't get condemned about that—become wise. When we *learn* from our wrestling episodes we grow more skillful. We become informed about what ungodly things may be lurking in our heart—things which are keeping us from God's best. Many times such revelations give us the opportunity to deal with areas in our hearts and minds that have given our enemy an advantage over us *(Proverbs 17:3)*.

So don't get discouraged or depressed about what appears to be wrestling "take downs." Remember you are in Holy Spirit training.

He is helping you become strong in every area in order to overcome!

POSSESS YOUR SOUL

The soul—the mind, will and emotions—will be the target of the enemy. Even though your mind, will and emotions will become an area of assault, the Bible tells us, *"In your patience possess ye your souls" (Luke 21:19)*. To possess your soul is to guard it as a precious and valuable possession. The Amplified version explains, *"By your steadfastness and patient endurance you shall win the true life of your souls" (Luke 21:19 AMP)*.

Keep in mind that the Holy Spirit desires to reveal Jesus to believers, and Jesus desires to reveal the Father to His people *(Luke 10:22)*. The more you have a revelation of who the Holy Spirit is, who Jesus is, and who the Father is, the more you will be equipped to apply pressure in the spirit realm.

AGAINST—DEFINED

The Apostle Paul emphasized the word "against" when listing each area of our warfare *(Ephesians 6:12)*. He said AGAINST principalities, AGAINST powers, AGAINST the rulers of darkness of this world, AGAINST spiritual wickedness in high places. Wrestling must be done against each of these divisions.

Strong's Concordance describes against as "motion towards, accession to, or nearness of." We need to aggressively charge against the enemy when under assault, with the intent to take back what has been stolen.

DON'T GIVE UP!
DON'T GIVE UP!
DONNNNNN'T GIVE UP!

Believers need to keep pressing, pressing and pressing against the pressure that is set against us from the enemy. Hebrews 10:32 describes the struggle that follows being "illuminated" or coming into light. *"But call to remembrance the former days, in which, after ye were illuminated, ye endured a great fight of afflictions."* There will be a fight of afflictions, reproaches and abuse.

We all become weary of the fight at times. In such a moment of weariness I complained to the Lord one day. He gently drew me to this verse and asked, "Do you want illumination or not? If you receive illumination, with it comes freedom that requires a fight. If not, you may choose to remain UNilluminated and remain in the bondage that accompanies it. It's your choice." I decided I would not murmur and complain about having to engage in spiritual struggles because my heart is set upon greater freedom and victory in every area of my life. How about you?

The Bible promises we will be rewarded if we don't give up. *"Cast not away therefore your confidence, which hath great recompense of reward. For ye have need of patience, that, after ye have done the will of God, ye might receive the promise"* (Hebrews 10:35-37). Like Paul, we are called to have confidence and patience and to PRESS TOWARD the mark for the prize of the high calling of God in Christ Jesus *(Philippians 3:14)*. Why do we need to press? The prize of the high calling of God is an awesome fulfillment of the specific impartation of God placed within each of us. It does not come by natural or worldly endowment. The pathway to the prize requires pressing—pressing against the pressure that comes with wrestling.

SATANIC PRESSURE OR DEMONIC PRESSURE

Remember that *satanic* pressures produced by fallen angels can only endure as long as they feel they are making progress in their goal and they are encouraged to continue. They keep records of past successes and failures and how long their target was able to endure. The key to success is to OUTLAST the enemy's assault with godly pressure.

Satanic record keeping which shows their defeat over and over will tend to weary *them* of wanting to be defeated again. The result is greater day-to-day victory for the believer.

Demonic pressures endure for as long as demons are tolerated, ignored or unidentified. They are the nagging type of spirits that flee under command but try to worm their way back if allowed. If not, they must move on.

Recognize the difference. Pressure against satanic influences is different than pressure against demonic forces. Pressure against the *satanic* realm must be done with a knowledge of our place and position in Christ Jesus. Pressure against the demonic realm means casting demons out in the Name of Jesus Christ of Nazareth, and replacing the void with the Holy Spirit. For example, when we cast out the demon of jealousy, we need to replace the void with the Fruit of the Holy Spirit: Love and acceptance of the goodness of God. Both demons and fallen angels are subject to Jesus' authority through the believer!

FASTING

We apply pressure to the flesh by God-led fasting coupled with prayer. The fleshly nature of a person is an area of weakness common to the human race. Throughout the Bible, fasting afflicted the soul in order to draw the person closer to God. Fasting does not change God; it changes the person. The appetites and pleasures of the body demand obedience and attention, whereas fasting (and prayer) applies pressure against those demands and quiets the soul before God. Fasting is not performance before God, but a godly disciplining of the body and soul in order to gain spiritual strength and insight, as well as resist the effects of evil hindrances and manifestations.

JESUS IS VICTOR

Jesus is the Captain of our Salvation *(Hebrews 2:10)*. He is the Lord of Hosts *(Isaiah 54:5)*. He is seated far above principalities and powers. He has provided a pathway of success specific to each person. *Strength for wrestling comes from Jesus and our life in Him.*

We are not called to war or to wrestle in our own strength and ability. The groundwork is laid in the command, *"...be strong in the LORD, and in the power of his might"* *(Ephesians 6:10, emphasis added).*

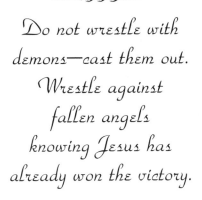

Do not wrestle with demons—cast them out. Wrestle against fallen angels knowing Jesus has already won the victory.

eavenly Father, I come in the Name of Jesus. I thank You for Your Holy Spirit whom You have sent to help me. I now ask for Your knowledge, wisdom and understanding concerning the words I speak. I ask for forgiveness for the times I have sinned against You with my tongue, and I ask You to cleanse me from all unrighteousness. I ask for forgiveness for unwise or foolish words I have spoken over others or myself. I ask for the Blood of Jesus to cleanse me from all defilement that I have allowed because of the words I have spoken. I ask You Lord to set watch upon my tongue and teach me according to truth. Make me wise and powerful in the words of life by the Word of Life, the Bible. I ask You to strengthen me and teach me how to possess my soul so that my mind, my will, and emotions glorify You. I ask You to cause my tongue to be an instrument for Your use. I call upon the Holy Spirit to help me be obedient to Your counsel. I desire that my lips declare Your praises and give You glory in my words and in my deeds.

Lord, I ask You, by the power of the Holy Spirit in me, teach me how to wrestle the enemy in wisdom and in truth. Give me spiritual eyes to receive Your spiritual revelation and direction. Give me counsel from Your heart how to apply what I learn and how to carry out Your instructions. Give me mercy to endure and overcome. I acknowledge that You are faithful, and give me abundantly what I need to succeed. I ask for the mighty hand of God to strengthen me and establish me on Your solid foundation of truth and faith. In Jesus' Name. Amen.

CHAPTER 5

HOW TO BE STRONG IN THE LORD AND IN THE POWER OF HIS MIGHT

T he battle against the enemy cannot to be fought with earthly weapons. Children of the King of kings are warriors along with the hosts of heaven, and do not use carnal, or fleshly, weaponry. Our weapons *"are not carnal, but are mighty through God to the pulling down of strong holds"* (II Corinthians 10:4). When we enter spiritual battle, we are not entering with resources within our own human nature.

The spirit realm is unseen with our natural eyes, but is experienced through forces and laws as real as gravity. You cannot see the law of gravity, but you understand and respect its power when you near the edge of a cliff. The spirit realm is real, and the manifestations of the forces operating in it can be seen in the natural realm.

For instance, the moment you asked Jesus into your heart, you were equipped and "issued" everything you needed in order to overcome satan and his host. During that instant you also received God's Communicator and Arsenal Chief, the Holy Spirit. Everything within Jesus is now available for your life, godliness and warfare. The difficulty is getting it from your spirit to your mind and understanding. Each of us must endeavor to not just learn *about* Jesus, but to continually gain greater understanding and personal fellowship with the person of Jesus Christ. Jesus wants to have personal relationship and fellowship with each of us.

How do we strengthen fellowship with each other? By talking to one another, sharing struggles and victories, showing mutual acceptance and respect, and expressing love and commitment. Jesus wants us to draw close to Him and allow Him to impart Himself to us. His great love is awaiting expression in our lives, desiring to meet needs and give gifts. He wants to enable those who are weak to find strength, those who weep to find comfort, those who wander in darkness to find their pathway in light, those who are confused to find truth, and those who are afraid, to find peace. He is ALL IN ALL.

The Lord has given us many ways to learn and grow, such as

through inspired preaching and teaching of those in ministry, the testimonies of believers, Bible studies, books, music and many more ways. He has equipped pastors, teachers, evangelists, apostles and prophets to <u>equip the saints</u>. Servants of the Lord are all endowed with a measure of Himself in order to benefit all.

Loving the Lord is the most powerful force we have to enable us to overcome. We obey because we love Him, and when we comprehend the love with which He loves us, we receive the provision He has made for us to overcome.

THE LORD'S PRESENCE

It is often during worship that the Lord reveals the facet about Himself that will defeat the enemy in our lives. Distractions, time constraints, interruptions, physical appetites and desires, as well as error, seek to keep us from entering into the presence of the Lord. These distractions keep us from pressing in to hear what the Lord is saying. Evil strategists are fully aware that when we press past them into the presence of the Lord, they suffer defeat. Examples are Daniel coming under persecution when he opened his windows to pray three times a day *(Daniel 6:10-13)* and Peter being harassed by the damsel possessed by a spirit of divination on his way to prayer *(Acts 16:16)*.

Pressures were applied from the spiritual but manifested in natural circumstances. What family has not had the same type of buffeting and harassment when they prepare to worship or pray? Sunday mornings become war zones in many households.

WEAPONRY

When we consider that our warfare is comprised of confrontations between the kingdom of light and the kingdom of darkness, we must not be ignorant of the weaponry used by each kingdom's army. Just as an earthly army would not merely amass rifles when the enemy is amassing tanks, the army of the Lord must not be distracted with things that do not pertain to the battle in which they are engaged.

The Body of Christ needs to investigate and be aware of the enemy's arsenal (which will be discussed later) as well as to become educated about the resources and abilities endowed to them by their Lord and Commander, Jesus Christ. Otherwise, we could get overwhelmed at the appearance of the enemy's weaponry. When we are knowledgeable of the power and authority we have within us in Christ Jesus, we will have confidence as we go forth to defeat satan's arsenal.

The most important thing each of us must understand is Jesus has already won the victory. When He died on the cross, he stripped satan of all power and authority, *"...having canceled the written code, with its regulations, that was against us and that stood opposed to us, he took it away, nailing it to the cross. And having disarmed the powers and authorities, he made a public spectacle of them, triumphing over them by the cross"* (Colossians 2:14,15 NIV).

> *Believers are hid in Christ in the spiritual realm, and He is hid in believers in the natural realm*

Jesus ripped the keys of out of the hands of hell and of death, *"I am he that liveth, and was dead; and behold, I am alive for evermore, Amen; and have the keys of hell and of death"* (Revelation 1:18). He dwells within us to display His power in the earth, *"Ye are of God, little children, and have overcome them: because greater is he that is in you, than he that is in the world"* (I John 4:4).

All the power we have over satan and his cohorts is in Jesus Christ and HIS victory. We, as people, have no authority of our own which compels satan to give heed to our commands. Believers must understand we are IN CHRIST.

WORDS ARE WEAPONS

Communication in both the spirit and natural realms is accomplished through words. Our words confirm that Jesus is abiding in our hearts to the natural world around us. Our words tell if we are abiding IN CHRIST when we speak to the spirit realm. Our words are the indicator of where we stand. Out of the abundance of the heart, the mouth speaks *(Luke 6:45)*. Again, whatever is in the heart is revealed by what is said—under pressure.

Putting into our hearts the knowledge of who Jesus Christ is, what He has done, and what He will do in our behalf is basic training to the believer who chooses to participate in the Lord's army.

TRAINING GODLY SOLDIERS

Wise military leaders know good soldiers need training, discipline and strategy planning techniques. They know soldiers gain experience and confidence through drills, drills and more drills. The better trained and disciplined soldiers are, the more capable they are at tackling hard assignments, being successful—and staying alive. The more strategic the assignment, the greater the need for qualified, disciplined and motivated personnel.

Recruits come in on the same basis, each bearing their individually unique background, character traits, talents and aspirations. Each is needed and each will find his or her position within the workings of the unit. When it comes to the training sessions and obstacle courses, each one must take what they have and attempt to succeed to the best of their ability, whether it is as a commissioned officer or raw recruit. Drill instructors know their efforts to shape and mold these trainees will greatly determine their success on the battlefield. The Holy Spirit is our "Holy drill instructor" who determinedly teaches us, encourages us, and prods us to continue. He dutifully trains us in preparation for the inevitable confrontation that is ahead.

People who are reluctant soldiers in any army tend to murmur and complain, find fault with their fellow soldiers, and despise following orders and authority. Many don't really comprehend the value of their training and how it can be used for their benefit, that is, until they face an enemy. Likewise, even though every born-again person is in the Lord's army, many do not realize that they will engage in battle against the enemy who seeks to kill, steal from and destroy them in any way he can.

Each believer needs to direct the fighter spirit against the enemy—satan —and not at fellow soldiers. It is not for the soldiers on the front lines or the soldiers in the officer's tent to question one another's importance. From cook to rifle expert, from sailor to Admiral, from private to General, each is needed for his or her unique and valued role. Likewise, whether pastor, layperson, intercessor, or babe in spiritual things, every person is valuable and necessary in the war of the kingdoms.

What is in the arsenal of the Lord? There are more weapons in the Lord's arsenal than any one soldier can use in a lifetime, and all are available to the believer. Each weapon is available to the measure and extent a person wants to be trained, disciplined and sent out on assignment. The foundation for warfare is given to us by Paul in Ephesians when he said, "be strong in the Lord and in the power of His might." When we learn "who I am *in* Christ, and who Christ is *in me*," we have the foundation to begin.

BASIC TRAINING

Basic for every warrior of the cross is an understanding and confidence in (1) the Name of Jesus, (2) the Word of God, (3) the Blood of the Lamb (4) the anointing imparted to each believer by the Anointed One (5) the Fruit of the Holy Spirit, (6) the Baptism of the Holy Spirit, (7) the gifts of the Holy Spirit, (8) the whole armor of God, and (9) the host of heaven of the Father's holy angels. Each area alone could fill volume upon volume. We have many rich and powerful teachings that can help us to grow in the things of God.

We should learn and wisely apply the benefits given us in Christ Jesus. These are basics upon which our faith and confidence is founded. I cannot overemphasize the importance for each of us to become knowledgeable and skillful in each of these areas. There are numerous worthwhile books and teachings that will help in becoming strengthened and equipped in mind and spirit. The Bible is the most important and effective.

FACING A GIANT

Consider the shepherd boy, David, when he went to meet a mighty foe and enemy of Israel, Goliath. As he prepared to face his enemy, he was offered King Saul's armor. As impressive and formidable as it appeared, David said, *"I cannot go with these; for I have not proved them. And David put them off him"* (I Samuel 17:39). David would not go to battle with armor and weapons in which he did not have confidence in and experience with. He had previously fought a lion and a bear and prevailed. Likewise, there will be lions and bears to fight before we encounter our Goliaths. We are in training orchestrated by the Holy Spirit to develop our faith and experience in what has been given to us in Christ Jesus, equipping us for future confrontations.

When we take from the arsenal of Heaven and learn more of what the Lord has equipped us with, we are filling ourselves with the

Lord's ability. Plan for war in peacetime. We can build a fortress of the Lord BEFORE the enemy attacks. Anticipate his attack. Do not be ignorant of his devices. Do not be ignorant of his intent to kill, steal and destroy.

———❦———

Plan for war in peacetime

———❦———

Furthermore, go after what he has already stolen or tried to kill or destroy. In some cases, seek resurrection for those things that have lost life. It could be a relationship with a relative or mate, or a business idea, talent or gift. The Lord has overcome all the power of the enemy. He will help us take back what satan has stolen.

BASIC TRAINING: THE NAME

One day every being created in the universe will do one thing—confess that Jesus Christ is Lord. He is before all things and by Him all things consist *(Colossians 1:17)*. He has created all things, and there will come a time when it will be acknowledged by all of heaven, earth and hell that Jesus is Lord of all. *"Wherefore God also hath highly exalted him, and given him a name which is above every name: That at the name of Jesus every knee should bow, of things in heaven, and things in earth, and things under the earth; And that every tongue should confess that Jesus Christ is Lord, to the glory of God the Father"* *(Philippians 2:9-11)*. Our Heavenly Father will be glorified for the sacrifice of His Son. Satan, the fallen angels and all the demons will bow their knees for all to see. When Jesus ascended from hell into heaven, He made an open show of His defeated foes before the spirit realm. The next time it happens, it will be before all humankind, to both the natural and spirit realms alike. Our Heavenly Father will be glorified for the fulfillment of His sovereign plan. Satan and his entire host will once again be made an open show of disgust and shameful humiliation before those he wished to see him as god.

The Name of Jesus is given to us as a gift of authority for the fulfilling of God's purposes. Jesus went about doing good and healing all who were oppressed of the devil *(Acts 10:38)*.

The Pharisees kept asking Him by what authority He did miracles and preached in the synagogue. They did not want anyone but themselves to have authority in spiritual matters. Satan works similarly today trying to challenge us and raise questions about the authority we walk in.

Jesus complimented the centurion because he recognized the authority He walked in. The centurion implored Jesus to simply speak to the sickness and his servant would be healed *(Matthew 8:5-13)*. His understanding of authority as a Roman officer helped him to realize Jesus' great authority. It is interesting that he was able to see that such authority could affect such things as sickness and disease. He saw beyond natural authority to spiritual, supernatural authority.

—◦◦◦—

Jesus was and is the embodiment of the authority

—◦◦◦—

AUTHORITY IN THE NAME OF JESUS

Jesus has been given a Name that is *above every* name *(Philippians 2:9)*. Jesus has given His Name to us so that we can carry out His work in the earth. *"Then he called his twelve disciples together, and gave them <u>power and authority</u> over all devils, and to cure diseases. And he sent them to preach the kingdom of God, and to heal the sick" (Luke 9:1, emphasis added)*.

What does Jesus give us to walk in His authority and to represent Him in the earth? *His Name.* His Name represents His position, privilege and place of power. Believers are His representatives and go forth in His Name. Jesus has given His Name to those who have asked Jesus into their heart. Those who call Him Lord will desire to walk as He did in the earth.

We must come to the Father in the Name of Jesus. Jesus made it possible for us to come to the Heavenly Father. It is through Jesus that the Father bestows His blessings according to His will, *"...Whatsoever ye shall ask the Father in my name, he will give it you" (John 16:23)*.

As the representatives and ambassadors of our Lord, He tells us, *"And these signs shall follow them that believe; In my name shall they cast* out devils; they shall speak with new tongues; They shall take up serpents; and if they drink any deadly thing, it shall not hurt them; they shall lay hands on the sick, and they shall recover" *(Mark 16:17-18, emphasis added)*.

Miracles happen when we know the power that is in His Name, "... *In the name of Jesus Christ of Nazareth* rise up and walk...And his name *through faith in his name* hath made this man strong, whom ye see and know..." *(Acts 3:6,16, emphasis added)*.

Cleansing and giftings happen in His Name, "...Repent, and be baptized every one of you *in the name of Jesus Christ* for the remission of sins, and ye shall receive the gift of the Holy Ghost" *(Acts 2:38, emphasis added)*.

The authority of Jesus is in His Name.

NAMES OF JESUS

Jesus has Names that reveal and describe hundreds of facets of His personality that carry power and divine authority. Within each one of His Names is the fulfillment of His wonderful gift to all who believe. Each Name carries with it the ability to manifest the aspect of all He is to meet our needs.

Studying and experiencing the Names of Jesus causes faith to form. As we become established in the powerful Names of Jesus, we will gain confidence and spiritual strength against methods and tactics of the enemy. Consequently, we will discover the power, not only in the mighty Name of Jesus, but also in His Names as Savior, Redeemer, Purifier and Refiner, Word, Shepherd and Bishop of our Souls, Passover Lamb, Lion of the Tribe of Judah and hundreds more. Believers will then bombard the heavenlies with abundant praises to God and bring embattlements against the enemy's host.

Jesus has many names that war against every plan of the enemy. As you study and learn about Jesus, watch for names available to you as you grow in your walk of faith.

When you run into the Name of the Lord, you are surrounded by the tower of the Lord and can depend on the "tower" to protect you, *"The name of the Lord is a strong tower: the righteous runneth into it, and is safe"* *(Proverbs 18:10)*. It does not say to run to, but into. By running "into," you are fully protected on all sides and can fully trust in Him. In times of stress, you can merely call upon His Name and let faith bring the tower of protection around you. In assurance of safety, there is peace. Let's look at a few examples.

SAVIOR

Jesus, our Savior, has saved us from our sins. We were in need of a savior who came to deliver each of us from sin. When Adam sinned, all humankind fell into a fallen nature and separation from God. In His Name as Savior, we proclaim His sacrifice for our sins. He delivered us from the destruction of eternal death and separation from God to eternal life *(Acts 4:12)*.

LORD OF HOSTS

Jesus is the Lord of all the hosts of heaven. It is a warring name, for He leads the entire host of holy angels in warfare on behalf of those who call upon Him.

The shepherd boy, David, carried only a slingshot, five smooth stones and the Name of the Lord when he faced Goliath, *"Then said David to the Philistine, Thou comest to me with a sword, and with a spear, and with a shield: but I come to thee in the name of the Lord of hosts, the God of the armies of Israel, whom thou hast defied"* (1 Samuel 17:45, emphasis added). Israel's enemy stood before them with formidable earthly weapons and a fearsome appearance, but David had "unseen" weaponry—faith in the Name and faithfulness of his Lord. We later read about David's adoration and praise in Psalm 24, *"Who is this King of glory? The Lord strong and mighty, the Lord mighty in battle... Who is this King of glory? The Lord of hosts, he is the King of glory"* (Psalm 24: 8,10). David knew things about the spiritual realm that gave him confidence and boldness. He had knowledge of a personal God who was involved in the battles of his life. As believers, we can know that Jesus is the King of Glory, that He is the Lord of hosts. We are able not only to have a personal relationship with the King of Glory but also have Him abide within us by the Holy Spirit. How awesome!

EMMANUEL

The angel announced to Joseph that the babe Mary was carrying in her womb was the One promised *(Isaiah 7:14)*. Emmanuel, meaning "God with us," is a powerful name that makes demons quake and satan shudder. Jesus, as the baby born to Mary in Bethlehem, was God in flesh form. God had prepared a body, a human form, to become the Lamb of God. His destiny was the cross of Calvary.

Jesus came in flesh form in fulfillment of the promise given to Eve when God told her that her Seed would crush the serpent's head. Emmanuel proclaimed that the promise had arrived.

Overcoming faith is founded on the belief that Jesus is God come in the flesh. He abides in and overcomes through those who call upon, rely and trust in Jesus Christ. He is God with us and in us. His Name proclaims that *"Whosoever believeth that Jesus is the Christ is born of God"* (I John 5:1), and *"Who is he that overcometh the world, but he that believeth that Jesus is the Son of God"* (I John 5:5).

DAYSPRING

In His coming, Jesus' light and life brought deliverance for all who sit in darkness and in the shadow of death. His life will lead His followers into the way of peace (Luke 1:79). You are promised a pathway out of darkness and death in His Name. You can proclaim the Name of "Dayspring" over loved ones who are sitting in darkness and in the shadow of death. Make statements over their lives that His light is dawning in their understanding and flooding their lives with truth and life.

HUNDREDS OF NAMES OF JESUS

I recommend you compose a list of every Name of Jesus that you come across as you study the Bible. Ask the Holy Spirit for knowledge, wisdom and understanding into the person of Jesus by His many Names. Belief in and relying upon each particular Name imparts into your life the ability, power and grace connected with that Name.

BASIC TRAINING: THE WORD

In the Gospel of John, Jesus is called the Word. *"In the beginning was the Word, and the Word was with God, and the Word was God. ...All things were made by him; and without him was not any thing made that was made"* (John 1:1, 3). The description of Jesus in Colossians 1 also explains this.

Jesus is God. He was in the beginning. Jesus Himself said, *"I am Alpha and Omega, the beginning and the ending, saith the Lord, which is, and which was, and which is to come, the Almighty"* (Revelation 1:8).

The Bible reveals Jesus. In revealing Jesus, the Heavenly Father is revealed because Jesus said if you have seen Me, you have seen the Father *(John 14: 9-11)*. The Bible sets forth words inspired by the Holy Spirit Who reveals a loving, merciful and long-suffering God. It shows God is just and forgiving, desiring that none be lost.

The Bible also tells of satan and the history of his destructive ways. It tells of the character of the evil one, his fall, his kingdom characteristics and his impending doom. However, if we do not read or delve into the truths of the Word of God, we cannot help but become disillusioned and confused when troubles, pain and sickness infiltrate our lives.

THE HIDDEN THINGS

The Word sheds light on things hidden in darkness. The Word shines a light on the Lord's path of safety. The Word reveals the person of Jesus Christ, His plan, His desire. The Word is a two- edged sword that causes us to see ourselves, show us our inner thoughts and motives, and yet tells us of the Lord's plan of forgiveness and restoration.

The Bible is a spiritual book pulsating the heartbeat of Jesus Christ. Those who know the words of His book will know more and more of the person Who was dead, resurrected and is alive forevermore. Jesus said, *"...the words that I speak unto you, they are spirit, and they are life"* *(John 6:63)*. The Word, Jesus the person, and the written Word will produce spirit and life to those who partake of Him.

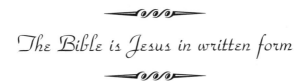

The Bible is Jesus in written form

We must also realize that the Bible is the legal book of both the earth and spiritual realms. The written Word of God sets forth legal statutes that bind and loose. Satan must honor the ordinances and statutes established in its words.

Those who remain ignorant to the rights and privileges given them by the Word of God will suffer the dealings of the enemy. Furthermore, those who know their rights may need to enforce their rights, as they stand strong in spiritual matters. We will discuss this further in future chapters.

BASIC TRAINING: THE BLOOD

Without the shedding of blood there is no remission of sin *(Hebrews 9:22)*. It was a condition of the sacrifice Jesus was to become. In the garden of Gethsemane, Jesus sweat great drops of Blood. Jesus knew what was before Him—the torture, anguish and shame, the bearing of all sin. In His humanity, He sought the Father for the cup to pass by Him if there were any other way than His crucifixion and the burden of all sin upon Him. His will was released into the hands of the Heavenly Father. He chose what His Father willed *(Matthew 26:39-45)*.

His victory over the will avails every believer a promise of freedom from the will of satan. *"And that they may recover themselves out of the snare of the devil, who are taken captive by him at his will"* *(II Timothy 2:26)*. Wrong choices, wrong decisions, a weak will before God or a strong will toward things of evil were overcome in the Blood shed in Gethsemane.

REDEEMED FROM THE CURSE

Jesus' Blood was shed when they placed the crown of thorns on His head. As they spit on Him, they struck Him on the head with a rod. The crown of thorns was not a round halo type of circle but was more the shape of a helmet that had thorns protruding which pierced the skin over the whole skull. Thorns represent curses. Blood flowed through the punctured places of broken flesh in Jesus' head and brow. His shed Blood broke curses of generations, curses brought by evil leadership or headship and every other curse. He broke the curses satan tries to lord over those who do not know that the price of God's own Blood has paid for their freedom. Curses spoken by someone in a leadership or authority position in your life can be nullified and cleansed by the Blood of Jesus. Because of the Blood, curses have no effect—for all those who believe and apply its benefit to their lives. Galatians 3:13 says, *"Christ hath redeemed us from the curse of the law, being made a curse for us: for it is written, Cursed is every one that hangeth on a tree."* In whatever way curses have been laid against people, Jesus has redeemed and broken the power of every curse—by His Blood and by the cross.

Jesus was led away to be scourged. Scourging was a beating with cords that had jagged pieces of metal attached to the ends. Each blow tore into the flesh of His body, ripping away pieces of tissue, muscle and flesh. Jesus knew such would be His pathway of sacrifice because Isaiah foretold of His suffering in chapter 53, verse 5, *"...and with his stripes we are healed."* Jesus willingly took the brunt of the terrible whipping in order to bring healing from injury, sickness and disease. The Blood and flesh hatefully ripped from Jesus' body makes it possible for healing wherever it is needed in your life.

Jesus was led to Golgotha, "the place of the skull," where He was placed on a cross, attached there by nails in His hands and His feet. The Blood, which flowed from His hands and feet, bore the punishment for sins of commission and omission. The chastisement of our peace was placed on Him *(Isaiah 53:3-5)*.

Blood and water gushed out of His side. The emptying out of Himself, the piercing of His heart drew the last of His life-giving Blood. He had poured out Himself to redeem back to Father God what Adam lost.

IT IS FINISHED!

As Jesus spoke the words, *"It is finished,"* He fulfilled the sacrifice of His life for the redemption and ransom for the entire human race *(John 19:30)*. He had fulfilled every aspect of the prophecies spoken concerning His death. The life that was in His Blood had been shed to bring life to all who would receive His sacrifice.

The temple sacrifices under the Mosaic covenant were a pattern of the sacrifice that was to be fulfilled in heaven *(Hebrews 8:5)*. When Jesus arose on the third day, He triumphantly entered the temple on the Holy Mount of God and presented His own Blood on the altar *(Hebrews 9:12)*. In doing so, He redeemed humankind back to the Heavenly Father. *"And to Jesus the mediator of the new covenant, and to the blood of sprinkling, that speaketh better things than that of Abel"* *(Hebrews 12:24)*.

In Genesis, God said that the blood of Abel spoke *(Genesis 4:10)*. Today, the Blood of Jesus speaks from heaven, and it guarantees the power of God to those who believe.

BASIC TRAINING: THE ANOINTING

The Name "Christ" means "The Anointed One." Jesus said, *"The Spirit of the Lord is upon me, because he hath anointed me to preach the gospel to the poor; he hath sent me to heal the brokenhearted, to preach deliverance to the captives, and recovering of sight to the blind, to set at liberty them that are bruised. To preach the acceptable year of the Lord"* (Luke 4:18). The anointing is actually true love, true knowledge and true faith, empowered by God to accomplish His purpose.

Anointing always has a purpose

Those who believe in Jesus Christ are anointed ones, for the Anointed One has come to abide within them. The anointing which marks the new creation in Jesus Christ sets them apart as children of the Most High.

There are other anointings which are in addition to the presence of the Anointed One within the believer. There are specific anointings that come upon those through whom the Holy Spirit is manifesting various callings and giftings. The five-fold ministry gifts are anointings that the Lord has endowed upon individuals who need the grace of the Holy Spirit to evangelize, pastor, teach, prophesy and establish churches. There are anointings to heal, deliver from demonic oppression and control, anointings to administer or organize godly projects, create or perform music, and many more. The anointing will rest upon the person who moves in the purpose of its power.

ANOINTED ONES

All good proceeds from the Father, by Christ Jesus, through the Holy Spirit into believing vessels. The anointing is for each of us; as it was upon Jesus, for we are, *IN HIM*. We are also called to preach the gospel to the poor, heal the brokenhearted, preach deliverance to the captives, recover the sight to the blind, set at liberty them that are bruised and to preach the acceptable year of the Lord (Luke 4:18,19).

The anointing is to take believers TO the battle to overcome. *"How God anointed Jesus of Nazareth with the Holy Ghost and with power: who <u>went about</u> doing good, and healing all that were oppressed of the devil; for God was with him" (Acts 10:38, emphasis added).*

———❦❦❦———

The anointing does the battle

———❦❦❦———

The anointing seeks, attacks and destroys all oppression of the devil. The anointing takes the action. The anointing does the action. The Holy Spirit's power in and upon the believer goes forth and pursues. When we move in the purposes of God, our souls can rest in the Lord, as we cooperate with the anointing flow of the Holy Spirit. The Lord said to me "You BE and the anointing will DO."

The anointing is supernatural goodness, the lavish richness of God abundantly flowing upon and through receptive vessels. The anointing is the vehicle of the power force, the conduit to supply God's glory.

There are hurting people who are being held captive by the enemy. The Lord has equipped you and me to set them free. He will, by the power of the Holy Spirit resting on and working within us, direct the pathway and actions of those who will obey and follow Him.

BASIC TRAINING: FRUIT OF THE SPIRIT

The Lord told me one day, "The Fruit of the Spirit does warfare against the works of the flesh listed before it." Love, joy, peace, long-suffering, gentleness, goodness, faith, meekness and temperance—the Fruit of the Holy Spirit will war against adultery, fornication, uncleanness, lasciviousness, idolatry, witchcraft, hatred, variance, emulation (jealousy), wrath, strife, sedition, heresies, envying, murders, drunkenness, reveling (feasting with sinful acts and obscene music), and such like *(Galatians 5:19-24).*

The power of the Holy Spirit in you will enable you to walk in the character and attributes of the Holy Spirit. The things of the Spirit confound the things of earthly thinking. Satan has deceived many people into relying on their own understanding and natural reactions in order to deal with the trials and stresses of life. They end up with earthy solutions to heavenly activities.

There are many misconceptions regarding the *power* of the Fruit of the Spirit. On the surface attributes like love, joy, peace, long-suffering, goodness look like passive milk-toast attributes. It sometimes gives the impression of "Run over me and abuse me, but I will still love you." To some this can seem like a characteristic of weakness. The bold charge, "You try to run over me and I will get out my Mack truck and run over you," seems more indicative of warfare.

The difference is that the Fruit of the Spirit is the personality and empowering of the Holy Spirit to deal with <u>people</u>. It does not apply to satan and his band. Get out your spiritual Mack truck, shove it into overdrive and floorboard it when it comes to going after the devil and his deeds.

ISSUES OF THE HEART

The problem is satan uses people for his wicked purposes. All mixed together in the person is a valued creation of God, as well as, areas of their lives that have been used by satan for his evil purposes. Some people defend satan's territory within their lives and willfully carry out the works of the flesh with vigilance. They can be good in many aspects of their lives, but in other areas they are bent on attitudes and activities that are hateful and destructive. Some people become skillful in glossing over ulterior motives and workings; they disguise their evil objective with cunning and clever words.

You may have a "gut feeling" about a person or a situation even though nothing on the surface indicates reason for concern. The Holy Spirit is resident in believers to give guidance and counsel. He has been sent to us to be our Helper. He is helping us become mature in spiritual matters. *"But strong meat belongeth to them that are of full age, even those who by reason of use have their <u>senses exercised</u> to discern BOTH good and evil"* (Hebrews 5:14 emphasis added). Our senses will go through many spiritual exercises as we learn to discern between what is good and what is evil.

People are the vehicles of manifestation of spiritual matters on the earth, whether they are of God or the enemy. The warfare that goes on in the earth between the kingdoms will inevitably deal with the righteousness of God within us as well as the sin nature and satanic influence involved within our lives and the lives of those around us.

THE POWER OF LIFE AND DEATH

Within every person is the capability to speak forth good and evil, even within the course of one conversation. It has been the tendency of onlookers to swallow both evil and good and then wonder why their stomach is in a knot, or to throw out the baby with the bath water and reject both the good and evil.

Mature believers are being taught by the Holy Spirit to take every conversation, every personality, every situation and separate out what is good and what is evil. They take into themselves goodness and reject that which is evil. They are able to be at rest and experience a sense of safety because they have confidence that they can sort out and discern <u>both</u> good and evil.

We must realize the love God has toward those who are created in His image. God so loved the world that He gave His Son to die an excruciating and shameful death in order to purchase our redemption. We cannot war effectively if we are fighting against people in personal ways. Additionally, we are fighting against God when we use carnal practices against people. *"And they that are Christ's have crucified the flesh with the affections and lusts "* (Galatians 5:24).

—=∞∞=—

Without His help we are left with natural reasoning and carnal solutions

—=∞∞=—

THE HEALING BALM

The Fruit of the Spirit is the power of love, joy, peace, long-suffering, gentleness, goodness, faith, meekness and self-control to tap into the lives of hurting people and touch their deepest needs. Fear and past pain may make a person try to protect those innermost areas of need. The Fruit of the Spirit within believers helps them reach into lives with healing balm.

Don't become confused into thinking that a personality filled with the Fruit of the Holy Spirit would be the sugar-candy type of personality. A person can be rough and rugged around the edges but emanate acceptance, love and forgiveness. It is possible for people to have personality characteristics of gentleness, goodness and long-suffering but not have the power of the Holy Spirit propelling life-changing impact through them. The Fruit of the Spirit is reliance on the personality of the Holy Spirit within your life to meet the challenges and buffeting of the enemy when it comes to relationships and dealings with other human beings.

BASIC TRAINING: BAPTISM IN THE HOLY SPIRIT

Jesus told His followers to tarry in Jerusalem until they were endued with power from on high *(Luke 24:49)*. Jesus told them in Acts 1 they were going to be baptized with the Holy Spirit within a few days. They were already believers; they were already followers of Jesus; He had already given them power to deal with demonic forces. He desired an impartation of power beyond what they had previously. It would be an impartation of Himself by the Holy Spirit to enable His followers to walk in an ability and power that was supernatural.

The Holy Spirit baptizes believers into Jesus Christ and Jesus Christ baptizes into the Holy Spirit

---

Jesus brings a drenching in the supernatural endowment of power into the life of a believer. The evidence of speaking with other tongues is the sign of what is called baptism in the Holy Spirit. Speaking in other tongues is a supernatural event in people's lives because they are speaking in a language that is not learned or studied, but is imparted by the Holy Spirit. It is a language of words spoken by the Holy Spirit to communicate with the Godhead the innermost needs and desires of the person. *"For he that speaketh in an unknown tongue speaketh not unto men, but unto God; for no man understandeth him; howbeit in the spirit he speaketh mysteries"* *(I Corinthians 14:2)*.

John the Baptist preached that whereas he was baptizing in water (unto repentance), there was One coming who would baptize in the Holy Ghost. Jesus Christ is the Baptizer in the Holy Ghost *(Mark 1:8)*.

THE MYSTERIES OF GOD

Every time you speak in other tongues, you are experiencing a supernatural demonstration of the person of the Holy Spirit. You are able to speak in mysteries beyond your own human intellect. You speak to God in a language with words chosen by the Holy Spirit to express the innermost desires, needs, petitions and worship. Your own prejudices, ignorance, background, sinfulness and timidity are overruled as the Holy Spirit prays. The Holy Spirit is able to take your strengths and weaknesses and blend them into powerful prayer. He is able to pray the perfect prayer. He knows the mind of God, and He knows the mind of the person and will pray according to the will of God *(Romans 8:26,27)*. He prays in line with what God wants to do. The Holy Spirit is interceding, through Christ Jesus, between God and the believer, bringing agreement and avenues for answered prayer.

Lack of wisdom, knowledge and understanding within us hinders us from progress in spiritual things. Speaking with other tongues transcends that lack and speaks forth insight about spiritual matters beyond our own intelligence and information.

PRAYING DIVINE PROTECTION

For example, one night the Lord impressed on me an urgency to pray. I climbed out of bed and spent about two hours praying in other tongues. I did not know of anything particular I was praying about, but I prayed until a peace and rest settled into my being. I went back to bed and then carried on into the day with planned activities. When my husband and I returned home later in the day after a hiking outing, we received a message that my mother and father had been in a car accident. The setting sun blinded them. They had driven head-on into a power pole that was in their lane, placed there to divert traffic. Immediately, we jumped back into the car and headed to the hospital. I desperately prayed, "Oh Lord, please take care of them."

The Lord gently replied, "I already have." He reminded me of the hours I had prayed earlier. I did not know I had been praying for the deliverance and safety of two people very precious to me. When we arrived at the hospital, we found my dad had a minor injury to his knee and my mom was admitted because of a slight concussion. When we saw the extent of damage to the car, the caved in dash and broken windshield where my mom had been thrown forward, the immensity of the deliverance that occurred was profoundly clear. Speaking in other tongues had lifted prayer beyond my understanding. Their lives were spared because of the intercession of the Holy Spirit. Satan had devised a wicked plan for my parents' injury and possible death, but the Holy Spirit had changed the outcome. The Lord desires paths of safety, deliverance and blessing for us. He has given us power through the language of the Holy Spirit to pray divine prayers of God's goodness.

THE CALL TO PRAYER

We have the opportunity to be available to the will of God by praying in the Holy Spirit not only about matters that pertain to our own lives but also to pray for people and situations that are far beyond our sphere of life or understanding. The Holy Spirit may need prayer for someone in another state or nation. Or perhaps there is a known need but exactly what is required to meet the need is not clear. Speaking with other tongues allows the Holy Spirit to pray God's perfect solution. He uses available pray-ers to intercede for people throughout the whole earth.

When it comes to spiritual things, there is much that is beyond our capabilities or understanding. The spiritual events that reach through three heavens would be difficult for even the wisest person to comprehend. Activity is a bustle all around us, yet it is unseen because things are taking place in the spirit realm. There is so much going on that we do not know, but the Holy Spirit does. As we begin to understand the operation and tactics of satan's hierarchy, we cannot help but see the need for prayers beyond our own limited understanding and knowledge.

The same Holy Spirit who moved across the face of the waters in Genesis 1, the same Holy Spirit who came upon Mary as the power of the Highest overshadowed her, the same Holy Spirit who raised Jesus from the dead, is the same Holy Spirit who is praying about powerful matters in the heavens and in the earth.

COUNTERATTACK

Is it any wonder satan attempts to instill so many controversies and hindrances to the Holy Spirit's prayers? Satan has used fear of tongues, doctrinal pride and misunderstanding of its purpose to try to thwart God's work. Whatever the reason, the endowment of power offered by Jesus is set aside.

The Holy Spirit is not a tyrant. He does not override the boundaries of will that eliminate freedom of choice. The prompting of the Holy Spirit in our lives are graces of God for holy purposes.

Satan is a supernatural foe. The baptism in the Holy Spirit is supernatural power to overthrow satanic and demonic efforts. In spiritual warfare, the baptism in the Holy Spirit is not an option, *it is a necessity.* See Appendix B for reasons why the baptism in the Holy Spirit is important and a prayer if you want to receive your heavenly language.

BASIC TRAINING: GIFTS OF THE SPIRIT

The gifts of the Spirit listed in I Corinthians 12:8 are: The word of wisdom, the word of knowledge, the gift of faith, gifts of healings, working of miracles, prophecy, discerning of spirits; divers kinds of tongues and interpretation of tongues. The Lord imparts by his Holy Spirit what is needed when it is needed. It has been said, "Seek the Giver, and not the gifts," and rightly so. However, it is the desire of the Giver, Jesus, to impart gifts. It is to the advantage of the believer to be aware what these gifts are all about so when the Holy Spirit begins to move, ignorance does not stifle the work He desires to accomplish.

- ◆ Word of wisdom—information regarding future events, facts, and information.
- ◆ Word of knowledge—facts and information which pertain to past or present
- ◆ Faith—a supernatural impartation of faith to believe

◆ Gifts of healings—supernatural healings
◆ Working of miracles—miracles
◆ Prophecy—words which encourage, edify and reveal
◆ Discerning of spirits—able to see angels or demons
◆ Divers kinds of tongues—speaking a message in tongues in the course of a gathering of believers for the purpose of interpretation
◆ Interpretation of tongues—giving the interpretation in one's known language of the message spoken in tongues

The Holy Spirit works with us to bring about words and knowledge from the spirit realm into the realm of our understanding, *"But all these worketh that one and the selfsame Spirit, dividing to every man severally as he will"* (I Corinthians 12:11).

THE WORD OF KNOWLEDGE

Take for example the gift of the *word of knowledge*. The Holy Spirit may tell a pray-er that the child lost in the woods is on Blueberry Ridge, not at Juniper Creek where everyone is searching. Or, the Holy Spirit may reveal to the pray-er the name of the demon oppressing someone is Jealousy. The demon, Jealousy, is cast out and prayers are lifted up to build a protection around the person so Jealousy and any companions are halted. The person then is counseled on how to identify and resist jealous inclinations. The word of knowledge revealed what the Holy Spirit knew and wanted to tell the prayer participants in order to bring liberty and instruction.

DISCERNING OF SPIRITS

Discerning of spirits, which is a gift of the Spirit, is being able to actually see spirit beings. Some people may see angels or demons. This is different than the believer who has the inner knowing a demonic presence is present or has been told so by the Holy Spirit. Discerning of spirits is a temporal manifestation given by the Holy

Spirit for His specific purpose. It does not mean the person who has seen spirits will or will not see them again. It is the working of the Holy Spirit to manifest the gifts as He wills for His intended purpose at that time.

We are wise if we know about and desire to be available to the Holy Spirt's gifting. He desires to flow through vessels that want to glorify Jesus and exalt the Heavenly Father.

BASIC TRAINING: THE WHOLE ARMOR OF GOD

Ephesians 6 lists armor the Lord has provided to believers for their warfare of the heavenlies. We are instructed to "put on" or clothe ourselves by faith in the protective armor He has made available.

◆ Loins girt about with truth—knowing the truths of God's word and how to apply them consistent with the character and revelation of God.

◆ Breastplate of righteousness—being knowledgeable and confident in our guiltlessness before God because of Jesus becoming the sacrifice for our sin.

◆ Feet shod with the preparation of the gospel of peace—being rock solid in the gospel of Jesus Christ as the foundation of our faith and being able to profess the gospel of Jesus Christ in its purity and fullness.

◆ Shield of faith (to quench all the fiery darts of the wicked)—having assurance and confidence in the protection believers have when doing battle with the enemy (I John 4:4).

◆ Take the helmet of salvation—being fully persuaded that you are saved from eternal hell through faith in the death, burial and resurrection of Jesus Christ, as well as, deliverance and protection from the evil of this present age.

◆ Sword of the spirit—the written and spoken Word of God.

God's divine truth reveals that man cannot stand before God in his own righteousness. The righteousness of Christ is revealed by the gospel of peace. Faith is necessary to believe and receive the gospel. When the gospel's truth and the gift of faith grip our hearts and we receive Christ, salvation occurs. Our head is covered. The direction of our lives is set anew. The Lord has not left us empty-handed or helpless; He gives us power by His Word, which is the two-edged sword of the Bible, to stand bold and strong against the strategies of the devil. Every part of God's armor contains delivering power and saving strength.

BASIC TRAINING: GOD'S HOLY ANGELS

We need a glance at the throne of God. Jesus is seated at the right hand of the Father. Believers are seated together with Jesus Christ because they are *in* Christ.

We find that, *"The Lord hath prepared his throne in the heavens; and his kingdom ruleth over all. Bless the Lord, ye his angels, that excel in strength, that do his commandments, <u>hearkening unto the voice of his word</u>. Bless ye the Lord, all ye his hosts; ye ministers of his, that do his pleasure. Bless the Lord, all his works in all places of his dominion: bless the Lord, O my soul"(Psalm 103:19-22, emphasis added).*

God's holy angels are ever before the Lord. The Psalmist describes their waiting upon His word. They excel in strength and are waiting for the command of the Lord. They are ministers of His, doing whatever is the Lord's desire. They are continually before the throne praising the Lord and awaiting direction.

HEIRS OF SALVATION

We read earlier that Hebrews 1:14 speaks of angels, *"Are they not all ministering spirits, sent forth to minister for them who shall be heirs of salvation?"* It goes on to say in Hebrews 2:3, *"How shall we escape, if we neglect so great salvation...?"* Every believer is an heir of salvation and therefore the recipient of angelic assistance, but we can neglect the hosts that are before the Lord.

In the past, I wondered if angels could be sent forth by the believer or whether they needed to be sent on assignment by God. The above scripture gives us a glimpse into heaven, and we can picture angels waiting upon the word of the Lord.

Jesus told Peter, after he cut the ear off one of the soldiers coming to arrest Jesus, *"Thinkest thou that I cannot now pray to my Father, and he shall presently give me more than twelve legions of angels?"* (Matthew 26:53) Jesus indicated that His Father would send the angels. Jesus again spoke of the Father and *His* angels in Revelation 3:5. Our Heavenly Father is sending forth angelic messengers and warriors on behalf of those who *call upon Him.* The Father's holy angels are an unseen army available to carry out spiritual warfare proclaimed and directed by the Lord of Hosts.

Jesus is the Lord of Hosts. Jesus is the warrior who is Lord, leading the angelic host. He does not do anything apart from what He sees the Father do, so He is yet fulfilling the wishes of the Father when He goes forth as Lord of Hosts.

SO GREAT A SALVATION

Holy angels minister to heirs of salvation in many ways. They are a task force commissioned to minister the whole range of need from minor to mountain moving. Too many people do not avail themselves of the ministering desire of angels. Ministers love to minister. Anointed vessels love to move in the anointing. Likewise, angels love to do the Father's bidding. Believers have the awesome honor of calling upon their Heavenly Father, in the Name of Jesus, and request angels to be sent forth upon their prayers.

Two-thirds of God's holy angels remained faithful to God. That means there are twice as many angels available to work *for* us as satan has to work *against* us. Believers can come to the throne of God, by the shed Blood of Jesus, and request of the Father angelic ministers to bring about "so great a salvation." Not salvation from sin, which can only come through the shed Blood of Jesus, but salvation that comprises deliverance from every sort of evil instigated by the adversary.

WARNING ABOUT ANGELS

Any encounter with an "angel" that does not point to Jesus as Lord, or that draws any attention to itself or to the person, is not of God. "Visitations" which bring another gospel are not of God. II Corinthians 11:14 warns that satan himself is transformed into an angel of light. Satan is the chief ruler of darkness. Any light he seeks to be transformed into has to be fragile because he cannot maintain light. Truth is light. Jesus said of satan, *"...there is no truth in him" (John 8:44)*. Knowing the truth of the Word of God will reveal what kind of "angel" is being presented.

With all the attention given to angels recently, there are many opportunities for error regarding them. Read books by reputable authors like Billy Graham and Terry Law regarding angels. Not all books on angels are truth but are a seduction into error by the angel of light, satan and his deceivers *(II Corinthians 11:13-15)*. Some "angel" visitations have resulted in cult religions. If you have had any encounter with angels or angel visitation, challenge what was said or revealed against what is scriptural truth. If it does not line up with the Word of God, or in any way disagrees with the character and gospel of Jesus Christ, it was not of God. Satan is seeking an inroad into your life.

For example, I heard the word in my mind, "angel hand-maidens." Something did not set right in my spirit about it. I set my attention into deep study of the Bible. Are there angel handmaidens? I have not found in scripture angels of the female gender. Today's society has readily portrayed angels as babies and young women with wings. God's holy angels are not cupid-like. They are not dainty female personages. They are formidable beings with size and strength to enforce spiritual laws and wage spiritual battle against evil fallen-angel forces.

Beware of angel stories and encounters that do not exalt or glorify Jesus Christ. If they magnify the person, themselves or some new or ancient doctrine, beware!

FALLEN-ANGEL STRATEGISTS WORK TOGETHER

In the next few chapters, we will take a closer look at the individual divisions of satan's strategists and attempt to help believers identify the type of assault that may be confronting them. In so doing we will also better understand practical application patterns of how to appropriate being strong in the Lord and the power of His might.

DIFFERENT DIVISIONS

Even though satan's kingdom is divided into different divisions, the line of demarcation between them is not always clearly defined. Why? Because like any fighting force, the various divisions work together to accomplish common goals. One thing builds upon another. You will begin to understand how the coordination of evil strategists work if you imagine a structure with divisions each built upon the other, and yet working in coordinated cooperation.

RANK AND ORDER

The base, or foundation, represents *spiritual wickedness in high places*. This is the division that has to do with perpetrating error, false doctrine and perversion to the gospel of Jesus Christ. The level above it would be the *rulers of the darkness of this world*, whose job it is to hide, distract and confuse. Ranking above rulers of darkness are *powers or authorities* who wield assaults, accusations and demand control of all below them. Nearest the top would be *principalities* who are assigned by satan to maintain control over a specific area or region and select targets for assault or promotion depending on whether they war against or cooperate with their evil plans.

Satan is the god of the kingdom of darkness and all those below him are enslaved to his insults and commands. Their fate in satan's kingdom has been set, and they are doomed to remain there because of their rebellion with satan in ages past. Remember, fallen angels became satan's strategists. Groups of demons are assigned to each division and follow orders from their satanic leaders. We will look at each division beginning at their foundation.

Satan	Tyrant leader
Principalities	Geographical heads
Powers or Authorities	Enforcers and attackers
Rulers of darkness of this world	Maskers of evil deeds
Spiritual wickedness in high places	False doctrine experts

CHAPTER 6

SPIRITUAL WICKEDNESS IN HIGH PLACES

Spiritual wickedness in high places is last in the list Paul gives us regarding our spiritual foes, but in many ways this division of satan's hierarchy is the most dangerous and powerful. Satan's greatest effort will be given to this area because his target is the belief system of humankind.

FOUNDATION STRATEGISTS

What people believe is the foundation of their whole being. Each person's belief system threads its way into every aspect of his or her life. Just as the circulatory system of the body has large and small arteries and innumerable little veins and vessels that reach to every part of the body, so it is with the belief system. The larger beliefs carry the major weight in guiding what we do or don't do. But there are innumerable little seeds of beliefs that shape our personality, traditions, desires, attitudes, time commitments and basically effect our lives down to the smallest detail. The foundation of our beliefs directs our pursuits and shapes our core values.

The onslaught of these strategists is the mind of a person. If your mind can be seduced, coerced or controlled to any extent, then satan can manipulate you for his purposes. The warfare of spiritual wickedness in high places is strategies of *doctrine verses doctrine*. When the Lord began to teach me about the warfare of doctrines, I needed some clarification of what doctrine really was—a definition. I asked simply, "Lord, What is doctrine?" He replied, "DOCTRINE IS A STATEMENT OF WHAT YOU BELIEVE." Whatever you believe, whether it is true or not, whether it is a little or significant matter, what you believe about anything, forms a statement of belief which is doctrine and comprises the foundation of your being.

The individual belief system consumes the whole sphere of what people are and what they possess. Let's look at some beliefs that make a statement about their place in people's lives:

- Is there heaven?
- Is there such a place as hell?
- Is sickness a cross God wants people to bear?
- Is sickness of the devil?
- Are vitamins essential to good health?
- Is a little lie okay, if it serves a good purpose?
- Should skirts and dresses always be worn to church?
- Should one stay away from people with rings in their noses and bellies?
- Do purple and orange look good together?
- It's a waste of money to ...
- Do I apologize or should the other person apologize first?
- Does red wine always go better with steak than white wine?
- Should you always kick on the fourth down?
- Once saved, always saved?

THE BASICS OF BELIEFS

The question to any statement of belief is "Why?" Why do you believe what you do? What is the basis of the decision to believe? It affects what is done about it. Is it based on truth or error? How do you determine what is right and wrong?

Everything in people's lives is rooted in a vast and articulate belief system

Many people are not really sure what they believe for themselves. Some beliefs are formed by others, whether it is parents, friends, teachers, clergy, and in many cases media. Every area of communication attempts to give a view, but in most instances they are slanted one way or another, seeking to impact their opinions and beliefs on every one of us.

Newspapers, magazines, radio, movies, television, and now Internet information systems directly or indirectly shape people's belief systems. The information that pours into the hearts and minds of people will have a direct bearing on what they hold as the foundation of their lives.

DOCTRINE DIFFERENCES

Satan tries to present his doctrine as truth. In the absence of the knowledge of truth in the Word of God and discernment by the Holy Spirit, satan's truth appears acceptable and is received by many as a belief and foundation for living. In essence, the person has provided a foundation for satan to build upon, enabling him to kill, steal and destroy either the person, those around the person, or both.

These strategists are the most deceptive, seductive and convincing of satan's whole kingdom. They are articulate, knowledgeable and tenacious at their task. However, they are limited in their ability and to the extent they are able to deceive. They are only successful when they deceive someone into error or keep people in ignorance.

The warfare of the kingdoms will mean battle in the foundation belief systems of every person. Sometimes the foundations of people's lives are shaken and their belief systems challenged. That is good. We need to know what makes up our foundation. Even if satan challenges the foundation of our beliefs, those which are founded on solid biblical truth will not be shaken.

The foundation of satan's kingdom is based on the work accomplished by his strategists assigned to spiritual wickedness in high places

Sometimes the shaking of our foundation eventually purges that which is not solid or truthful. We do not need to fear looking at the foundations of our belief systems, how we arrived at them and how valid they are. It is a process that continues throughout our lives. Foundational beliefs should not be neglected or dealt with only at a point of crisis. That is a hard way to live life and find truth.

HIGH PLACES

Why did Paul describe this segment of satan's host as spiritual wickedness "in high places?" Throughout the Old Testament, there are many references to the term "high places." Although these high places were often located on higher ground, they were primarily places of belief and worship.

Paul was a scholar of scriptural writings and well versed in its terminology. He described areas of worship that were not holy to God but were filled with spiritual wickedness and disobedience. When Paul listed "spiritual wickedness in high places," he was referring to a whole realm of doctrinal error that was established in wickedness and had its driving focus on perpetuating and promoting error. Leviticus 26:30 says, *"I will destroy your high places, and cut down your images, and cast your carcases upon the carcases of your idols, and my soul shall abhor you."*

God's favor or disfavor rested upon each king throughout the Old Testament, depending on what he did concerning the high places in his kingdom. It was prophesied 322 years before King Josiah was born that he would tear down and destroy the priests and their high places *(I Kings 13:2, fulfilled II Kings 22 & 23)*. God planned destruction and judgment against wicked places of worship.

THE GLORIOUS LIGHT

Paul simply pointed out believers would wrestle against beliefs that are outright assaults against the knowledge of God and the gospel of the Lord Jesus Christ.

II Corinthians 4:2-4,6 tells us, *"But have renounced the hidden things of dishonesty, not walking in craftiness, nor handling the word of God deceitfully; but by manifestation of the truth commending ourselves to every man's conscience in the sight of God. But if our gospel be hid, it is hid to them that are lost: In whom the god of this world hath blinded the minds of them which believe not, <u>lest the light of the glorious gospel of Christ</u>, who is the image of God, should shine unto them...For God,* (the same God) *who commanded the light to shine out of darkness, hath shined in our hearts, <u>to give the light of the knowledge of the glory of God in the face of Jesus Christ</u>"* (explanation and emphasis added).

THE GOSPEL WARS AGAINST ERROR

According to Romans 1:16, the gospel is the power of God unto salvation, *"For I am not ashamed of the gospel of Christ: for it is the power of God unto salvation to every one that believeth; to the Jew first, and also to the Greek" (emphasis added)*. The gospel embodies the power of God that is able to discomfit the enemy. It has the capacity to bring light and understanding. Therefore, satan tries to pervert and counter the good news which the gospel proclaims. If our gospel is hidden, it is hidden by the god of this world who has blinded the minds of those who do not believe *(II Corinthians 4:4)*. It is hidden from their hearts and minds. But the same God who said, "Let there be light" in Genesis 1, again has spoken and said He would give the light of the knowledge of the glory of God in the person of Jesus Christ. The power is of God and not of individuals. God has given to every person a gift of faith to believe. It is deposited within them. Otherwise, God would be unjust in any being lost to eternal hell. Every person has been given enough faith to receive Jesus Christ as Lord and Savior. It is a gift of God *(Ephesians 2:8)*. However, that seed gift of faith has been clouded and hidden by many other factors that blind our minds. Such blindness keeps people from receiving, believing and relying upon the Lord Jesus Christ and the fullness of all He has provided through His death, burial and resurrection.

UNBELIEF MUST BE EXPOSED

As we discussed earlier, unbelief keeps us from entering into the rest of God and all that He has promised to us. Satan has devised strategies of unbelief that war against the knowledge of God. Jesus charged his followers to battle unbelief. One avenue for battling unbelief is through prayer and fasting. When the disciples could not cast out the devils in Mark 9:23-29, Jesus explained that prayer and fasting would be needed to displace unbelief.

MURMURING AND GRUMBLING

Unbelief kept the Israelites out of their promised land because *"... they despised the pleasant land, they believed not his word: But murmured in their tents, and hearkened not unto the voice of the Lord" (Hebrews 4:5,6 and Psalm 106:24,25)*. Such grumbling words produced unbelief that cost them their promised land and their lives. Murmuring fuels unbelief and wars against resting in Jesus.

The Holy Spirit works within each believer to root out areas of error, misunderstanding and unbelief. The Lord seeks to set believers abundantly free. True freedom usually comes only through "foundation" renovation by the Holy Spirit.

—✐✐✐—

Murmuring is actually a negative statement of belief

—✐✐✐—

The business of dealing with root beliefs can become a heart-rending experience as areas of unbelief, idolatry and rebellion are revealed. It is difficult to feel the shame and see the wickedness in our own hearts. As each detail of the purging comes into focus, we must not rely on our own resources, worth or excuse, but freely receive mercy and cleansing by the Blood of Jesus. As verse 1 of II Corinthians 4 relates, *"...as we have received mercy, we faint not."* The Holy Spirit will expose each satanic inspired belief and as we are able to receive mercy, we are able to receive cleansing without condemnation.

CONDEMNATION

Condemnation is one of satan's doctrines of control over people's lives. He seeks to perpetrate condemnation of good and acceptance of evil. He is continually going before the Heavenly Father accusing us, desiring to find an opportunity to steal faith and take advantage of our weaknesses *(Revelation 12:10)*.

In Job 1, we find satan accusing God, saying Job would curse God to his face if He removed His hedge of protection. Job endured many tragic trials during his affliction without knowing why. I believe at some point Job knew of satan's accusation. We have written record of what was said in the heavenly realm. Moses, who is believed to have written the book of Job, was his contemporary. Job very likely told Moses what God showed him of the conversation in heaven regarding his trials. We cannot get a true picture of the troubles Job experienced if we do not understand satan had accused both God and Job. Job received double fold blessings in the end.

Satan's tactic continues as we see in Luke 22:31, *"Simon, Simon (Peter), listen! Satan has asked excessively that (all of) you be given up to him—out of the power and keeping of God— that he might sift (all of) you like grain, But I have prayed especially for you [Peter] that your [own] <u>faith may not fail</u>; and when you yourself have turned again, strengthen and establish your brethren"* (AMP, emphasis added).

Jesus told Peter point blank that satan was after him and wanted to cause his faith to fail. Jesus also told Peter that He had prayed for him and that Peter would overcome and be able to strengthen others.

JESUS CHRIST OUR GREAT HIGH PRIEST

Jesus not only prayed for Peter, He also lives to make intercession for us. Hebrews 7:25,26 tells us, *"Wherefore he is able also to save them to the uttermost that come unto God by him, seeing he ever liveth to make intercession for them. For such an high priest became us, who is holy, harmless, undefiled, separate from sinners, and made higher than the heavens."* Those who come to Him can be assured they have a high priest who is not only able to keep their faith from failing, but to preserve them blameless until the coming of our Lord Jesus Christ *(I Thessalonians 5:23)*. Condemnation has no hold where a believer receives the promise of being blameless through the cleansing Blood of Jesus Christ. As we learned earlier, high priests were called of God to go before God on behalf of the people. Jesus is our Great High Priest who prays on our behalf to the Heavenly Father. Even though sin may be hidden to a person, it has not escaped the watchful eye of our God *(Hebrews 4:13)*. He is drawing believers to His holy calling by exposing satan's strategy against them. We can be comforted in knowing Jesus moves in love and compassion as He reveals our innermost motives, beliefs and desires.

THE HIGH PRIEST

By the Bible's own requirement, a high priest must (1) have compassion on the ignorant (2) have compassion on them that are out of the way or in error and (3) not take this honor unto himself (be puffed up) but realize that he is called of God *(Hebrews 5:2)*. Jesus glorified not Himself to be made a high priest but was called of God to be a priest. He is our high priest at the highest level before the holy alter of God in the heavenly temple and He is easily touched by our infirmities *(Hebrews 4:15 and Hebrews 9:23-26)*.

A priest was one who was called to teach people to discern. *"And they shall teach my people the difference between the holy and the profane, and cause them to discern between the unclean and the clean" (Ezekiel 44:23)*. Jesus, as our Great High Priest, through the Holy Spirit, enables us to overcome the lies that bombard our hearts and minds. He gives us holy foundations of faith. He wars against spiritual wickedness in high places and affirms Jesus as our foundation *(Isaiah 28:16)*.

THE WORD OF OUR TESTIMONY

In John's Revelation, the Lord again exposes satan's tactic, *"...for the accuser of our brethren is cast down, which accused them before our God day and night. And they overcame him by the blood of the Lamb, and by the word of their testimony..." (12:11)*. The word of their testimony refers to the confession of our beliefs and the experiences that relate to those beliefs. We overcome satan's accusatory rhetoric by profession and proclamation of our belief in Jesus Christ and His shed Blood. Our statements of belief wage an effective blow in the defeat of satan. Our statements of belief are ones that proceed out of our heart, not merely out of our mouth and mind.

> *When the combination of the three is established on sound doctrine—heart, mind and mouth—and is proclaimed or professed, the efforts of spiritual wickedness in high places are paralyzed*

EVANGELISTS—GOD'S DOCTRINAL SPECIALISTS

The Lord has placed evangelists as promoters and watchers of gospel truths. Often evangelists also work in miracles because of the gift of faith that flows through their ministry. Presenting the gospel against the mind-blinding effects of evil strategists requires extraordinary faith, for they continually have to "wrestle" against unbelief, error and satanic opposition. The Bible correlates the gospel to feet. Isaiah 52:7 says, *"How beautiful upon the mountains are the feet of him that bringeth good tidings, that publisheth peace; that bringeth good tidings of good, that publisheth salvation; that saith unto Zion, Thy God reigneth!"* (emphasis added) and Ephesians 6: 15 *"And your feet shod with the preparation of the gospel of peace."* The gospel is at the foundation, the footing, the place where we stand. Evangelists target the truth or error of our standing in Christ. Sometimes they ruffle feathers because they expose pet sins and challenge our belief systems. The profession of truth encourages those who know truth and desire to walk in truth. Truth also unsettles and stirs up the uneasy shifting ways of error.

II Samuel 22:33-39 encourages us, *"God is my strength and power: and he maketh my way perfect. He maketh my feet like hinds' feet: and setteth me upon my high places. He teacheth my hands to war; so that a bow of steel is broken by mine arms. Thou hast also given me the shield of thy salvation: and thy gentleness hath made me great. Thou hast enlarged my steps under me; so that my feet did not slip"* (emphasis added).

The Lord will establish a solid foundation. Evangelists and those who have a heart for soul winning present frontal attacks on the efforts of spiritual wickedness in high places—whose whole thrust of existence is to battle belief in God. Therefore, evangelists are bold and many times seem outspoken when it comes to the matter of what the gospel is and what we believe. They have an added anointing upon them to operate in strategic and supernatural impartation to thwart the error and lies of false doctrine.

FIVE FOLD MINISTRY

Our Lord speaks through all the ministry gifts given to the Body of Christ *(Ephesians 4:11)*. These gifts are apostles, prophets, evangelists, pastors and teachers who all have special anointing upon their lives and are established in speaking, preaching, teaching, correcting, encouraging, nurturing and equipping believers. They are called to be helpers in the hand of the Lord to edify, build maturity and bring the fullness of the gospel of the Lord Jesus Christ into the fabric of our lives.

ANOINTED TO PREACH GOOD NEWS

Many times the word "preach" in the New Testament is from the Greek word *euaggelizo*, the base from which we get our word for evangelist—a preacher of the gospel. However, the same word is used when Jesus said in Luke 4:18, *"The Spirit of the Lord is upon me, because he hath anointed me to preach the gospel to the poor..."* Every one who believes in Christ Jesus as their Lord and Savior has an anointing within them to declare the good news that unravels the lies of error, for themselves and for others. The anointing moves with the purpose of revealing truth and uprooting error.

Keep in mind strategists in high places set up doctrines that accuse and refute the doctrine of Christ. Believers may be challenged, questioned and harassed for their stand in Christ Jesus. *"But sanctify the Lord God in your hearts: and be ready always to give an answer to every man that asketh you a reason of the hope that is in you with meekness and fear"* (I Peter 3:15). We can always be ready to give testimony to the love and faithfulness of our Lord that we have experienced in our lives. We can be confident that the power of the gospel works salvation to us and those who hear us *(Romans 1:16)*.

COUNTERFEIT DOCTRINES

There are many teachings that war against the gospel of the Lord Jesus Christ. There are people who are radical and belligerent in their doctrines of error. The Spirit of the Lord is grieved by the rebellious mentality of these people. Their lost condition and their stubbornness to remain in conflict with the gospel of the Lord brings with it the pressure of confrontation of doctrines—a "wrestling" between those who know Christ and those opposed to belief in Jesus Christ as God.

Where satan has not prevailed by directly opposing gospel truths, he has taken a different course of action by bringing religious detours through doctrines that sound like truth but are not founded upon scriptural accuracy. These people base their belief system upon religious traditions and error *(Mark 7: 5-13)*.

The warfare of spiritual wickedness in high places is a realm of doctrines. Winds of doctrine are counterfeits to the wind of the Spirit of God. *"That we henceforth be no more children, tossed to and fro, and carried about with every wind of doctrine, by the sleight of men, and cunning craftiness, whereby they lie in wait to deceive"* (Ephesians 4:14). Satan will always attempt to introduce a counterfeit to God's genuineness. Strategists in high places arrange snares to entice and seduce a person into error.

Satan hates seeing the Lord exalted and revered as the Most High because it pronounces his diminished standing. He still wishes to be lifted up as god. However, our Heavenly Father is pleased and honored when we profess His wonderful position and personage as Most High God. *"I will praise the Lord according to his righteousness: and will sing praise to the name of the Lord <u>most high</u>"* (Psalm 7:17, emphasis added).

When we praise the Lord Most High, we are acknowledging the authority, power and position of God OVER the spiritual-wickedness-in-high-places strategists, *"I will be glad and rejoice in thee: I will sing praise to thy name, O thou <u>most High</u>"* (Psalm 9:2, emphasis added). We are giving honor to our God who is higher and more powerful than any and all of the enemy's power or position.

DESTINY DIRECTION

God has a wonderful plan for each of our lives. When believers have even small faith in the Lord's direction for their lives, there is a foundation. As the assurance of our destiny becomes clearer, the foundation becomes more secure. As the vision grows, the foundation is deepened and broadened. How can we stand firm on the turf of our destiny if we don't know what destiny we are called to? What do you *believe* is your destiny? It is a frustrating question to many because they feel so disheartened about not knowing their destiny in God. They feel the aimless drudgery of everyday living without knowing the deep purpose of their lives. God's desire is, *"That the God of our Lord Jesus Christ, the Father of glory, may give unto you the spirit of wisdom and revelation in the knowledge of him: <u>The eyes of your understanding being enlightened; that ye may know what is the hope of his calling</u>, and what the riches of the glory of his inheritance in the saints, And what is the exceeding greatness of his power to usward who <u>believe, according to the working of his mighty power</u>"* (Ephesians 1:17-19, emphasis added).

Spiritual strategists are tampering with the belief system of our lives trying to make us think we are not needed, not worthy or valuable in God's enterprises. There may be times when the Lord's grace dumps His destiny for us in our laps but we are so insecure in ourselves we reject it. We do not *believe* what God is saying to us. There may be others

—•◦•—

You will live out what you believe

—•◦•—

of us who desperately are seeking God's will for our lives and it seems like our purpose is hidden.

HIDDEN IN PLAIN SIGHT

You know, it is possible to hide something in plain sight. During World War II, one of the tactics used by the Navy was to camouflage ships by painting large geometric patterns on them. Enemy planes searching for the ships could not find them because the patterns blended with the water and light to make the ships obscure and effectively unnoticed. Rulers of darkness (which we will read more about in the next chapter) try to obscure what may otherwise be "in plain sight."

One way to combat work of evil strategists is to take the scripture written above and read it aloud, inserting yourself into it. "That the God of our Lord Jesus Christ, the Father of glory, may give unto *me* the spirit of wisdom and revelation in the knowledge of Him. The eyes of *my* understanding are enlightened, that *I may know* (be fully acquainted with and confident) what is the hope of *my* calling, and what are the riches of the glory of *my* inheritance in Christ Jesus. That *I may know* what is the exceeding greatness of *His power in me*, for *I believe and am able to receive* according to the working of his mighty power which He wrought in Christ, when he raised Him from the dead, and set Him at His own right hand in the heavenly places..."

Why do we read scriptures in such a way? Because *"The entrance of thy words giveth light: it giveth understanding..."* *(Psalm 119:130)*. In other words, the scriptures give light. We know that light dispels darkness; therefore, scriptures war against ruler of darkness activities and strategies—and understanding wars against unbelief.

Spiritual understanding helps us gain a secure foundation of belief upon which we can walk out God's destiny for our lives. We need to realize there is an enemy who is actively working to present an alternative plan for our lives, to bring a diversion from the holy purposes and calling of God.

DESTINY COURSE CORRECTION

Believers can get lured into beliefs that are not doctrinally wrong but stray off of God's destiny for their lives. There are many seductions in the world's system that lure us into any number of activities. There is nothing wrong with being a businessman instead of a pastor unless the Lord has called you to the ministry. There is nothing wrong with being a pastor unless the Lord wants your business genius to be used to help finance the gospel. Individuals may be within the field the Lord has called them but they have been lured into some deviation from what the Lord has truly purposed for their lives. Many sincere and dedicated people are living frustrated and unfulfilled lives because they have been ignorant to the wonderful purpose they are uniquely fashioned to accomplish. It is the exception rather than the rule to have someone say, "I love what I am doing. I am fulfilled in what I do every day. I believe I am living within the plan God has for my life." There is a God-given passion within every one of us to fulfill a unique and specific plan designed for us by our Heavenly Father. If the Lord is involved in our lives enough to monitor the hairs on our heads *(Matthew 10:30)*, how much more does He desire to help us accomplish the wondrous purpose He has designed for each of us. It doesn't mean that the path the Lord has for us is carefree and unchallenging, but in the midst of obstacles and frustrations there is a sense of purpose and inner fulfillment.

There can be minor deviations in our path that can get us off course. If left in place, these will have an impact on our long-range destination. If we take a wrong turn on the thoroughfare and do not make a course adjustment, we may end up in a city or an area where we don't belong. The bottom line is—we need to know where we are going and what purpose God has for us *(Habakkuk 2:2-4)*. Otherwise, how will we even know if and when we get off course?

It is a good idea to regularly do "course" checks. There are many obligations, opportunities and responsibilities that come from the different areas of our lives (social, employment, family, personal, and so forth.) The Holy Spirit will help us discern the daily path of our steps. The Lord, by the Holy Spirit, will take off our blinders and reveal His heart for our lives. We have personal access to the Heavenly Father in Jesus Christ who desires intricate involvement in our destinies. We can come to Him to receive counsel for direction and for our needs. Psalm 32:8 promises, *"I, the Lord, will instruct you and teach you in the way you should go: I will counsel you with My eye upon you"* (AMP).

MATURITY TAKES TIME

Not one person has come to Christ as a mature and seasoned believer. Every person has within them many beliefs that are not scriptural or biblically sound. For example, I grew up believing that the Bible said, "God helps those who help themselves." As I matured in the Lord, someone told me that statement was not scriptural. I fervently searched the scriptures to see if it were so. I never found it. On the contrary, I learned that the Lord's strength is made perfect in weakness *(II Corinthians 12:9)* and that apart from Him we can do nothing *(John 15:5)*. The more we grow in Christ, the more we find there are deeper areas of cleansing and uprooting which the Holy Spirit performs to build us into the image of Christ.

As a not-so-new believer, I had reached a point of burnout. I tried to live the Christian life as the "super-Christian, super-Mom, super-wife, super-daughter, super-friend, super-this, super-that"

What do you believe so strongly you are willing to die for it?

until was I super-wasted. I was exhausted and desperate for truth. The Lord took me back to the basics. He counseled, "Find out what you *know*" with the explanation, "Find out what you believe so strongly that you are willing to die for it." He led me to the scripture, *"For I determined not to know any thing among you, save Jesus Christ..."* (I Corinthians 2:2). He stopped there. For the next year, each day I studied one Name of Jesus and learned of His character, His ability and His promise to me. I found there were over 365 Names of Jesus or descriptions of His character that help us *know* Jesus. The word know means "to be fully acquainted with, and assured of, putting confidence into." When that happens, it results in faith.

The following year, when I asked the Lord what would be my focus for the new year, He spoke in such a way that the previous year passed in a second and He continued as if there had been no time lapse. He simply said *"...and Him crucified."* That year was a study in the powerful book of Hebrews, which sets forth Jesus' heavenly ministry and why the crucifixion was so important.

The Lord took me back to basics and caused me to find out what my foundation was made up of. In many instances he replaced error and fear with truth. There was dying to be done. Dying to self, dying to tradition, dying to unrealistic expectations of myself and others, dying to fear of man and dying to the need for approval. I came to understand the scripture which says he who will save his life will lose it, and he who will lose his life will find it *(Matthew 16:25)*. I entered into a new depth of faith and freedom. It would not have happened without subtle conscious and subconscious belief systems being exposed and dealt with by the Holy Spirit. Hebrews 4:12 describes the Word of God as dividing asunder the soul and spirit and discerning the thoughts and intents of the heart. The Bible helps us sort out what is valuable to keep and what is to be discarded.

> *The intent of satan is to make one seek to know anything and everything BUT Jesus Christ and Him crucified*

STORM-PROOF FOUNDATION

What we believe comprises our foundation for life. Jesus gave the illustration of the house built on a foundation of rock that withstood life's storms, whereas the house, which was built on sand, fell and *"great was the fall of it"* *(Matthew 7:27)*. The foundation that is sound can have great things built upon it, and it will resist the buffeting of satan's winds of doctrine and oppression. A foundation that is not based on truth shifts, compromises and changes with whatever wind is blowing at the time.

In his letter to the young convert Timothy, Paul admonishes him to *"...give attendance to reading, to exhortation, to doctrine...Meditate upon these things; give thyself wholly to them...Take heed unto thyself, and unto the doctrine; continue in them: for in doing this thou shalt both save thyself, and them that hear thee" (I Timothy 4: 13,15,16).* And then to Titus, Paul speaks, *"Holding fast the faithful word as he hath been taught, that he may be able by sound doctrine both to exhort and to convince..." (Titus 1:9).* Sound doctrine is a statement of truth founded on the Word of God. The Bible is the only basis of truth. It points to and reveals Jesus Christ.

When Paul instructs us to take heed to ourselves and to doctrine, he is telling us to compare the beliefs we hold to the Word of God and the doctrine of the gospel he has preached. Paul speaks his message again to the Corinthians *"...I have laid the foundation, and another buildeth thereon. But let every man take heed how he buildeth thereupon. For other foundation can no man lay than that is laid, which is Jesus Christ" (I Corinthians 3: 10,11).* A believer's foundation is true (correct) knowledge of, and faith in, Jesus Christ.

Speaking to the Galatians, Paul marveled that they had removed themselves from Christ's gospel unto ANOTHER gospel. He even goes so far as to say every person who brings another gospel shall be accursed, *"But though we, or an angel from heaven, preach any other gospel unto you than that which we have preached unto you, let him be accursed. As we said before, so say I now again, If any man preach any other gospel unto you than that ye have received, let him be accursed" (Galatians 1:8,9).* WHO brings another gospel to seduce believers into error or endeavors to keep precious souls from hearing the true gospel? It is spiritual strategists with a false message. In Galatians 3:1,3, Paul scolds them. *"O foolish Galatians, <u>who hath bewitched</u> you, that ye should not obey the truth, before whose eyes Jesus Christ hath been evidently set forth, crucified among you?...Are you so foolish? having begun in the Spirit, are ye now made perfect by the flesh?" (emphasis added)*

How are we going to know if another gospel is being presented? None of us should rely totally on the revelation and instruction given us by others about the Word of God. Jesus is a personal Savior, a personal help in time of trouble, a personal friend and a personal God who has a desire to love each and every person in a relationship uniquely specific to them. When someone begins to read the Bible with the intent of personally discovering Jesus for himself, then error and deception is uprooted and the person is set free. It is in the pages of the Word of God that the deepest need of love, acceptance and forgiveness is met and abundantly exceeded.

JESUS IS THE WORD

Jesus is the Word. That was His Name in eternity past. *"In the beginning was the Word, and the Word was with God, and the Word was God" (John 1:1).* His Name is eternally the same, *"And he was clothed with a vesture dipped in blood: and his name is called The Word of God" (Revelation 19:13).*

Writing is an eternal characteristic. There are books in the spirit realm. One of God's books is the Book of Life. Through the ages there has always been the written word. From the beginning Jesus has been laying Himself as the foundation through the Word of God. One cannot separate the Word of God from the person of Jesus because He is the Word.

The Lord has chosen to bring Himself to the world through His written word, the Bible, as well as through words *spoken by the Holy Spirit* in people's lives called *rhema* words. Rhema words are words or *revelation* the Lord gives to people to grip the inner man with truth and reveal the answer to their petition and cry.

TAKE HEED TO FOUNDATION

The Lord, however, requires each of us to take heed to the doctrine we have laid at the foundation of our lives, and be wise about what is built upon it. King David humbled himself before the Lord. He petitioned the Lord with *"Examine me, O Lord, and prove me; try* (refine and purify) *my reins* (thoughts) *and my heart,"* and again, *"Search me, O God, and know my heart: try me, and know my thoughts: And see if there be any wicked way in me, and lead me in the way everlasting" (Psalm 26:2, 139:23, 24 explanation added).* King David yielded himself to the work of the Holy Spirit to purge out every error and wicked thing within his thoughts and heart.

Likewise, the Lord honors those who yield themselves to the work of the Holy Spirit to purge and purify. He is able to cause each of us to look at our foundation beliefs and show us what is being built upon them in the spiritual and natural realms.

One of the reasons I reached the point of burnout in my

Christian walk was that I was ignorant of what was false in my foundation. One day the Lord gently spoke to me the word "Pharisee." I asked what a Pharisee was. He replied, "A Pharisee is one who does the spiritual thing in the flesh." How many of us walk out our spiritual lives with actions and beliefs that are merely extensions of our fleshly nature?

In Matthew 16, the Sadducees and Pharisees came to tempt Jesus. Jesus rebuked them by calling them a wicked and adulterous generation. Later, His disciples questioned him about this. Jesus warned them to *"...Take heed and beware of the leaven of the Pharisees and of the Sadducees" (Matthew 16:6)*. The disciples thought He was talking about not bringing bread with them. Jesus explained what He meant and in verse 12, Matthew relates what they were taught, *"Then understood they how that he bade them not beware of the leaven of bread, but of the doctrine of the Pharisees and of the Sadducees" (emphasis added)*.

THE ROCK

Later Jesus asked his disciples, *"...Whom do men say that I the Son of man am?"* They said, *"...Some say that thou art John the Baptist: some, Elias; and others, Jeremias or one of the prophets."* Then Jesus asked them a powerful question. *"...But whom say ye that I am?"* When Peter replied, *"...Thou art the Christ, the Son of the living God," (Matthew 16:13-16)*. Jesus explained flesh and blood had not revealed that Name to him, but that the Heavenly Father had revealed it to him. Then Jesus said something that is powerful in the context we are discussing in this chapter. Jesus said, *"...That thou art Peter (a rock fragment), and upon this rock I will build...and the gates of hell shall not prevail against it" (Matthew 12:18, explanation added)*. Peter had established in his belief foundation a Name, character and anointing of Jesus that was revealed by God. Upon such a foundation, Jesus would build. When spiritual truth is laid at the foundation, then the gates of hell shall not prevail (apply overcoming pressure) against it. It is the same scenario discussed earlier where the house built on the rock foundation withstood the storms (gates of hell) beating against it.

This is a vital truth. If our beliefs and guidance are not founded on the Word of God, Jesus Christ and Him crucified, then we are being led and controlled by something or someone other than the Spirit of God. Satan can only operate where there is ignorance of or rebellion to the Word of God. Therefore, the foundation of satan's kingdom is a warfare of well-laid plans of deception, seduction, coercion and control against the Word of God and the gospel of the Lord Jesus Christ. Wherever believers have a solid foundation on biblical truths, satan is hindered, if not halted, in that area. Where there are beliefs and thoughts of an unrenewed mind, that person is subject to being bound, depressed and emotionally imprisoned.

DOORWAY TO THE HEART

The main onslaught of spiritual-wickedness strategists is on the *mind*; but their *target is the heart*. What the mind decides will rule the emotions and actions of the individual. The mind makes the decision on what comes out of the mouth, where the body will go and what will occupy the person's time. The mind determines the attitude for the whole being of a person. However, scripture states, *"... with the heart man believes..."* (Romans 10:10). Spiritual belief does not come out of the mind but out of the heart. When belief comes out of the heart, its expression is faith—faith in what God has said or what the enemy has planted (Hebrews 10:22).

From the beliefs laid at the foundation will flow all the issues of life

The mind is a doorway to the heart. Believers are instructed to renew their minds. They are cautioned to take heed to what they hear and how they hear. Proverbs conveys wisdom to us with *"... attend to my words; incline thine ear unto my sayings. Let them not depart from thine eyes; keep them in the midst of thine heart. For they are life unto those that find them, and health to all their flesh. Keep thy heart with all diligence; for out of it are the issues of life"* (Proverbs 4:20-23). We must guard our hearts and minds to keep our belief foundation established on sound doctrine.

BIBLE BATTLEFIELD

There are many who have tried to read their Bibles and seek God's answers but did not understand or recognize the attack against their mind and soul. The pressure and confusion they encountered was a satanically orchestrated deterrent from entering into knowledge and direction. Demonic voices were assigned to speak, repeating lies like, "The Bible is too hard to understand;" "God doesn't talk to people personally;" "It's going to take too long to get an answer, if there will even be an answer;" "God doesn't want to talk to you because of this sin or that sin," on and on it goes until they find one lie that works. Those seeking truth must discern what is being said and recognize it as a lie if it discourages reading and understanding the Word of God.

> *When satan tries to trip you—he is trying to make you stumble at a biblical truth*

Remember, the mental picture of the wrestlers of pressure verses pressure? Whoever maintains the more consistent and increasing pressure overcomes. Press through the confusion, even panic, that God will not give His answer in time to meet the need. Apply the persevering pressure to press in and hear from God by the spoken (rhema) and written Word of God.

The same thing applies regarding prayer. When distractions come, press in until you hear His voice in prayer. The distraction that keeps you from reading and believing is not a thing but a *who*. Why? Because ignorance gives way to being manipulated and controlled.

JESUS, OUR FOUNDATION

Why is Jesus the believer's foundation? Because no man can come to the Father except through Him *(John 14:6)*. Jesus is the only way by which humankind is redeemed from sin, the only means of righteousness before a powerful and just God, the only victor over the devil. Whenever people get in trouble in their spiritual walk, they need to go back to basics—back to what is laid at the foundation. They need to ask themselves: "Is my foundation founded on solid truth, sound doctrine—on the unfeigned truth of faith in Jesus Christ and His gospel? What do I know? What truth am I willing to die for? What truth am I willing to suffer loss for?" Find out what you know. What beliefs make up your foundation?

Error and false doctrine is not a characteristic of our DNA at physical birth. Error, idolatry and false doctrine are learned. There are evil strategists and people used by them to impart lies and error.

False teaching, error and confusion can be uprooted. *"He that refuseth instruction despiseth his own soul: but he that heareth reproof getteth understanding"* *(Proverbs 15:32)*, and *"By mercy and truth iniquity is purged: and by the fear* (reverence) *of the Lord men depart from evil"* *(Proverbs 16:6, explanation added)*. Idolatry is a learned belief, *"When thou art come into the land which the Lord thy God giveth thee, thou shalt not learn to do after the abominations of those nations"* *(Deuteronomy 18:9, emphasis added)*.

———◦/◦/◦———

The gospel is your weapon of warfare against spiritual wickedness in high places. Whether by word, action or proclamation, the power of the gospel overcomes the deception of error.

———◦/◦/◦———

The Gospel of Mark encourages believers. *"These signs shall follow them that believe…"* *(Mark 16:17, emphasis added)*. Powerful things follow what you believe. Beliefs bring things to pass. What you believe is able to bring blessing. Negative beliefs bring things that do not bless. Examining your foundation and becoming grounded in the love of God for yourself and for others, will bring signs and wonders which follow the one who believes.

ather, Your Holy Spirit has revealed that there has been error, unbelief and perversion to the gospel of Your dear Son, Jesus Christ in my life. I repent and ask Your forgiveness. I call upon the Blood of Jesus Christ to cleanse me from all unrighteousness, all uncleanness, all defilement and every effect of error and unbelief in my life. I now renounce and uproot every lie, every error and every strategy of the enemy that has sought to ensnare me. I proclaim truth into my heart and mind. I proclaim the gospel, the good news, over my life and call upon the Holy Spirit to teach me and bring me into all truth and establish my faith in sound doctrine—upon the wisdom, knowledge and understanding of Jesus Christ and Him crucified. Lord Jesus, You are the Purifier and Refiner. I submit my heart to You and ask for Your compassion and power to cleanse my heart and cause it to become a reflection of You. In Jesus' Name. Amen.

Also, as the Holy Spirit directs:

1. Proclaim the Light of the glorious gospel against the doctrine of error—known and unknown.
2. Bind up the lying spirits of error. Proclaim the Truth of Jesus Christ into the situation or to the person. (Prayer can be done for a person not present with you by praying for them as if they were in front of you. There is no distance in the Spirit. The Holy Spirit will close the distance between you.)
3. Speak words into the situation that are founded on the truth of scripture. Read the scripture that states the godly statement of belief with the intent and "applied pressure" —pushing ungodly statements of belief out of minds and out of the situation.
4. Proclaim the Blood and the broken body of Jesus Christ against the defilement of evil thoughts, desires and actions that have caused what is holy to become unholy.

A partial list of some of the ways false-doctrine strategists have deceived precious people is found in Appendix A at the end of the book. Also listed are some of the ways they work their wickedness.

In the following chapter we will look at some of the ways satan's emissaries have intruded into the lives of people and sought to obscure the lies of the enemy.

CHAPTER 7
RULERS OF DARKNESS—EXPOSED!

Rulers of darkness of this world are fallen-angel strategists who have within their personalities a ferocious desire to rule. They desire to seize, imprison, detain, obstruct, hinder and exercise their strength. Their purpose is to hide, camouflage, distract from discovery, blind and work strategies to keep satan's tactics, workings, purposes and motives from being brought to light.

Satan is the god of this world who has set out to blind the minds of those who would believe *(II Corinthians 4:4)*. Satan probably employs greater numbers of strategists and demons in this area than in any other because of the effort it takes to hide things and keep them from being exposed. Great effort is given to keep satan's plans hidden, hiding truth from those seeking truth, setting up distractions and keeping people in positions where they sit in darkness

Whenever the light of God is manifest, darkness is rendered helpless

and in the shadow of death *(Luke 1:79)*. Rulers of darkness are very active and expend great energy and activity in their warfare against us.

Rulers of darkness are masters in the art of confusion, vexation, frustration, affliction and diversion. Rulers of darkness have the charge of keeping darkness away from light (which reveals truth). They have the duty of formulating strategies of lies, distractions, diversions and seductions that will be implemented to keep people in darkness. It is important to realize that demons assigned under the command of rulers-of-darkness entities are the ones who are actually used to carry out the orders designed by the rulers of darkness.

LIGHT RULES

Whenever the light of God is manifest, darkness is rendered helpless. How is it, then, if darkness is helpless where light is, that there can even be "warfare" between light and darkness? The Heavenly Father dwells in the kingdom of light. He is the Father of Lights and there is no darkness at all in His presence and in His kingdom. When satan was cast out of heaven, he was relegated to a kingdom without light. The earth, however, was restored in such a way that there was light, but not light in the measure and intensity of God's heavenly kingdom; nor is the darkness God allowed on the earth of the blackness or density experienced in the kingdom of darkness.

The human race is sovereignly placed in such a position where we may choose light or darkness. We are given a free will. The war of the kingdoms is the battle for the decision of each individual. The Bible describes our journey on this earth as but a vapor in the scheme of eternal things *(James 4:14)*. God is preparing a people who will reign with Him who have willfully chosen Him and desire to serve Him, honor Him and worship Him throughout eternity.

Jesus will rule with a rod of iron during His Millennial reign *(Revelation 19:15)*. Believers are called to overcome in this world and thereby become equipped to rule and reign with Christ. Rulers of darkness are greatly threatened by believers who are learning to rule and reign in Christ.

LIGHT VERSES DARKNESS

The most obvious and logical warfare of darkness is, of course, light. Light in every aspect of the physical as well as the spiritual realm overcomes and overpowers darkness. Darkness has no ability to overcome or displace light. Even in the darkest of nights, one tiny candle or lighted match pierces the darkness so much so that it can be seen for miles. With light and darkness, one must give way to the other. Darkness cannot put out light. Darkness can only take a place that has been vacated by light.

ARMOR OF LIGHT

Believers are "the light of the world" in Christ Jesus. They are called and commissioned to walk as children of light. Ephesians 5:8

tells us, *"For ye were sometimes darkness, but now are ye light in the Lord: walk as children of light."* The sworn task of rulers of darkness is to do everything possible to keep believers from walking as children of light.

Believers who engage in spiritual warfare have an armor that has been given to them which was purchased by the Blood of Jesus Christ. Armor of light was made available to them when they became citizens of the kingdom of light. Paul, in speaking to the Romans, said, *"The night is far spent, the day is at hand: let us therefore cast off the works of darkness, and let us put on the armour of light"* (Romans 13:12). To cast off the works of darkness means to take our hands off of whatever we are doing that keeps us from picking up the armor of light, putting it on and wielding it as an weapon against darkness. Armor denotes both protection against attack and assures confidence when going on attack.

DELIVERED FROM THE POWER OF DARKNESS

What is it and how do we use the armor of light? Colossians states that the Father has *"...delivered us from the power of darkness, and hath translated us into the kingdom of his dear Son: In whom we have redemption through his blood, even the forgiveness of sins"* (1:13, emphasis added). Believers have been delivered from the power of darkness.

When we were washed in the Blood of Jesus, we received a cleansing that produced a luminous effect that is visible to the spiritual realm. Believers are the children of light; there is a radiance or light that is given off from them. Some years ago I read an article about scientific tests that revealed born-again believers had more light in their bodies than unbelievers, and those with the infilling of the Holy Spirit had an even greater measure of light. In the scientific realm, as well as in the spirit realm, there is verification of such light in the "children of light." So in a very real sense, as people grow in the things of the Lord, the "wattage" of their light grows and their walk in spiritual things becomes more and more evident. The light of their lives in Christ is a threat to the kingdom of darkness.

To wield the weapon of light is to walk boldly in the knowledge that the Blood of Jesus produces an immense light—a dynamic light—a glory light that shatters the darkness. We will see with eyes of faith that as we walk in the "glory" light, it overcomes satan at every turn. Believers can wield the light in any direction their faith points. It will overpower the darkness wherever it is pointed because by every law of nature and of spirit, light overpowers darkness.

———◦◦◦———

Darkness cannot put out light. Darkness can only take a place that has been vacated by light.

———◦◦◦———

LIGHT OF THE WORLD

Jesus desires for His light to radiate through His people, *"Ye are the light of the world. A city that is set on a hill cannot be hid. Neither do men light a candle and put it under a bushel, but on a candlestick; and it giveth light unto all that are in the house. Let your light so shine before men, that they may see your good works, and glorify your Father which is in Heaven"* (Matthew 5:14-16). Jesus counseled His followers that <u>He</u> did not want the light in them to be hindered. Rulers of darkness try to "put a bushel" —to restrict believers or try to make them draw back from walking as children of light. Jesus said it wasn't from Him. He desires to put His believers upon the lamp stand of the world to have them glorify God.

We must be continually reminded the Lord desires to impart wisdom, knowledge and understanding to His people. Daniel, in his thankful praise said, *"He revealeth the deep and secret things: he knoweth what is in the darkness, and the light dwelleth with him"* (Daniel 2:22). The Lord even places Himself in covenant with His servants, *"Surely the Lord God will do nothing, but he revealeth his secret unto his servants the prophets"* (Amos 3:7). Paul, in I Corinthians 14:1, exhorts his listeners to *"Follow after charity, and desire spiritual gifts, but rather that ye may prophesy."* God reveals hidden things to His people, to those who press through the trappings and stumbling blocks of the rulers of darkness of this world.

God wants to reveal the "why" of things. Why did this happen? Why should I obey? Where did I go wrong? In understanding the why, we find security and confidence. The Lord wants to answer the questions that rise up in your soul. Many times, my best Bible revelations were when I went into study with a question upon my heart.

ROADWAY OF REVELATION

The warfare of the believer against the rulers of darkness of this world is not an event, but a roadway of events in an ever-increasing knowledge and faith in the power of the Light of the world, Jesus Christ, His truth and His love. When believers are translated into the kingdom of Jesus Christ, they have things available that are in the kingdom of light, like truth, love, revelation and life. Jesus said, *"I am come a light into the world, that whosoever believeth on me should not abide in darkness"* (John 12:46).

When believers are informed and understand the tactics of the enemy, they will be wise! When we realize the power of God in Christ that is in us—we can be bold!! *(I Corinthians 1:24-31)*

Rulers of darkness have set plans of discouragement, distraction and diversion even before our birth. For anyone that desires freedom, the Lord said, *"And I will bring the blind by a way that they knew not; I will lead them in paths that they have not known: I will make darkness light before them, and crooked things straight. These things will I do unto them, and not forsake them"* (Isaiah 42:16).

MISSION IMPOSSIBLE?

There was a program on television some years ago called Mission Impossible. A team of specialists was called together for a mission. Their mission, "if they chose to accept it," was to work in such a way that their task would be accomplished with the Mission Impossible team being undetected. Most of the time their enemy was defeated by manipulating the person, or through people and circumstances around them. The team used disguises and impersonations to play on the weaknesses and vulnerable areas of their target. Of course, they were always against the bad guy.

Rulers of darkness work their evil plans similarly. The realm of strategists of the second heaven work together in a team effort to set up situations, manipulate circumstances and work through disguises of all sorts in order to achieve their desired end. It has been the task of rulers of darkness to work in such a way that every one else BUT them and their cohorts are blamed for the evil that occurs. They actively try to set blame and accusation upon God, His people and on holy purposes and callings.

CONFUSION (INCLUDING FEAR AND WORRY)

Confusion reigns when there is partial truth. Confusion brings oppression against the mind in the form of stupor and clouding of the mind. Rulers of darkness pour in false information and withhold facts. Confusion occurs when "unknowns" weigh heavier than what is known. Rulers of darkness will allow just enough truth to make their offering a consideration to the mind of their target.

Psalm 119:105 tells us, *"Thy word is a lamp unto my feet, and a light unto my path."* The Word of God is light. It wars mightily against the oppressive pressures of darkness.

Confusion attacks and tries to set the mind in a whirl. Those who fasten their faith in the faithfulness and compassion of the Lord toward them are not easily tossed about by confusion. Psalm 112:7 tells us, *"He shall not be afraid of evil tidings: his heart is fixed, trusting in the Lord."*

Psalm 27:1 reveals, *"The Lord is my light and my salvation; whom shall I fear? the Lord is the strength of my life; of whom shall I be afraid?"* Fear and confusion work hand in hand. However, believing and speaking forth verses like these in the face of fear and confusion will settle our minds and redirect our attention to God's desire for us.

STUPOR

Confusion occurs when the mind is clouded and dulled. Stupor is an evil personality that places a fog over the mind and makes us feel like we are drugged even though there is nothing in the natural that would produce such an effect. Stupor seeks to immobilize and dull the senses much like a drug would. A drugged state of mind makes us feel like we can't lift one finger to fight anything—it is almost like a dream where we are trying to talk and nothing comes out of our mouths. There is a helpless feeling that we are not in charge of our own faculties, or ability to resist.

There was a time when I experienced such a state of mind. I don't recall anything happening to bring such a feeling, but the stupor effect was a definite reality. It was hard to explain to anyone, and it had been present for a number of weeks.

I received a newsletter in the mail from Oral Roberts. As I read it, he told about four spirits the Lord had revealed to him had been loosed in the land. One of them was called Stupor, which described perfectly what I was experiencing. There was hardly one ounce of fight or energy in me to do anything about it, but I knew my enemy had been exposed. With the lowly ounce of fight left in me, I weakly spoke the prayer written out in the newsletter which went something like, "By the Name of Jesus Christ, whose I am and whom I serve, I renounce the spirit of stupor and command it to leave my life, my mind and my home." Then I went on about my day. Two hours later, the fog of my mind broke. It did not drift away but *broke*. It was not gradual but instant. It was a testimony to me of the power of the word spoken, even in a thimble of faith. In my weakness, I had spoken and the Lord guaranteed its power.

TERROR

Terrorism tactics produces confusion and is the initial step of dividing and attacking. Terror that attacks believers challenges their righteousness in Christ Jesus and questions the faithfulness of the Lord. Terror and oppression can rule where righteousness has not been established.

ARMOR OF RIGHTEOUSNESS and BREASTPLATE OF RIGHTEOUSNESS

The breastplate of righteousness given to the believer *(Ephesians 6)* is compared to an armor situated over a warrior so that it covers the vital organs of heart, lungs and stomach. Some warriors in past armies used their breastplate in battle by polishing its smooth surface into such a sheen that when the sun shown off it, much like the reflecting of light off a mirror, it reflected a blinding light into the eyes of the enemy. It caused confusion in the enemy because they could not see the approaching activity of those who wore the armor. So it is with the brilliance of believers in their righteousness in Christ. *"In righteousness shalt thou be established: thou shalt be far from oppression; for thou shalt not fear: and from terror; for it shall not come near thee...No weapon that is formed against thee shall prosper; and every tongue that shall rise against thee in judgment thou shalt condemn. This is the heritage of the servants of the Lord, and their righteousness is of me, saith the Lord"* (Isaiah 54:14,17, emphasis added). The believers who put on their armor of light and tactically use the breastplate of righteousness given them in Christ will bring blinding torment to the rulers of darkness.

The Blood of Jesus cleanses us from all unrighteousness; therefore those who have been washed in the Blood of Jesus are righteous before God. *"For he hath made him to be sin for us, who knew no sin; that we might be made the righteousness of God in him"* (II Corinthians 5:21). Paul speaks of this righteousness, *"By the word of truth, by the power of God, by the armour of righteousness on the right hand and on the left"* (II Corinthians 6: 7). The Lord equips believers with His armor of righteousness for spiritual battle.

IGNORANCE

Rulers of darkness hide truth or make truth obscure. They reinforce false doctrine by setting forth strategies that seek to authenticate error. They are only able to rule where there is ignorance.Therefore, ignorance is one of the most powerful weapons against people.

Lack of knowledge is dangerous

The Book of Proverbs talks about the benefits of wisdom, knowledge and understanding. People perish for lack of knowledge. The fear of the Lord is the beginning of wisdom. Reverence for God and His Word will bring knowledge into your life. Colossians 1:9 says, *"...to desire that ye might be filled with the knowledge of his will in all wisdom and spiritual understanding."*

- ◆ Knowledge—gives information, facts
- ◆ Wisdom—shows the "why" of things
- ◆ Spiritual understanding—shows the "how" of things

The more believers learn about God and His will, the more they know how He works and why He does what He does. They can walk with specific purpose in God's will.

Psalm 119:130 says, *"The entrance of thy words giveth light: it giveth understanding unto the simple."*

IGNORANCE MEANS IGNORE

Rulers of darkness seek to promote ignorance of the power that is in the Name of Jesus, the Blood of the Lamb, the indwelling presence of the Holy Spirit in believers and the bondage breaking force of forgiveness. They seek to distort the attributes and character of God through lies and accusations. The root word for ignorance is "ignore." Many ignore the workings of satan and his impact upon their lives. The Word admonishes every person not to be ignorant of satan's devices *(II Corinthians 2:11)*. Do not ignore them; do not be ignorant of them. Satan is a defeated foe. He has been rendered powerless by the resurrection of Jesus Christ. Satan doesn't want anyone to know that.

Neither can we ignore the counsel and warnings of God. God commanded the Israelites to destroy all their enemies in certain cities *(Deuteronomy 7:16)*. He commanded King Saul to destroy King Agag when he went to battle *(I Samuel 15:2-9)*. In both instances, God's command was not followed and the enemy was not destroyed to the measure set forth by God. Consequently, for them and for generations to come, their enemy became a thorn in the side of Israel.

Timidity is a by-product of ignorance. Where there is a lack of confidence, knowledge or assurance of the things of God, the person will draw back and even cower when rulers of darkness challenge them. Some translations replace fear with timidity; in II Timothy 1:7 we are told, *"For God hath not given you the spirit of fear* (timidity); *but of power, and of love, and of a sound mind"(explanation added)*. Ignorance produces fear; fear produces powerlessness, hate and confusion. God gives the opposite—power, love and soundness of mind.

ISOLATION AND DIVISION

Isolation and division have kept many ensnared in loneliness and personal prisons. Tactical rulers-of-darkness strategies are implemented to divide and to isolate. In the division and isolation of a person or persons, they are cut off from sources of assistance, information, encouragement and even deliverance. In isolation there is weakness and vulnerability. This is not referring to seclusion when you are shut in with the Lord, seeking His will and purpose. Rulers of darkness fear the power of the prayer closet. The isolation referred to here speaks of separation from God, from believers, from any who might possibly bring acceptance and restoration.

Think of the wildlife documentaries of predator and prey. For instance, a lion will stalk a whole herd seeking a prey. He is powerless against the herd. The lion causes confusion and panic so the herd will take off running. His purpose is to get everything so confused and scattered that there are some who end up separated. Before the prey can be rejoined to the safety of the group, the lion leaps upon its victim to devour it. The one that becomes separated is left to its own resources and strength for survival, whereas in the group safety is almost guaranteed.

When we stay within the protective boundaries of godly fellowship and counsel, *"The old lion perisheth for lack of prey"* (*Job 4:11*). The lion (satan) that goes about seeking whom he may devour will come up starved of his purpose and weakened in his plan.

RULER OF DARKNESS WOUNDS

When people become isolated, something has scattered them from safety. A satanic strategy of rejection most likely is the culprit. Rejection itself is not the greatest danger, because every person encounters rejection as a part of life. However, rejection that produces isolation is a damaging and dangerous plan wrought in the second heaven to paralyze and immobilize.

People who have become isolated can identify (by the revelation and power of the Holy Spirit) the event that brought about their isolation. They can allow the power of the love of God to fill the wounded place. Isolation cuts people off from the blessings and purposes of God. They are separated, almost as if a knife has sliced them away from tangible provision and fellowship. People end up hiding themselves away from one another. In so doing, they are hidden from those who are able to help.

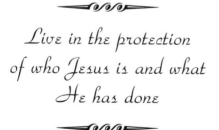

Live in the protection of who Jesus is and what He has done

Rulers of darkness seek to keep individuals unknown from one another. They manipulate circumstances and pervert information in order to reinforce isolation. That is why the Lord commands believers to forsake not the assembling of themselves together *(Hebrews 10:25)*. There is safety and protection in being with other believers. There is guidance and encouragement in fellowshipping with one another in the Lord.

The truth of the love of God draws us into freedom that displaces rejection and isolation. People who are founded in the knowledge of the awesome love of God toward them do not have to battle the effects of rejection dealt them by man. They are better able to forgive and not remain wounded.

LURED AWAY

Those who have asked Jesus Christ into their hearts have received an anointing from the Anointed One. As we have learned, Christ means "Anointed One." Christians have an anointing upon their lives designed to fulfill their part in the Body of Christ. Whenever we are cut off from believers, we are lured away from those who have been given power to overcome the work of satan. Aggressive involvement of believers through prayer and Holy Spirit led action may be needed in order to counter the false security offered by isolation.

Isolation not only includes the individual who is separated from other people, but it can also include satan making every effort to keep people isolated from people and places where the gospel is preached and the miracles of God are in operation. Rulers of darkness want unbelievers to stay separated physically, emotionally and spiritually from those who would bring the gospel of the Lord Jesus Christ to them or testify of the wonderful works of God.

Even people in groups can suffer from isolation because of hidden sin and fear of exposure. The power of the love of God and the revelation of the His grace for each person brings restoration and healing to those seeking deliverance from isolation.

- ◆ Perverted truth fosters rejection
- ◆ Half truths bring injury and rejection
- ◆ Pure truth brings freedom and healing

Before we continue further into our investigation of rulers of darkness, let's take a moment to receive the Lord's goodness as He ministers His grace and healing to us in this area of need.

*L*ord, I call upon You by the power of the Blood of Jesus Christ of Nazareth to come and heal the wounds that have been revealed. Father, pour Your love into the soul, mind, and emotions of Your hurting vessel and cause peace and restoration to make me whole again. I sever any attachment I may have with isolation and any demons who have brought false counsel or comfort. I cast them out in the Name of Jesus Christ of Nazareth. I speak truth into my life, and I call for the Light and love of Jesus Christ to flood my being. I declare I am free from the bondage of separation and isolation. I proclaim that I am RELEASED from the enemy and RESTORED into the life of the Lord Jesus Christ and the Body of Christ. In Jesus' Name. Amen.

SELF PITY (PITY AND FORMS OF DEPRESSION)

Self-pity is a powerful method used by rulers of darkness to introduce or intensify isolation. Self-pity is a stronghold that imprisons many. Fallen-angel strategists weave intricate nets to ensnare a person, usually by instilling error, lies and rejection. Familiar spirit demons play a major role in people who suffer self-pity over their lives. The person can even develop affection towards the familiar spirit because it gives comfort, even if it is false comfort designed to entangle one's soul.

There is a difference between self-pity and depression. Depression seeks answers. Depression seeks hope. Depression grasps opportunity for freedom. Depression acts upon avenues of deliverance and refuses the coddling of self-pity emotions. One can be depressed and not be in self-pity.

SELF PITY OPPOSES HOPE

A person controlled by self-pity is continually rehearsing all aspects of situations where they were wronged. Some receive consolation from dark rooms, isolation and "inner" conversations, which justify their actions, give reasons not to forgive, to hold onto hate, or various reasons why they should remain separated from others. Self-pity refuses hope and is critical of any consolation given. Self-pity argues against hope. Self-pity refuses truth. Therefore, people controlled by self-pity will refuse their source of deliverance. Sometimes the self-pity demons even raise their head in outright anger at those who bring counsel or truth. Self-pity controlled people have their attention on self rather than on God or godly principles, and usually are angry with God. Rulers of darkness and their demons relish in their work. Self-pity will seek to dominate and manipulate people and situations. To give up self-pity strongholds, the person must give up the controlling, manipulative power they have exercised. Because of the intertwining of familiar spirit demons in the person's life, the person needs an understanding of how such demons work in order to break the hold leveled against them. See the segment on familiar spirits in Chapter 10.

NEGATIVE PRIDE

Because I had to confront self-pity myself, I know it can seem like a formidable foe. You will discover it is not formidable once its *method of operation* is revealed. I was deceived into false humility. I had grown up with it and when I came to the Lord, He began dealing with me about my pride. My question to Him was, "How can someone who is so down on themselves have so much pride?" He answered, "You do not have the puffed up type of pride but the opposite kind, which is really negative pride." It was a self-degrading type of attitude that fed self-pity. Self-pity feels it can change circumstances around it through manipulation and control of people and situations. It entertains demonic ideas of how to bring people to feed self-pity. Self-pity demons encourage one to injure or allow injury to oneself either directly or indirectly.

A DEADLY FORCE

My wake up call came when the Lord most emphatically and clearly spoke to me and said, "Self pity is a death-dealing force." He showed me how my thoughts of self-pity were making way for an opportunity to oblige satan in his plans for injury. Satan was planning a wicked scheme, and I was developing an attitude of "acceptance" rather than resistance and warfare against his plan.

Self-pity is a force working toward its end result—death. Death can take on any number of forms, like divorce and separation, unhealthy eating habits, death to dreams and goals and even physical death.

Once the Lord revealed to me there was a "who" (a being who was speaking the words of self-pity into my mind), I was able to recognize the demon spirit. I was then aware how dangerous it was to cooperate with its evil scheme by allowing the demonic words to roll around in my thinking. The Lord had also revealed its intent. The powerful emphasis with which the Lord spoke assured me this was a serious matter. A whole area of my thought processes took a dramatic turn. I found a freedom in my mind that brought God's opportunity and strength.

I repeat—*self-pity is a stronghold.* Any thought of self-pity cannot be entertained or played with. It is a thief that seeks devastation of its victim. Again, we must understand demon voices will speak into our minds satan's evil desire for our lives. They identify their success by watching our actions and listening to our words. We must discern the words being spoken within our thought processes. If those words feed self-pity, we must deny their entrance and instead speak forth the faithfulness and goodness of God over ourselves and over the situation.

When thoughts of self-pity strike your mind, you should speak out loud what God says—speak the Word. God's truth will then bombard the thoughts planted in your thinking by evil rulers of darkness, thereby causing the Word (Jesus) to rule your mind.

LIES

As with every area of satan's kingdom, lies saturate the fiber of ruler of darkness workings. Rulers of darkness are infused with the nature of their master, the father of lies. Rulers of darkness wield the weaponry of lies with wild abandon like a sower tossing evil seed to the wind. They know there will be "takers" somewhere along the line. They also use lies in masterful and strategic implementation. Lies are a force—a force of deception that carries with it an ability to divert, control, manipulate and seek to change the course of a person's life and the course of peoples and nations. Truth is also a force—a force that neither lies or troubles can bind, *"...the word of God is not bound"* (II Timothy 2:9-15).

Hate is a product of darkness. Lies are a product of hate. One does not lie to a person if a root of hate does not exist. Where there is light there is truth, and where truth is there is love. Love has free expression where there is truth and light.

LIES WOUND

Most people have a hard time believing that people lie. However, experience teaches otherwise. We are ignorant of the capability spawned within people to cover truth, misinform or to outright lie. Even those who are caught up in the web of lying want to believe that they will not be lied to.

We must recognize that within the fallen nature of human beings, the father of lies, satan, had his root. His whole kingdom is founded upon lies, so his followers will also lavishly propagate a vast array of lies. He will play upon the sinful nature within every person to keep each one bound by lies and will continually instigate lies in and through people.

Rulers of darkness intimidate by words, threats, lies and imagination

Lies cause wounds. Whenever someone finds out they were lied to, the person has a sense that they have been somehow violated, abused or injured, which indeed they have been. Rulers of darkness desire to cause woundedness, for in it, doors open for further pain and control into people's lives.

Rulers of darkness desire to inflict pain and torment, whether mental, emotional, physical or financial. Pain and torment cause one to look inward and to consider their suffering more than anything else around them. Their whole attention can become focused on eliminating the pain or torment that has entered their lives.

Truth is our defense against the lies of the enemy, John 8:31-32, *"...If ye continue in my word...And ye shall know the truth, and the truth shall make you free."* Truth brings freedom. Truth brings lasting peace *(Psalm 119:160)*. Spiritual truth cannot be found apart from the Word of God. Rulers of darkness war vehemently against the written and spoken scripture because the words of God bring a direct line of defeat to their work. If we do not maintain fervor into the Word of God, we are vulnerable to the inevitable lies of satan's workers.

DEALING WITH LIES

How do we deal with the lies that have infiltrated our thinking and beliefs? Believers and unbelievers alike can have their understanding darkened and their hearts blinded. We can hide from our own fleshly motives and desires *(I Corinthians 4:5)*.

Ephesians 4:18-20 explains, *"Having the understanding darkened* (by rulers of darkness), *being alienated from the life of God through the ignorance that is in them, because of the blindness of their heart: Who being past feeling have given themselves over unto lasciviousness, to work all uncleanness with greediness. But ye have not so learned Christ; If so be that ye have heard him, and have been taught by him, as the truth is in Jesus"* (explanation and emphasis added).

The Psalmist declares, *"Try me...And see if there be any wicked way in me, and lead me in the way..." (Psalm 139:23,24)*. This request of the Lord is for each of us who is seeking to root out evil within us by not letting any darkness abide in the inner thoughts and motives *(Psalm 26:2)*.

Those with the heartfelt desire for truth will pray and the Lord will enlighten their darkness *(Psalm 18:28)*. The Lord will make darkness break up so shafts of light or the dawning may come forth. Jesus is our Dayspring to give light to those who sit in darkness and in the shadow of death *(Luke 1:79)*.

SEEKING TRUTH

The Bible speaks about seeking—seeking with one's whole heart and mind. Seekers must do so with a determination that cannot be shaken when they desire the best from God. Why does the Lord require such tenacity? Because He knows rulers of darkness inhabit the battleground between the person and the blessings of God. That is why we must

Revelation without obedience brings confusion

continue in the Word of God, because there is a pathway punctuated with signposts of direction for those who seek to be free.

Revelation without obedience brings confusion. The danger in making that statement is that satan would like to imply that EVERY blessing, every need, every answer must go through a strenuous and arduous process to receive from God. No! No! No! The mercy and lovingkindness of our Heaven Father brings His provision and blessings abundantly and at every opportunity. He is *seeking* opportunity to pour out blessing and to answer needs. Rulers of darkness want to portray God as a pious overlord withholding good things from us.

Whenever the Lord can pour out blessings that do not have a requirement on our part, He abundantly provides. The Word says He pours out the rain on the just and the unjust. The Lord will sometimes bless just because He cannot restrain himself. His blessings spill over because He cannot contain His great love. Supernatural answers come to needs even without being prayed for (at least to the knowledge of those receiving the answer). The Lord reveals Himself, even without being sought after in any tangible way. Sometimes there is minimal effort taken to seek God and He swiftly complies.

Then there are other times when answers do not come, provision is delayed and revelation is seemingly withheld and must be earnestly sought in prayer, fasting, repentance and forgiveness. Prayer places the focus on God for what is sought; fasting shuts down the power of the flesh that wars against the spirit; repentance removes the blockages to God; and forgiveness removes the hindrances of receiving *from* God. Will not God rejoice when we press through such stumbling blocks (placed there by the enemy) to grasp what He desperately desires to endue?

There can be a wrestling with our flesh, as well as wrestling against unseen forces before breakthrough manifests. Such requirements are necessary not because GOD is withholding or that He needs to be appeased like some ritualistic god, but because spiritual forces have set themselves against those who will do exploits in Jesus Christ.

God sees what is in the darkness. Light dwells with Him. He will expose that which is hidden by darkness. There must be a commitment to be freed from the strategies of darkness. It is a pathway, not an event. However, it can be eventful. But until we actually arrive at our heavenly destination in the kingdom of God, we will wrestle with rulers of darkness. *"Therefore judge nothing before the time until the Lord come, who both will bring to light the hidden things of darkness, and will make manifest the counsels of the hearts: and then shall every man have praise of God"* (I Corinthians 4:5).

CHAPTER 8
RULERS OF DARKNESS—PART 2

Believers must not be naive enough to think that once they attack the kingdom of darkness there will be no counterattack. The territory guarded by rulers of darkness is so important that their very place of domination depends on their efforts. Christians, by skillfully standing and being tenaciously confident of Christ's victory and abiding authority within them, are able to take treasures out of darkness *(Isaiah 45:3)*.

RULERS OF DARKNESS COUNTERATTACK WHEN EXPOSED

In Hebrews 10:32-36, the Lord counsels those who engage in the battle. When they were illuminated (with spiritual revelation and impartation), believers endured a great fight of afflictions. They endured the fight—they met the measure of the attack and endured to victory. The Lord commands us not to draw back, because if we do not draw back, we shall overcome. He is delighted in our victory.

The truth is not bound; the Word of God is not bound *(II Timothy 2:9)*. Satan cannot overcome when truth goes forth. We must build our faith in the power of truth—the power of God's truth. We must open our eyes into the spirit realm

The Bible shows satan's defeat

that reveals how proclamations of the Word and truth pierce darkness and scatter demons as glorious light bursts forth into the situation.

DISTRACTIONS

The objective of strategies of distraction is to divert our mind and attention away from a certain subject, focus or intent. They make every effort to keep people in their present state of darkness or ignorance—they know what control they have had and have spent time and effort getting there.

Having a strong focus is a valuable attribute of a person's makeup.

The one who can deal strongly and wisely with distractions meets goals and achieves success. This is especially true in the walk of godly paths. Most distractions, whether in the natural or in the spiritual, are stealers. They steal time, energy and achievement. There are diversions and distractions at every turn. There are a myriad of things that contribute to the stumbling block efforts of distraction.

Some distractions, on the other hand, are just the happenings of every day life, the demands of responsibilities of home, family, jobs and God-lead commitments. Those will happen and are necessary.

There are some instances where we think we are being distracted, but really are opportunities. Sometimes it seems like a fine line between opportunity, proper obligation and distraction. What is being addressed here are the distractions set up by rulers of darkness to draw us away from God-ordained destinations and activities, our call or purpose. We want to address distraction that draws us away from entering into the place where we will be exposed to God's acceptance, truth, revelation and direction.

The Bible exposes satan's character and works

Rulers of darkness divert our attention to other activities and tug our emotions toward what they want to showcase. Entertainment of all sorts, physical and mental pursuits, and many other things aggressively seek our attention. We are not to be lovers of pleasure more than lovers of God *(II Timothy 3:4)*. Problems can also summon physical, mental and emotional attention and sap strength, thereby luring the person away from a pathway designed by the Lord to bring him into a safe and fruitful haven.

Distractions can also draw our heart away from seeing the results of past sin or error. Rulers of darkness seek to make one numb to sin's consequences. They desire to rationalize error, false doctrine or disobedience. Rulers of darkness desire to block our hearing. Distractions cause us to not listen. We may be seeking to hear from God, but demon voices make a racket, clamor for attention, make suggestions, accuse and offer alternative solutions. The Word admonishes us to "have ears to hear" *(Mark 4:23,24)*. Faith comes by hearing and hearing by the Word of God *(Romans 10:17)*. Hearing is <u>not</u> a passive activity. Hearing, with discernment, is active and brings revelation and wisdom.

GOD DOES NOT KEEP US IN THE DARK

Rulers of darkness also use distraction and divisive strategists to accuse. They accuse God for our problems; they accuse us or those around us. Their plan is to place attention on what they want us to see, making every effort to keep our attention off *their* deceptive work.

Military strategists know the value of setting up diversions and distractions. The purpose is to take attention off what is really "coming down." They know if their enemy saw them coming an expected way, they would prepare and reinforce. The effect of diversion and distraction is to weaken or eliminate resistance to the intended plan. Demons, who are dispatched to cause distractions, seek to create an open door for what satanic planners want to achieve.

The problem with most of us is that we don't see the "big picture." Our day-to-day existence does not readily reveal the bigger plan of our lives. The bigger plan is seen through the eyes of vision and of faith. The visionary sees the plan afar off. The Lord has placed within every one of us the visionary attribute for fulfilling our part in the plan of God. Vision—godly inspired vision grounded in faith and truth—protects us from the thievery of distraction. Vision is defined as "divine revelation, it often involves a supernatural appearance and/or prediction, direction, or instruction" *(taken from Guidepost Family Concordance, p. 754)*.

Habakkuk 2:2 instructs us, *"And the Lord answered me, and said, Write the vision, and make it plain upon tables, that he may run that readeth it."* Set the vision before your eyes and before others who will assist in achieving and maintaining the goal.

According to Proverbs 29:18, *"Where there is no vision, the people perish: but he that keepeth the law, happy is he."* The Hebrew word for perish is *para*. It describes the effect of "setting at naught, to expose, dismiss, make bare, uncover." Where there is no vision, distraction will cause us to become uncovered, unprotected or made ashamed. But the rest of the verse offers a solution. He that *keepeth* the law is happy (successful). The Hebrew word for keep is *shamar* which means to "hedge about, guard, protect, attend, take heed to." The one who keeps, protects, attends to and stays focused on what the Lord says will be happy and fulfilled. Distraction loses the day!

STEALERS OF VISION

Rulers of darkness want to bring a division or a di-vision, a dividing from our vision. They are stealers of vision. Spirits of error introduce a lie that says our dream or vision is not from God and that it will never come to pass. Little by little, darkness covers the vision until it is placed so far back from our view we do not clearly see it any longer. We become convinced it was not to be, and our energies are diverted to other things.

—————

A thief only comes for what is valuable

—————

Jesus wants to restore dreams and visions. He placed them there initially anyway. He is the Way, the Truth and the Life. Call upon Him. He will make a way for those dreams and visions to again have their pathway of priority in your life. He will cause you to understand how error and darkness have obscured your eyes from beholding the prize that awaits you *(James 1:23-25)*. He will reveal what He wants to do from this point forward. And He wants to breathe renewed, refreshing life into the dreams and vision for your life. He abides within the believer. Listen to His counsel as He speaks to your heart. Cooperate with His direction. Sometimes such counsel is as simple as breathing in deeply (to receive refreshing renewing life) or symbolically taking off blinders from the eyes (unseen by the natural eye). Don't worry about starting small. It is much easier to walk in sunlight than it is in darkness. A simple act of obedience can make the difference between walking in light or darkness. Flipping on a light switch is really not a big deal in and of itself, but by doing so, it sets in motion principles that are in place to cause light to fill the room. Being faithful in little things gives way for mature faithfulness in big things.

Darkness strategists cause division between those of common purpose and vision. Beware of the tactics of the adversary to divide and isolate believers from one another. Proclaim light and truth into the situation. Listen with spiritual ears to what is being said. Speak forth scripture that fills the situation with life and truth.

SEDUCTION—(AND VEXATION)

Seduction is an allurement that entices in order to control or to draw away from a right path. Mark 13:22,23, warns, *"For false Christs and false prophets shall rise, and shall shew signs and wonders, to seduce, if it were possible, even the elect. But take ye heed: behold, I have foretold you all things."* James relates, *"But every man is tempted, when he is drawn away of his own lust, and enticed"* (James 1:14). Rulers of darkness seek a vulnerable spot, a weakness that they target for purposes of seduction. Seductive spirits lure, prod, question and vex in order to gain control.

To illustrate the methods satan uses here, let's look again at the story of Samson and Delilah. As we read the account of their story, we see several methods used to overcome a powerful and chosen vessel of God. Samson's weakness was women. Knowing this, his enemy employed a seductive temptress to discover the secret to his great strength. Armies could not defeat him but seduction would. Day after day Delilah prodded and accused Samson. She accused him of lying to her, of mocking her by not telling her his secret. She accused him of not loving her. She played on every emotion he had. She wasn't even too vague about her request, *"And Delilah said unto Samson, Tell me, I pray thee, wherein thy great strength lieth, and wherewith thou mightest be bound to afflict thee"* (Judges 16:6). Samson unwisely thought he was able to play with fire and carelessly handle the call of God upon his life.

The Delilah type of seducing spirit will:

- ◆ Want you to reveal how you can be bound.
- ◆ Try to get you to reveal secrets in order to control.
- ◆ Use seduction that dulls the mind and emotion to potential danger.
- ◆ Use a false security in your own abilities and gifts.
- ◆ Use vexation, accusation and project guilt in order to control.

EVIL SOUL TIES

Seduction draws people into evil soul ties. The purpose of satanic inspired soul ties is to cast a snare into the life of one set on a God ordained path. Romans 6:12 says, *"Let not sin therefore reign in your mortal body, that ye should obey it in the lusts thereof."* Lust oriented strategies are seeking to obtain rule, and in so doing they control the destiny of the person. *"Be not deceived: evil communications corrupt good manners" (I Corinthians 15:33)*. Ungodly relationships are set up by satan to keep us from fulfilling God's purpose for as long as they remain an influence in our life.

VEXATION

Vexation wears down with toil in order to overcome your will or resistance. Vexation, manipulation and seduction work closely with one another. Vexation is a type of harassing spirit that rattles the mind and wears down emotional strength.

Demons, who are skilled in the art of agitation, cause the actual torment to the mind, but behind it is the strategy of broken resistance. Rebuke the harassing demon but also seek out the *strategic* reason for it being there. It guards its hiding place, but the Holy Spirit will reveal it and give counsel for its defeat.

SEXUAL SEDUCTION

Sexual seduction is rampant in today's society. It is almost impossible to avoid every aspect of the multitude of sexual advertisements, sexual content in movies and television, seductive apparel accepted as the norm of today's fashion and the proliferation of pornography. There are multitudes of men and women who are struggling with the effects of sexual impurity. Demons of sexual perversion are freely trafficking the earth because people have accepted the sexual freedom attitude as the up-to-date version of today's society. Many people have ignorantly allowed demons of sexual uncleanness to invade their lives and homes. Much of the turmoil in the home is spurred on by the presence of spirit forces. Sexual uncleanness is an isolating and tormenting spirit.

Demon forces may be present, but believers have authority to cast them out. Demons cannot remain where they are cast out and every attempt at their reentry is diligently repelled.

Whenever believers exercise their authority against an unclean (sexual) spirit in the Name of Jesus and fervently stand against its return, demons must obey. Demon spirits actually handle the body in order to challenge resistance to the seduction strategy. They want people to believe they have chosen the seduction or they have again fallen into its trap. Unholy sexual habits may be the permissive presence of a demon spirit that manifests against the person at the slightest suggestion or stimuli. Recognizing a demon spirit is present and knowing it must leave in the Name of Jesus can help you become free. Realize, however, when an unclean spirit leaves, the place it left must be filled with the presence and power of the Holy Spirit and the saving knowledge of the Lord Jesus Christ *(Luke 11:24-26)*. How can you "fill your house?" Jesus said, *"If you love me, keep my commandments" (John 14:15)*, and *"If ye keep my commandments, ye shall abide in my love..." (John 15:10)*. Love the Lord more than the sin. Filling your life by loving Jesus and allowing Him to love you gives you power to overcome. Love enables you to keep His commandments. Love of the Lord enables you to turn from sin and have strength to walk away from the bondages and snares of the enemy, *"The wicked have laid a snare for me: yet I erred not from thy precepts" (Psalm 119:110)*.

Jesus has given believers power over all the power of the

The Bible tells of our pathway back into right standing with God through Jesus Christ

enemy. In Him is the victory. Greater is He that is in us than the enemy that is in the world. Jesus said, *"... for the prince of the world cometh, and hath nothing in me" (John 14:30)*. When we are filled with the power of God and His Word, we, too, can say, "though the prince of the world may come in various and varied disguises, he shall find nothing in me, no door of entrance, no avenue of seduction." We are free.

FLATTERY

Flattery can have constructive attributes, and it can also have a destructive motive. All people need encouragement and desire to have good things spoken to them and about them. Encouragement builds up people and propels them forward. It is a necessary ingredient for well-being.

Flattery that is satanically inspired is manipulative and desires control over its recipient. We are told in Proverbs 29:5, *"A man that flattereth his neighbor spreadeth a net for his feet."*

Psalm 5:9 says, *"For there is no faithfulness in their mouth: their inward part is very wickedness; their throat is an open sepulchre; they flatter with their tongue."*

Sexual seduction reeks with flattery but wisdom is able, *"to deliver thee from the strange woman, even from the stranger which flattereth with her words"* (Proverbs 2:16).

The Bible tells us of our weaponry against satan's kingdom

The Pharisees used flattery in their attempt to entangle Jesus in His own words. *"...Master, we know that thou art true, and teachest the way of God in truth, neither carest thou for any man: for thou regardest not the person of men. Tell us therefore, What thinkest thou?..."* (Matthew 22:16,17). Now, if that isn't a catch phrase for the spirit of flattery to entice. "What do you think"... our ego kicks in, we start to expound and the snare is laid. *"But Jesus perceived their wickedness, and said, 'Why tempt ye me, ye hypocrites?'"* (Matthew 22:18). We need to discern between flattery and sincerity. There is nothing wrong with seeking the counsel of the Lord about flattering words that come our way. The indwelling presence of the Holy Spirit is there to help us discern between wicked flattery and godly encouragement or counsel.

The important thing to understand is manipulative flattery is seeking an avenue of control. Knowing its motive will help us resist the smooth stroking of flattering words that are impure.

We can also perceive when uplifting, encouraging words are genuine. Words often come from grateful people who are expressing appreciation and admiration. The Lord does not begrudge this but rather admonishes believers to encourage one another daily (Hebrews 3:13). Accurate discernment grows as we mature in spiritual matters. Mature people understand every believer is at different levels of growth in their lives. We need help from each other to cover and protect areas where we may be vulnerable.

TIME

The dimension called time came into being at the restoration of the earth in Genesis 1. God's kingdom has no darkness. In eternal life there is eternal light and in that light time does not exist. It is a scientific fact that at the speed of light, time ceases to exist. God is the Father of Light and in Him is no shadow of turning *(James 1:17)*. Heaven is not pressured by time. Time itself is an earthly characteristic.

Time limits, deadlines and related time demands are pressure opportunities for rulers of darkness. Many times when we wrestle with tormenting time demands, we are actually wrestling with rulers of darkness. Rulers of darkness even create the illusion of deadlines or time restraints. How many times have we reeled at the pressure of a deadline only to have it change or be insignificant?

Rulers of darkness use time deadlines to apply pressure against waiting for the answer from God. Psalm 106:13 explains, *"They soon forgat his works; they waited not for his counsel."* They pressure us to make decisions outside the counsel of God.

The Bible builds faith in us

The Israelites waited for Moses to return from the mountain. Moses was on Mount Sinai 40 days fasting and communing with God. Forty days and nights was a long wait for the impatient Israelites. They thought Moses was surely dead. They knew Moses had gone to the mountain to hear from God. They did not have sustaining faith in Moses or in God, even though mighty miracles and the powerful hand of God had brought them out of their place of bondage. Instead they took matters into their own hands. They made a god of their own handiwork and were making their own future plans. They forgot they walked on dry ground as the Red Sea made walls along their path. They disregarded the mighty works that God did for them and were not willing to wait on the counsel of God. Waiting was a tremendous pressure to their souls. Hence, <u>time pressure</u> became one of the steps that diverted their path from the Promised Land to a lifetime in the desert.

We can learn from some New Testament saints the value of waiting. When Jesus was ready to ascend unto heaven, He left instruction, *"And, behold, I send the promise of my Father upon you: but <u>tarry ye in the city of Jerusalem, until</u> ye be endued with power from on high"* (Luke 24:49, emphasis added). For fifty days, there were 120 followers of Jesus waiting to receive the promise given to them. What they did during their waiting time was crucial. *"These all continued with one accord in prayer and supplication..."* (Acts 1:14). They continued with one accord; and they continued in one accord in prayer and in supplication. They were in agreement; they were focused on receiving the promise, and they continued to wait until...the promise came.

SUDDENLY, there came a sound from heaven...and they were filled...and began to speak. They were changed from weak to bold and endued with power from on high. Their waiting became the conditioning time for them to receive what God wanted to give them. The Lord had ordained the time for Jesus to baptize His followers, to endue them with power and the supernatural ability to speak with other tongues. Pentecost was the Jewish Festival of First Fruits. It was fulfilling prophetic events of Jesus Christ the Messiah. The promise was sure. The waiting had a specific timetable to obey. Those who waited for it were never the same.

TIME HASTE—A TRAP

Time pressures cause carelessness and tempt us to take chances. Many times shortcuts can actually be snares. The voice of the Holy Spirit might direct us not to go a certain way, or to slow down or to stop. When this happens, He is providing an escape from danger or loss. You can tune your spiritual ears into the realm of the spirit and receive counsel. Make a conscious decision to listen to the voice of the Spirit when time is pressing against you.

DEAD WORKS

Rulers of darkness divert us from good works to dead works. The simplest way to explain this is the way the Lord explained it to me. I was ruled by the demands of many things. I had a high expectation of what I wanted to accomplish, mainly because accomplishment gave me a sense of self-worth. I made my lists and breathed a sigh of victory with every item I marked off. The trouble was that my lists became unmanageable. They became a testimony to my unfinished tasks. It was becoming a way of life. I complained and complained. One day at a Bible Study, I showed them my lengthy list and murmured, "Do, do, do, there is so much I have to do." In prayer some days later, the Lord said, "Look up Philippians 4:9," and I dutifully obeyed. The Apostle Paul was speaking in the verse, but the Lord made it personal to me. *"Those things, which ye have both learned, and received, and heard, and seen in <u>me</u>, <u>DO</u>: and the God of peace shall be with you"* *(emphasis added)*. He went on to say, "To do anything less than what I tell you to do is slothfulness or disobedience. To do any *more* than what I tell you to do is <u>dead works</u>." As I pondered on the things on my lists which were mine and those that were directed by the Lord, I discovered I had a lot of dead works which had weighed me down. There were burdens the Lord had not desired but ones I had placed there to feed my own ego and spiritual reputation. I began to say "No" to things if I did not have the witness of the Lord in my inner man—in my gut. A refreshing peace came, the God of peace was indeed with me.

As I began to study dead works, I found it is an area that must be guarded against by all believers. Dead works seek their own glory. Good works give glory to the Lord. *"Let your light so shine before men, that they may see your good works, and glorify your Father which is in heaven"* *(Matthew 5:16)*. This scripture says good works do not have to be hidden away but are to shine before men in such a way as to glorify the Heavenly Father. Rulers of darkness seek to hide good works, to pervert their message or to substitute other works for good works.

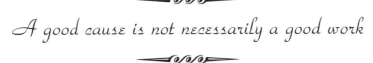

A good cause is not necessarily a good work

Discernment is needed to identify good works. Good works are those God has instituted, ones He has directed. Believers can be busy with many things, but unless they are divinely orchestrated, they will not be fruitful. Time is a valuable commodity which we should not waste. Rulers of darkness steal time by drawing us into fruitless endeavors.

GREATER WORKS

The Lord desires for us to do His works. *"Then said they unto him. What shall we do, that we might work the works of God? Jesus answered and said unto them, This is the work of God, that ye believe on him whom he hath sent"* (John 6:28,29). Basic to anything believers do is their knowledge of and relationship with Jesus Christ, the One whom the Father has sent. Jesus said, *"Verily, verily, I say unto you, He that believeth on me, the works that I do shall he do also; and greater works than these shall he do; because I go unto my Father"* (John 14:12). Jesus desires to impart to us powerful works, the works he did, and even greater works than He did. No wonder rulers of darkness are busy suggesting any other work, because at every turn Jesus was about the work of destroying satan's efforts. We are called to make ourselves available to the Spirit of God Who has called us to good works and IN JESUS CHRIST will know, *"How God anointed Jesus of Nazareth with the Holy Ghost and with power: who went about doing good, and healing all that were oppressed of the devil; for God was with him"* (Acts 10:38). In Jesus Christ, we do likewise!

PREDICTABILITY

While I was watching a Superbowl football game some years ago, a commentator made a very interesting comment. He said the losing team was being trampled because they had become predictable. The winning team anticipated the maneuvers of their opponent. They were able to block and tackle aggressively because they knew exactly where to send their strongest players or repeatedly "read" the play.

The Bible teaches us how to war

Whenever we become predictable, the enemy is able to block, tackle and halt any forward motion. The Bible says to put on the whole armor of God in order to stand against the wiles or methods of the devil. Satan's plan is to get us into a method. The word method, in Webster's dictionary, is defined as "a rule of accomplishing an end, orderly procedure, orderly arrangement." Satan would like to get us in such a predictable state of mind and of activity that he is able to set up traps and ambushes.

The Lord's Prayer says, *"Give us this day our daily bread. And forgive us our debts, as we forgive our debtors. And lead us not into temptation, but deliver us from evil..."* (Matthew 6:11-13). Bread has to do with not only daily provision, but Jesus also relates bread to doctrine. So daily bread also means daily beliefs of purpose and direction.

His mercies are new every morning, *"It is of the Lord's mercies that we are not consumed, because his compassions fail not. They are new every morning: great is thy faithfulness"* (Lamentations 3: 22, 23). His plan of protection and guidance is fresh every morning. Satan cannot implement plans on such short notice. The Lord sees every strategy of the devil and will safely guide His beloved away from danger.

CHAPTER 9

WORSHIP AS WARFARE

One of the issues that needs to be dealt with regarding books and teaching on spiritual warfare is the matter of getting out of balance. When I first began learning about demons and spiritual warfare, I spent a great deal of time casting out demons. I met every uncomfortable and hurtful situation by casting out this or that demon. It happened over and over again. Finally, the Lord gently counseled me, "You sure are giving satan a lot of attention." I realized I had been spending more time rebuking satan than worshipping and praising the Lord. The Lord told me satan loves all the attention, even if we are ranting and raving against him. If it steals worship away from God, he will relish any attention his kingdom gets. It gives to him a sense of power to gain our undivided attention.

At the time, I thought demons were the only personalities in satan's kingdom. Satan would like to see believers waste time and effort trying to cast out one demon at a time. Just think how long it would have taken Jesus to cast out 4,000-6,000 demons from the maniac at Gadara if such a process were the norm. Satan hates his own demons and will sacrifice any of them to steal away worship and adoration from Jesus, the Holy Spirit and the Heavenly Father. Satan hates the praises and worship that travel the heavenlies to the throne of God. It is torturous to him.

The Lord gave me a frame of reference to understand how satan feels when praise and worship to God go forth. It makes me shiver to have someone run his fingernails down a chalkboard. The screeching sound makes me cover my ears. The Lord equated that same feeling with how satan experiences the sounds of God's people raising their voices and instruments of music, their clapping hands, their dancing feet in praise unto God. It makes satan miserable and it hurts his ears.

Walking in our authority and taking our stand against the workings of satan's evil kingdom is a vital and necessary part of life in Jesus Christ. Casting out demons is part of, but not the majority of the focus believers should have. Who is getting the greatest time and attention? If most of our thoughts are on satanic or demonic issues, then we are out of balance.

OUR GREATEST WARFARE WEAPON

We wage our greatest spiritual warfare by glorifying, honoring and worshipping the Father, Jesus Christ His Son and the Holy Spirit. We wage warfare by proclaiming marvelous works and wondrous attributes of the Godhead—not by giving our undivided attention to satan and his works. Dealing with satan and his followers needs to have its proper priority and place.

The heavens proclaim the glory of the Lord. Worship which proceeds from believers on earth penetrates and shatters the barriers in satan's kingdom. They are woefully inadequate to resist the force that praise and worship carries. Holy Spirit orchestrated praise and worship cause second heaven restrainers to stand aside as holy angels usher provision and impartation from the throne of God to those in His presence.

In private and corporate times of prayer, praise and worship, the Lord reveals Himself to those seeking His face. When He reveals a facet of Himself to us, we receive an impartation of Christ Himself to abide in and to overcome.

Being strong in the Lord and the power of His might is a matter of the heart—not just of the head. It is important to be knowledgeable and to have facts, but strength and dynamic perseverance come when we meet with our Lord face-to-face, experience the presence of the Heavenly Father and know the Holy Spirit as our companion.

We cannot meet Jesus, hear His voice and feel His presence without being impacted with His love. We cannot enter the presence of the Father without revelation of penetrating love. God loves us. The Holy Spirit will help us have an understanding of the God embodied love toward believers and unbelievers that will establish a foundation for solid standing in spiritual matters.

HOLY ANGELS WORSHIPPING

The Heavenly Father's kingdom radiates worship and praise unto the Father, to His Son, Jesus Christ and to the Holy Spirit. Angels continually offer worship unto God and glorify the God of Heaven. They, together with the saints who have died in faith, worship and adore their God. Angels have always worshipped Elohim, the Creator God. They continually proclaim before the throne adoration and the joyous shouts of "Alleluia" *(Revelation 19:1, 4-6)*.

It was this glorious worship which satan desired be directed toward himself when he fell from his position as the Anointed Cherub. He offered all the kingdoms of this earth to Jesus if only Jesus would worship him.

Our Heavenly Father seeks those who would worship Him in spirit and truth *(John 4:24)*. Worship and praise are actually proclamations of doctrine which exalt the Names, character and attributes of God. They express adoration and glorification of God.

Praise will affect first and foremost the pray-er. Praise sets the attitude and focus of the one who is praying; it exalts the Lord in the soul of the pray-er and strengthens the inner man. When we magnify the Lord, it is not to make the Lord "bigger" but to acknowledge the Lord IS bigger than any problem, failure, injury or evil strategy.

A HEART OF PRAISE

The believer needs a heart of praise, not merely a mouth of praise for long-term, effective warfare. We can lift a sacrifice of praise when our heart is gaining its foothold in faith, but long-term praise is grounded in understanding the power and purpose of praise and worship. Understanding means knowing WHO is praised and WHY to praise. Actions of any sort without understanding will eventually lead to misunderstanding.

The Lord desires that we praise Him with all of our heart, soul, mind and strength. The heart of the praiser is strengthened and encouraged because the Holy Spirit bears witness that the One who rules the heavens has received blessing, honor and glory. The presence of the Lord fills the heart of the one who worships Him. In His presence is fullness of joy and in His joy is strength *(Psalm 16:11, Nehemiah 8:10)*.

Worship focused on the Lord removes attention from ourselves, our problems, and more importantly, from the enemy. Worship centers on the One who is able to fulfill every need. Worship magnifies the One worthy of all praise and honor. Worship is songs and words which come from the innermost being that give reverence, honor and blessing to the Heavenly Father and to Jesus by the Holy Spirit.

WORSHIP SONGS

Songs, dance, uplifted hands, tambourines, instruments of music, flags, clapping and the various ways we convey our worship, exalt and glorify the God of Heaven. If you browse through the Psalms, you will find verse after verse praising the greatness, compassion and faithfulness of God, ones like, *"O Lord our Lord, how excellent is thy name in all the earth! who hast set thy glory above the heavens"* (*Psalm 8:1, emphasis added*).

The second heaven is lower than the third or highest heaven. When we extol the God who is *most high*, the God whose glory is *above the heavens*, we are acknowledging the God who is above all, most powerful, most glorious, most honored. It reminds the enemy he is subordinate and <u>under</u> the foot of Almighty God. God is exalted when we believe in our hearts and speak with our lips *that we know* God is higher than our problems, our fears and every plan the enemy can devise.

True worship is speaking truth, acknowledging the true character and identity of a holy God. It professes and proclaims what He has done to redeem and bless. True worship always takes us to a place where we acknowledge the love given to us and in turn we love the Heavenly Father, Jesus Christ His Son and the Holy Spirit. It proclaims the victory of the cross of Calvary and exalts Jesus Christ who paid redemption's price. It resounds thankfulness for the gift of Jesus Christ to the world by the Heavenly Father in His majesty and love. It is there that believers are redeemed and brought into right standing before the Heavenly Father. It is there that healing, restoration and redemption were established. It is in the remembrance and declaration of the victory of Jesus Christ on the cross, and the believer's new life in Him, which ravages satan of his evil doctrines of deceit.

WORSHIPPING THROUGH THE CROSS

Satan fears the cross. That was where his eternal doom was set. God's prophecy of the ages was fulfilled when Jesus, who was the Seed of the woman promised in Genesis, was lifted onto the cross. It was on the cross where Christ's heel was bruised and the head of the serpent, satan, was crushed (*Genesis 3:15*).

Through the cross came the way for more "Jesus-es" or little anointed ones (Christians) in the earthly kingdom—more of the same Jesus who would declare satan's defeat and humiliation before the spirit realm. Since Jesus' death and resurrection, satan must contend with those believers who have the same Spirit abiding within them which raised Christ from the dead. The same Holy Spirit lives within us to teach us, help us and give us the grace to be transformed into the image of Jesus.

In acknowledging Jesus Christ's work on the cross in worship, believers herald the One who has overcome all the work of the enemy. They build up within themselves a confidence and assurance of what they believe. Speaking and singing statements of belief that exalt Jesus Christ and His work at Calvary is actually warring against unbelief, error and ignorance.

Jesus said, *"...the words that I speak unto you, they are spirit, and they are life" (John 6:63)*. Whatever truths are believed, spoken and acted upon will produce life within us. We profess to a spirit world who witness what is said and done. God's holy angels are present to obey the voice of the Father, and demons are present to bear their defeat.

DECLARING WORKS

Spiritual wickedness in high places seek to declare the works and power of their master, satan. Satan requires it of his subjects. He demands homage and honor. His desire to be worshipped as god has not changed since his original thought of rebellion.

One day, someone told me about their spiritual walk and all the areas of satan's success. The person proceeded to explain <u>briefly</u> about promises God had given, and then went into <u>great depth</u> and dramatic display of how satan had done this and that to hinder those promises from happening. As I was leaving the building, the Lord counseled me, "You have just heard that person proclaim the mighty works of satan." I sensed the grieving of the Holy Spirit over the defeat expressed in the person's words and attitude wrapped in a spiritual cloak of false martyrdom.

God is exalted when people expound on who He is and what He has done. When we declare *His* marvelous works, we are exercising weaponry against rulers of darkness who want to hide the wonderful works of God. *"Remember his marvellous works that he hath done; his wonders, and the judgments of his mouth" (Psalm 105:5)*; and *"I will speak of the glorious honour of thy majesty, and of thy wondrous works. And men shall speak of the might of thy terrible acts: and I will declare thy greatness. They shall abundantly utter the memory of thy great goodness and shall sing of thy righteousness"* (Psalm 145:5-7).

Satan continually presents an evil counterpart to holy things. If declaring God's marvelous works honors Him, satan wants his works declared. Believers who discipline themselves to examine who is exalted in their circumstances and situations will draw the favor and provision from the Lord as their words honor the Lord and acknowledge His marvelous works. *"Oh that men would praise the Lord for his goodness, and for his wonderful works to the children of men! For he satisfieth the longing soul, and filleth the hungry soul with goodness"* (Psalm 107:8,9).

What mighty and powerful things has the Lord done in your life? Declare them. Speak forth praise and adoration. Declare his marvelous works; declare what He has done. Be specific. It ministers glory to the Lord and builds up faith in us and in those that hear us.

Speaking Holy Spirit breathed words that explain, express and describe what you have learned and believed about the Lord establishes a solid foundation. The creativity of God has given us many ways to express our praise to Him. Reading the last 15-20 chapters of Psalms, or for that matter all of the Psalms, gives a virtual feast of worship for anyone who needs help in expressing worship to the Lord.

SOUNDS OF PRAISE

The sound of our voice is very important. The Lord loves to hear the voices of His people as we praise. When statements of adoration and praise to Him flow out of our mouths, it is a place where the Lord draws close.

Paul and Silas had been beaten and thrown into prison. They did not murmur and complain about the day's events by rehearsing between themselves the injustice they were experiencing. Instead they prayed and sang praises unto God. They were making statements in word and song regarding their God. They lifted their voices loud and strong, for the Word says, *"and the prisoners heard them"* (Acts 16:25). In the midst of their praying and praising, the prison doors were opened and all the prisoners' chains were loosed. Paul and Silas' proclamations not only set them free but the chains of all those who heard them were released. Their words did not free the prisoners to escape and then continue on their own sinful ways; instead Paul cried out to the keeper of the prison, *"...Do thyself no harm: for we are all here"* (Acts 16:28, emphasis added). The prisoners who filled the dingy, dirty prison cells stayed to learn more of the God Paul and Silas worshipped. Even the prison keeper asked, "Sirs, what must I do to be saved?" How would he know to ask such a question, except statements of doctrine, statements of truth, and adoration of their God filled Paul and Silas' prayers and songs?

THE POWER OF WORDS

Worship is not just songs, but words spoken to magnify and exalt God. Lifting up your voice in prayers of worship and speaking words of devotion unto God has a powerful impact on the spiritual realm. Out of the abundance of the heart, the mouth speaks. *What the heart believes, the mouth will speak.* When the heart filled with love of God expresses itself in worship, it makes a statement that fills the atmosphere around the person. It activates God's holy angels and causes demons to tremble or flee. Persistent and continued prayers, praises to God in times of worship, as well as in daily events and circumstances, unravel satan's plans.

WORDS OF WORSHIP

Satan understands the power of words, especially words of worship to God. Therefore, he has attempted to introduce songs and phrases that speak negative statements over our lives. There are even songs sung within the framework of church services which are really songs that do not glorify God. They may project a concept or view of God that is erroneous. Satan tries to dress up his error in religious clothing. Unknowing individuals will profess over themselves words and songs of error, thereby causing bondage to hinder them. If songs, as well as creeds and other statements, are not founded on biblical doctrinal truth, do not speak them. Words are powerful. They set a course for your life.

The Holy Spirit will bear witness to truth and cause you to question statements made or songs sung. The Bible will always verify its truths to those who seek truth. *"By mercy and truth iniquity is purged: and by the fear of the Lord men depart from evil"* (Proverbs 16:6).

The Lord loves the music of worship as the sounds of trumpets, timbrels, stringed instruments, organs, cymbals, tambourines and as everything that has breath praises Him. Music that has the anointing of God upon it wars against the heaviness of satan's burdens. There were times when my kids, recognizing a heavy weight of oppression on me, would put a praise and worship tape in the stereo to play. It wouldn't be long before my foot would start to tap, then before long I would bounce to the beat of the music. My countenance would change and joy would displace darkness. The music, wisely chosen by young children, was sufficient to do battle on my behalf. It worked and they knew it. The anointing destroys the yoke. Satan's yoke of heaviness is removed through praise. My kids did their own paraphrase of "put on the garment of praise for the spirit of heaviness" *(Isaiah 61:3)* with "put on the tape of praise against the spirit of heaviness."

WE WORSHIP WHAT WE SET OUR ATTENTION UPON

Satan continually tries to fill our minds with his evil dialogue. There are many opportunities for the airwaves to perpetuate evil gossip, lyrics and rhetoric. Satan offers many alternatives for people to set their affections and attention upon. Music is a powerful spiritual motivator.

Those who know they are in right standing before God can rest, refusing to cooperate with confusion, strife or offense

Teaching and music media, Christian radio and TV have been ordained of God to fight for His people and to help keep us filled with doctrines of truth.

Be wise! Be discerning! Doctrines of error and evil are constantly being broadcast or published through media sources.

You can allow the power of praise to fill your home and in so doing the anointing (which is on godly music, preaching and teaching) will actually do warfare in the atmosphere of your home, car or business. You may be "at rest" while the anointed Spirit of God is waging war against evil words, actions or intentions. Putting godly CD's or music on in the room of a rebellious child or loved one will project godly words against evil words which may hang in the atmosphere of the room. The Lord's warfare of worship stands on the line of battle and will prevail.

WORSHIP IS PROTECTION

The presence of the Lord's glory, which rests upon the one who has been in the Lord's presence, will by its very nature do battle without the person even realizing it. When Moses came down from the mount, there was such radiance in his countenance the people pleaded for him to cover his face because it made their sinfulness and unworthiness painfully apparent. They were afraid of the power of God.

Believers today enter the Lord's presence and the unction (or smearing of glory upon the person) causes sinfulness and darkness around them to quake and tremble, *"But ye have an unction from the Holy One, and ye know all things...But the anointing which ye have received of him abideth in you, and ye need not that any man teach you: but as the same anointing teacheth you of all things, and is truth, and is no lie, and even as it hath taught you, ye shall abide in him"* (I John 2:20, 27). Many times things are exposed and answers flow easily because of the powerful presence of the Lord upon a person who has had an encounter with God. This is the glorious privilege of every person who will press in to meet with God.

MANY FACETS OF PRAISE AND WORSHIP

Music, songs, dance, flags and banners, intercessory prayer, laughter, travail and fervent words of adoration—all have their place in glorifying God. I heard one person say that he felt studying his Bible was worshipping the Lord. I agree, for we are drawing into ourselves words of spirit and life. Our body is the temple of the Holy Spirit. Bible study is pouring in life and truth through which the Holy Spirit can express the things of God.

Colossians adds another facet when it speaks of teaching and admonishing one another in psalms and hymns and spiritual songs, singing with grace in their hearts to the Lord *(Colossians 3:16)*. Spiritual songs, sung in the Spirit with or without the understanding, greatly edify both the Lord and the believer.

THE SACRIFICE OF PRAISE

Any person who is a Christian will realize his new life in Christ is not free from struggles. Indeed, being a Christian means we were snatched out of the grip of satan. Satan *fears* both the new and the seasoned believer, therefore he brings challenges and afflictions that try to make us feel like our minds and emotions are being put through the wringer. We learn Jesus is always with us; the Holy Spirit abiding within us will help us; and God's faithfulness is intimately involved in what we are going through. Afflictions and discouragement may come from our enemy but our Lord promises us victory. *"Many are the afflictions of the righteous: but the Lord delivereth him out of them all"* (Psalm 34.19).

There are times when we do not feel the closeness of the Lord's presence or quickly hear His counsel. Perhaps you have been through an especially trying time. Maybe you have been persecuted and ridiculed because of your life in Jesus Christ. Perhaps people and spiritual forces have buffeted you. Paul, the writer of Hebrews, understood the place you stand. Hebrews 13:15 says, *"By him therefore let us offer the sacrifice of praise to God continually, that is, the fruit of our lips giving thanks to his name."* Sometimes praising the Lord in the middle of great times of stress and struggle is not what we feel like doing. The Holy Spirit will help us. When it seems impossible for any good to come from the circumstances you are in—praise. When it seems like the most illogical thing to do—praise anyway. God sees it as a sacrifice of praise. It has cost you something—the right, you think, to be discouraged. Instead you are choosing to praise the One Who is above your circumstances. When you lift up your heart in words that tell the Lord He is worth any and all the rejection, ridicule, confusion and disappointment you are suffering for His sake—that is worship.

Loving and worshipping the Lord (whether it is in words or in songs) during the tough times not only deeply blesses the Lord, but it causes strength and fortification within your faith foundation—a foundation that becomes more and more solid. Storms that beat against your life can work for you instead of against you. The storms will pass, but the foundation remains.

WORSHIP PUTS US IN AGREEMENT WITH GOD

All of heaven, including the holy angels, and the saints who have entered into heaven, give praise and glory to Jesus the Christ and to the Heavenly Father. There is a corporate event happening when we praise, for we are joining the host of heaven and generations of believers in adoration of The King of kings and Lord of lords. All of heaven and earth declares His glory.

The work of the Holy Spirit brings honor and glory to the Lord Jesus Christ. Whenever you have an attitude and propensity to worship the Lord, you make yourself available to the Holy Spirit. At a moment's notice, you can be used by the Holy Spirit to bring glory to Jesus Christ.

Those who carry on continual fellowship and worship also will be ones who are quick to repent for any wrongdoing that occurs in their lives. They value their oneness with the Lord so highly they will not let the least little sin threaten their communion with their Lord. The purity of their hearts before God enables the Holy Spirit to freely work through their lives and the Father delights in sending angelic assistance whenever necessary.

THE HIGHEST FORM OF FELLOWSHIP

The Bible says if we do not praise the Lord the stones will cry out *(Luke 19:40)*. The earth travails and awaits its redemption from its present state *(Romans 8:22)*. The earth itself declares the glory of the Lord; how much more shall those who are created by the Lord in His own image, give praise and worship.

Lucifer, as we have read, was the Anointed Cherub. He had tabrets and pipes within him which produced beautiful music in praise to Elohim; that is, until his heart turned against God. The one who was leading worship in heaven was deposed and cast out. Lucifer desired to be worshipped, but when Adam and the following generations worshipped God, satan's jealousy only increased. I heard someone say that God created human beings with the ability to offer praise to Him which would replace the worship (and supersede the worship), which was lost when Lucifer fell. It is an interesting thought.

Praise brings believers before the throne in mutual love. King David had such a precious heart for God. His Psalms are saturated with words and songs of exaltation, praise and worship. The Lord fervently desires our worship—worship that springs from our innermost being. Our conversations with God reflect that we truly know Him. Father God is seeking out those who desire to worship Him and want to have intimate fellowship.

John 4: 23, 24 reveals that, *"But the hour cometh, and now is, when the true worshippers shall worship the Father in spirit and in truth: for the Father seeketh such to worship him. God is a Spirit: and they that worship him must worship him in spirit and in truth."*

Jesus said the hour was coming, and it was ready to be fulfilled, when it would be possible to worship the Father in spirit and in truth. Not only that, but the Father was actively, expectantly seeking those who would worship Him in intimate fellowship. Up until the time that Jesus died, there was separation between the Father and the fallen human race. They could worship Him, but not in the same way as those who can now come boldly into His presence because of the Blood of Jesus *(Hebrews 10:19)*. The Father has long awaited the time when there could be ones to worship Him as He desired. God can now be truly worshipped— worshipped in spirit and in truth.

TRUE WORSHIP STEMS FROM LOVE

Sin separated humankind from God. Until Jesus' Blood was shed, and His Blood taken to the altar in heaven to cleanse us from sin, true worship could not be attained. The inhabitants of heaven must have become absolutely ecstatic with praise when they saw

The Bible tells us how much God loves us

Jesus bring His own Blood to the Holy Place of heaven. How it must have blessed the Father's heart when Jesus made the way for the worship of billions of people to rise before Him! How much love emanates between Our Heavenly Father, Jesus and the Holy Spirit as Their love for one another pours out into the lives of those who will worship the Father in spirit and in truth!

When we glorify the Father in true reverence, it is worship that is above the carnal level. It is worship which rises out of our spirit, out of our heart to a place where we speak heart to heart in spiritual understanding and agreement. This can only happen when there is true understanding of who God is, what His character is, His attributes and personality, as well as having some comprehension of Him as the God of love. The more we know and experience the love of God, the more we are able to worship Him in spirit and in truth.

JESUS' LOVE MADE A WAY

No man can come unto the Father except through Jesus Christ *(John 14:6)*. Jesus made it possible for believers in Him to come to the Heavenly Father—to even come *boldly* before the throne of grace *(Hebrews 4:16)*. Read through the Gospel of John and drink in the love relationship between the Heavenly Father and Jesus. How much Jesus wants the Father to be worshipped; how much the Father wants Jesus glorified. How much the Holy Spirit wants to strengthen us in the inner man that we might comprehend and know the deep love of God *(Ephesians 3:14-21)*.

Our Heavenly Father, whom the Holy Spirit has told us is Love—God IS love—has so desired to express His love to us *(I John 4:8)*. The scripture which is the best known verse of all time is John 3:16, *"For God so loved the world, that he gave his only begotten Son, that whosoever believeth in him should not perish, but have everlasting life."* We need to look at this verse in the context of understanding what was lost when Adam fell. Intimate fellowship was set aside. God walked in the garden with Adam, and there was closeness and warm fellowship beyond anything we can imagine. But sin caused a breach to separate humankind from the once close bond and fellowship between Adam and God.

The Heavenly Father, with the Blood of Jesus paying the penalty for sin, is now seeking Blood-bought, sin-cleansed, redeemed believers to draw close to Him and receive the love He desires to impart in a personal way.

WE CRY ABBA—FATHER

It is amazing how our Heavenly Father in His mighty power and magnificent presence encourages us to call him Abba, an endearing name used in affection, close relationship and adoring fellowship. It carries the similar affection we use when we say Papa, or Daddy.

When we worship our Heavenly Father, we must keep ever present in our minds and hearts the price that was paid for us to be able to come to Him—the shed Blood and the broken body of God Himself in the person of Jesus.

We need never draw back from coming to the throne of the Heavenly Father and His Son, Jesus Christ, because they desire us to boldly enter Their presence. In Hebrews 10:19 we are told of our awesome privilege, *"Having therefore, brethren, boldness to enter into the holiest by the blood of Jesus."* They are honored and blessed when we appropriate the Blood of Jesus to enter the holy place of Their presence. They greatly desire our coming before them; otherwise the scriptures would not encourage believers to boldly enter. The greater the understanding we have of the Blood, the greater the boldness in reverent adoration we will have as we draw close to our Lord.

Your Heavenly Father awaits your worship. Desire to know Him as He truly is. There are numerous names that tell of the attributes of the Godhead and describe their being. The Father is Sovereign, long-suffering, great in mercy, the Almighty, the Ancient of Days. Jesus is Savior, Redeemer, the Lamb of God. The Holy Spirit is called the Comforter, the Spirit of Grace and the Spirit of Truth. The more we know our God, the more our worship lifts out of thankful hearts.

Seek to worship the Lord in spirit and truth. God will make it worth your while, for He promises to reward all who diligently seek Him.

CHAPTER 10

DEMONS

Before we continue with the descriptions and personalities of other fallen angels, we will deal with the matter of demons so readers can more readily see the differences between the two.

Demons are spirits that always seek a "house" to occupy, *"When the unclean spirit is gone out of a man, he walked through dry places, seeking rest; and finding none, he saith, I will return unto my house whence I came out..." (Luke 11:24).* They are spirits that exist in a form of spiritual suspension—this is, until they can find a host to whom they can attach. Because of the discomfort and torment they experience apart from being connected to a host, they permit themselves to crowd together. Many demons can occupy a small space that was evidenced by the group of approximately 4,000-6,000 (which is the number in a legion) demons in the madman at Gadara *(Mark 5:13)*. To the degree they occupy or adhere to a person, they may have expression and exercise their personal attributes and personality.

Demons have personalities, attributes, faculties of desire, decision-making abilities and some aptitude. We find this in the account of the unclean spirit that was cast out *(Luke 11:24-26)*. When the demon came back and found the "house" (or body) clean, it found seven demons more powerful than itself and returned to occupy the "house."

The unclean spirit (demon) reasoned, made a decision and functioned with a certain amount of intelligence. It also shared its habitation with others greater than itself in order to insure its place of residency. Demons have a measure of power and knowledge; have feelings, doctrines, desires, preferences and personalities specific to their abilities. For instance, a demon that promotes fear will itself be intensely fearful. A demon of lust promotes lustful desires. A demon is identifiable by the characteristics it manifests.

Demons do not die. Therefore, demons that inhabited the earth in Abraham's day are still operating against some person today. Many are permitted to operate in the earth for the present time.

However, they are destined for the lake of fire along with satan and his fallen angels.

The description of demons is as vast as the variety of ways people sin. Some demons are ugly and fearsome-looking while others appear seductive and beautiful. They may speak with fierce intimidation to instill fear or with sugary sweetness to lure.

Because they are limited in intelligence, they group together to cover one another's lack. They function together to accomplish their task, but there is no allegiance to one another. They are as their god, satan. They are selfish, jealous and will displace one another if the opportunity arises.

DEMONS, THE LOWEST OF SATAN'S KINGDOM

Because demons are the lowest form of beings in satan's kingdom, they carry out satan's schemes in people's lives *(Mark 6:13)*. They are the ones who actually implement the instructions of their superiors (who are the fallen angels of the second heaven). Because there are many of them, there can be a variety of satanic strategies in operation against a person. You do not need to fear this. Satan's wisdom and his intelligence, as well as his information systems, are limited.

Some demons are assigned to operate under the control of *principalities*. Others carry out orders after the character of *powers or authorities*. Some others are skilled in the diversionary tactics of *rulers of darkness of this world*. There are those who are seductive and convincing, so they are used to promote doctrines of error according to the dictates of *spiritual wickedness in high places*.

Because two of satan's greatest weapons are <u>deception</u> and <u>ignorance</u>, it seems likely that the largest number of demonic spirits are employed within the realms of the rulers of darkness and of spiritual wickedness in high places. Their assignment is to keep the operation of the kingdom of darkness—in the darkness. Wherever the light of the glorious gospel breaks forth, they are discomfited and set to confusion; therefore, they work diligently to keep their presence unknown.

DEMON TYPES

There are types of demons such as unclean spirits *(Matthew 10:1)*, tormenting spirits *(Matthew 8:6; Revelation 9:5)*, familiar spirits *(Leviticus 19:31)*, foul spirits *(Mark 9:25, Revelation 18:2)* religious spirits, seducing spirits *(I Timothy 4:1)* and others.

Demons and fallen-angel strategists work together attempting to establish an open door for demonic presence and influence within a person's life.

In the case of <u>spiritual wickedness in high places</u>, they seek to give a *doctrine or belief* for the demon's existence *(Revelation 2:14,15)*. These demons speak into the minds of people and give reasons why demonic influence should be allowed to stay in their lives. Of course the people are ignorant of the fact that they even have demons present in their lives. For example, a doctrine strategist instigates a belief of hate against individuals. Demon(s) of hate will goad, accuse and speak into the receptive mind hateful lies, seeking to overtake their thought processes. They begin to talk about the hateful feelings and thoughts they have had. Demons continue to prod, harass and speak into the mind more reasons or justification for hate and add hateful actions to their list. If the people getting all the hateful input in their minds do not respond with rebuttal or resistance, then the emotions and actions will follow suit. The demons will either find acceptance of their hateful presence or resistance to their intrusion into the people's lives. If people believe they have a right to hate, they have accepted within themselves a doctrine of hate as part of their belief foundation. *Strategists of false doctrine* have promoted the doctrine of hate and demons facilitate its propagation and expression.

DISTRACTION AND DIVERSION

Demons assigned to <u>rulers of darkness</u> are busy with every sort of distraction and activity that draw people away from light, love and truth, *"And have no fellowship with the unfruitful works of darkness, but rather reprove them. For it is a shame even to speak of those things which are done of them in secret. But all things that are reproved are made manifest by the light: for whatsoever doth make manifest is light"* *(Ephesians 5:11-13)*. Demons in this realm will be the ones who actually bring the prescribed distraction, stumbling block or diversion assigned by evil strategists. A demon of this sort could be used to hide the needed answer to a problem. They even hide the fact that there is a problem, and unknowing souls suffer under hindrances beyond their realm of facts and understanding. For instance, a business has an employee stealing from it who has covered his or her tracks well. Demons of theft and concealment are working against the embezzler spiritually and the owner, financially. The thief wants to keep his activities from being exposed and the ignorance by the employer leaves such thievery unhindered. Satan wants both of them to lose.

MISUSED AUTHORITY

Demons assigned to <u>powers or authorities</u> are used to harass, degrade, agitate, prod and apply pressure to their target *(II Peter 2:7-9)*. They seek to justify their behavior as they continue to torment through abuse from a position of authority. For instance, a demon may influence a parent to belittle and degrade a child. The demon of criticism operates through the parent who demands control through criticism and emotional degradation. That person is outside the boundaries of the character of God and godly guidance. The child is emotionally injured and confused. These demons are used against humankind under the guise of authority. People who misuse their authority are being manipulated by demons assigned to evil strategists in the authority sector of satan's kingdom.

LAWLESSNESS

Demons delegated to the realm of <u>principalities</u> are used to influence people who make laws that will promote satan's evil agenda and permit or excuse demonic activity. Murdering demons have been allowed to legally bring death to millions of babies through legalized abortions. The principality strategist instituted the law; the demons carry out their work through those who actually do the killing of innocent victims.

Psalm 106:35-38 tells us, *"But mingled among the heathen, and learned their works. And they served their idols: which were a snare unto them. Yea, they sacrificed their sons and daughters unto devils, And shed innocent blood, even the blood of their sons and of their daughters, whom they sacrificed unto the idols of Canaan: and the land was polluted with blood."*

CHIEF DEMON

Demons are task specific. They aren't well-rounded individuals but must rely on one another to accomplish a purpose because they have limited capabilities. They are arranged under levels of rank.

Apparently, there is one chief demon who rules over other demons. When Jesus addressed the maniac at Gadara, He spoke to the unclean spirit and asked him what his name was *(Mark 5:1-20)*. The unclean spirit answered saying his name was Legion. His name indicated his task. He ruled over a great number of demons that tormented the man continuously. The man lived naked among tombs crying night and day. Legion was the spokesman for the rest, but when the rest of the demons realized they were going to be cast out of the country, they all began to plead with Jesus asking rather to be sent into swine feeding nearby. Legion and his subordinate demons were ordered to leave the man's body and they entered the swine. The swine ran violently down a steep cliff into the sea, where the water drowned them.

I wondered why being cast out of the country was such a dramatic punishment for Legion and the other demons. I asked the Lord. He said demons must learn languages just as human beings do. If they were in a foreign land, they could not communicate. They would have to stay in their suspended state until they could learn the language, locate an unsuspecting host and manipulate their way into the person's life.

I suspect that demons, who are cast out of the country, would then be under the authority of a different principality. Satan's kingdom is vicious, toward human beings and toward one another. This may be another reason for their not wishing to leave familiar surroundings.

FREE AT LAST

The man at Gadara who had been possessed with the demons was changed. He not only sat with Jesus, clothed and in his right mind, but Jesus told him to go home and tell his family and friends what had happened. He became a preacher, telling of the compassion of Jesus to those bound by the enemy. More importantly, he did not desire to be free of the demons and then live life apart from Jesus Christ.

Those desiring deliverance from demons cannot flirt with ungodly attitudes and influence in their lives. The person who wants to be healed of a hangover, or delivered from a DUI charge, but refuses to give up drinking, will not get free.

When the unclean spirit left the house (or human) in Luke 11, the Bible says the house was swept and garnished, or cleaned. Whenever demons depart, their defiled foul presence leaves and the person is clean. The person is aware they are clean and something awful has departed. The problem with the "house" of the person in Luke 11 was the house was left empty—there was nothing there to repel or resist the reentry of evil tenants.

The Name and presence of Jesus Christ, by the Holy Spirit, is the only power which demons recognize as greater than themselves or their satanic superiors. They don't want to leave, and they don't want to be left wandering in the spirit realm. Therefore, they must be forcibly evicted and not given any opportunity for return.

Those who seek deliverance from demonic influence and control need understanding of the wonderful gift the Lord has given. He will fill every empty space with Himself. The power of the Holy Spirit is available for every person who desires to be free from demonic influence and control.

FAMILIAR SPIRITS

Familiar spirits cover a wide range of demonic personalities. They are perhaps the most deceptive of the demonic kingdom. Satanic strategists are extremely dependent upon the information supplied by these informants.

For example, fallen-angel authorities gain information from their demon operative in order to find out who in a person's life can be used to buffet, harass or undermine their targeted person. The fallen-angel strategist then devises a strategy whereby the person will be besieged in a vulnerable area. The fallen angel's purpose is to challenge the individual's strength, position, standing, self-worth, but especially their faith. (We will learn more about evil strategists called "power or authorities" in the next chapter.)

Familiar spirits are demonic beings who are intricately involved in people's lives in order to gain insight into their behavior, weaknesses, areas of ignorance, personality traits and responses. They keep detailed records of actions, events, people and behavioral patterns. They communicate with other demon spirits, giving them pertinent information on what may succeed against the person and potential areas for invasion or assault. They relay information regarding a person to the fallen-angel strategist over them. They work aggressively to keep the lost from drawing close to believers, and they keep believers from drawing close to God. They endeavor to steal or shake a person's faith and their acceptance of the Word of God. They are afraid of being revealed and evicted.

Since familiar spirits are satan's secret agent employed to watch and collect information, their most important trait is their ability to remain undetected and to be able to operate in secrecy. They actively protect their anonymity. They call upon other demons who are skilled in ruler of darkness schemes to set up distractions and circumstances to keep them "under cover."

Familiar spirits are the ultimate spies of satan's kingdom

Familiar spirits are often referred to as family or friendly spirits. In their deceptive nature, they portray themselves as friendly and valuable to their host. "Familiar" is taken from the root word, family. Familiar spirits are ones who live with or have lived within the family. They know all about them. They have taken a person's time and resources and developed a relationship with them. They can be "friendly" spirits because most people don't care to develop a relationship with someone who isn't friendly. Familiar spirits want to get buddy-buddy with the person. They want to become a substitute for a genuine relationship. They can become a companion to the person. In reality, it is an evil liar. Its association with the person is based upon lies. Familiar spirits use flattery designed to ensnare a person. Every person desires approval, acceptance and praise. Flattery is a powerful tool that the familiar spirit uses to insure its ability to stay in someone's life.

ACCUSATIONS

Demons speak accusing words that demean other people and exalt the person's flesh. The person being manipulated takes on an attitude of pride and haughtiness perpetrated by demon voices. Psalm 36:2 counsels us, *"For he flattereth himself in his own eyes until his iniquity be found to be hateful."* Self-flattery and demonic flattery will bring you to a place of bondage and unhappiness. Flattery is satan's counterfeit to godly honor and approval.

FAMILY SPIES

There are demonic spirits that join themselves in a family setting. They promote themselves as part of the family and seek to establish a place of acceptance and influence, if not control. The part they play within the household indicates the division from which they were dispatched. Because of the importance of the "spy" activity within the family unit, the identity of the dominant familiar spirit will be tightly guarded.

How do familiar spirits develop this relationship? Through speaking their lies into a person's mind. They carry on a conversation in the mind that is so subtle *the person thinks it is his or her own thoughts.* Depending on the extent of such conversations, the familiar spirit may have limited, or perhaps controlling, influence in a person's life.

Consider, for example, heated words that flare between you and another individual. Have you ever muttered something to yourself under your breath about the situation? Chances are those words were actually conversation with demonic agitators who fueled your thoughts and actions with more hateful suggestions. What do your actions reveal? Are your words and actions indicative of past behavior?

A familiar spirit tries to entwine itself so masterfully into our activities, personality and desires that we don't recognize anything strange about their activities and involvement in our daily lives. We may have an inner sense that there is something amiss, but the meshing of personalities and circumstances are so camouflaged that detection is not obvious. In some instances, familiar spirits are accepted as hereditary characteristics, or personality traits, but are actually demons contrary to life in God.

Demons want to stay in surroundings where they know people and are already accepted—places where they have a foothold. When someone in the family dies, the demons that lived with their host will "identify" with a family member and seek acceptance from them. There have been instances where a surviving family member has felt the "presence" or even had glimpses of the deceased loved one. They believed the presence was that of their loved one, when it was the presence of a demon spirit attempting to establish a relationship and abiding place.

FAMILY LIES

Demon personalities which stubbornly resist eviction or are un-challenged in their activities may be passed down from generation to generation. They are as their name indicates—famil(y) liar. Their lies have been accepted. As such, their presence is not refuted, debated or changed. A lie is only as powerful as the hold it has on those who believe it. Truth sets us free. Continuing in the Word of God reveals truth, and walking out truth will bring freedom.

Demons, remember, are the lowest of satan's forces. However, without demons doing the legwork, satan cannot accomplish his plans.

FORTUNE-TELLERS

Fortune-telling, palm reading, and tarot cards reek of familiar spirit activity. Unknowing people seek knowledge about future or past events from demon spirits who relay information from their files to the evil spiritualists. It is information given which seems to verify the fortune-teller's knowledge of past histories and seduces vulnerable people to believe they can foretell future events. Fortune-tellers merely set forth satan's plan for the person's life. It is a plan based on lies and deception. Someone hears a plan for their future and consciously or sub-consciously walks out that plan. The person does not understand that they have opened a door into their lives for demonic activity with its final goal of destruction and death.

Isaiah 8:19 advises us, *"And when they shall say unto you, Seek unto them that have familiar spirits, and unto wizards that peep, and that mutter: should not a people seek unto their God? for the living to the dead? To the law and to the testimony: if they speak not according to this word, it is because there is no light in them."*

God has warned us against familiar spirits throughout genera-tions. Some people may actually encourage you to go to palm readers, tarot card readers, fortune-tellers, mystical games (like ouija boards, Dungeons and Dragons), horoscopes, or seek after power in magic or wizardry. Such activities are all seductions into the demonic realm. Demons seek receptacles for their present and subsequent operations. They do not speak truth according to the Word of God because they are of the kingdom of darkness and there is no light in them. Isaiah goes on to say *"And they shall look unto the earth; and behold trouble and darkness, dimness of anguish; and they shall be driven to darkness" (Isaiah 8:22).* The kingdom of darkness will imprison those who seek counsel and guidance from familiar spirits.

—ᴓᴓᴓ—

The Bible gives counsel and hope

—ᴓᴓᴓ—

Past association with such practices must be renounced and every influence evicted and resisted. Any tentacle, which finds a resting place, will hinder you from gaining freedom and growth. If you need freedom in this area, seek out those who will pray with and counsel you by the revelation and direction of the Holy Spirit.

ather God, I come to You in the Name of Jesus Christ of Nazareth. I ask for and acknowledge Jesus Christ to be the Lord of my life. I repent of any participation I have had with fortune-tellers, tarot cards, palm reading, horoscopes, witchcraft, mystical games or spiritism of any sort. I recognize and call it sin and I ask for Your forgiveness. I ask for cleansing by the Blood of Jesus Christ that washes the filth and defilement of such activities from my life. I declare my mind and belief system to be purged and cleansed by the shed Blood and broken body of Jesus Christ. I acknowledge Jesus is God come in the flesh and has overcome all the works of the enemy. I ask to be filled with the Holy Spirit, and seek Jesus Christ, the Son of the Living God to have rule in every area of my life. The gates of hell shall not prevail over me, for I determine to become fully acquainted with Jesus Christ and His sacrifice for me. In Jesus Name, I claim and proclaim release and victory. Amen.

ACCEPTANCE

Acceptance is vitally important and is a basic need in every person's life. Demons play on this basic need. The necessity of acceptance draws people to relationships and companions who accept them. The Bible tells us that evil communications corrupt good morals. Why? Because relationships require agreement, whether the terms are godly or evil. Those who desire to be godly are uncomfortable around those who want to do evil. Those who wish to do evil do not want those who are godly around them, because they hate the discomfort that light brings upon their evil deeds.

Relationships develop where there is acceptance and agreement—whether good or bad. Familiar spirits offer acceptance and flattery in order to maintain their influence in the person's life. Acceptance is sometimes the only hold gangs, cults and negative relationships offer. The sense of belonging and the need for acceptance can be so great a person can fall into the trap of those who offer any form of acceptance, even if it results in damage to them. Familiar spirits lure wounded souls into a false web of acceptance.

The need for acceptance is a vulnerable spot for every person. You need to examine where, and from what you gain acceptance as you grow in spiritual things. Your acceptance will increasingly need to be grounded in Jesus Christ; everything else will hinder you from true acceptance and freedom.

COMMANDING FAMILIAR SPIRITS

Because the spirit world is a world that is not seen with the natural eye, we need a "spiritual eye" to see spiritual things *(I Corinthians 2:10-12)*. Familiar spirits are spirit beings that must be dealt with spiritually. Believers are able to have supernatural eyesight to "see" how we have been manipulated, hindered and brought into bondage.

I had been blind to the enemy's tactics in a situation, and I slowly become ensnared within his net. I knew there was something wrong in the situation, but I was unable to see clearly what was truth and what was error. I sought the Lord for an answer. The Lord told me, "Command the familiar spirits to become *un*familiar." When the Spirit of the Lord gave me counsel, I obeyed His instruction, not really understanding at the time what it meant.

I began to see the persons involved and the situation with "new" eyes. I saw ways in which I was being manipulated and controlled. The Holy Spirit within me was saddened by my bondage and ignorance to the manipulation. It was His prompting that showed me something was wrong. When I looked for specific truth, the Holy Spirit gave me counsel and guidance on how to deal with the people in the situation.

Command familiar spirits to become unfamiliar

The simplicity of the solution to familiar spirit deception is amazing. When the Lord said, "Command the familiar spirits to become unfamiliar," it set forth principles of His Word. God spoke saying, *"Let there be light" (Genesis 1:3)*, and Proverbs 18:21 says, *"Death and life are in the power of the tongue..."* Words are powerful. Words are the power tool of the spirit realm. Demons are cast out by words commanding them to leave in the Name of Jesus. The character of God Who abides within believing vessels has the capacity to command the lying spirit to be stripped of its "familiar" ability to hide.

UNCLOAKING HIDDEN SPIRITS

God gave me revelation on how to change the character of familiar spirits so they could no longer hide under the cloak of familiarity as in times past. Why didn't the Lord just say, "Cast out the familiar spirit?" Familiar spirits need to be exposed and *recognized* as evil. We need to renounce the familiar spirit and all its tentacles of intrusion and control in the Name of Jesus. Then when they try to regain their former place they will be again recognized and repelled.

It can be hard for the soul to have "friendly" and "family" types of familiar spirits exposed. Those who have been trusted may not be as trustworthy as you were lead to believe. What is promoted as love, concern, or caring relationship may be emotions tainted with impure motives and influence. We can also have sincere, genuine relationships born out of a pure heart, *"Seeing ye have purified your souls in obeying the truth through the Spirit unto unfeigned* (without hypocrisy) *love of the brethren, see that ye love one another with a pure heart fervently" (I Peter 1:22, explanation added).*

Seeing the shortcomings, failures or deceitfulness of people we care about is hard emotionally and mentally. The very desire to *maintain* trust, love, and fellowship with those being used by familiar spirits is the reason the familiar is so hard to discern. When the *pain of the bondage is greater than the fear* of changing the status quo, or rejection from those involved, then the quest for exposing and expelling familiar spirits will be easier. Complacency and fear of change have kept many people in the grasp of familiar spirits.

A friend asked me if this could be done long distance when praying for someone many miles away? Yes. In the spirit realm, distance is not a hindrance. If an evil influence came through a person, even years ago, declare that satan's familiar spirit must become unfamiliar and his strategy against you halted. In some cases, the person is deceased. You can pray that any familiar spirit influence cannot continue. Wash your mind, will, emotions, your soul, spirit and body in the cleansing Blood of Jesus Christ. Diligently affirm your freedom in Christ Jesus, *"Now the Lord is that Spirit: and where the Spirit of the Lord is, there is liberty"* (II Corinthians 3:17).

DISENTANGLE YOURSELF

How about those who are used by familiar spirit influences in your life? You must become disentangled from the familiar spirit itself, and then do not cooperate with those who continue with the familiar spirit patterns that have been revealed. The counsel of the Holy Spirit will guide you regarding how to handle the people involved. It may be that you confront the person, and perhaps not. Overcome evil with good. Allow grace to keep bitterness from finding roots (Hebrews 12:15). Obey the Holy Spirit who is establishing freedom from this subtle entrapment.

It is also wise to examine our lives to see if there are areas where familiar patterns or influences are being expressed through *us*. When the Lord began revealing the subtle ways these spirits work, I examined whether there were generational patterns that I may have been operating in myself. I commanded "familiar spirits to become unfamiliar." I definitely did not want to cooperate with any demonic influences that would hinder my family and others from growth and freedom in Jesus Christ.

SOUL TIES

Sometimes soul ties need to be severed with the familiar spirit and any evil soul ties with people they have operated through.

What is a soul tie? The soul of a person is the part of their being which comprises the mind, the will and the emotions. The soul is the part that has connection with the world around you. We relate to our surroundings through the faculties of our soul. Even the body follows the directions that the soul dictates. The soul is what initiates the interaction with people and receives back the responses from others.

Sometimes, a bond between the souls of one or more people can become so strong it becomes a powerful connection. It should also be pointed out here that there are good soul ties as well. There are souls ties that are ordained of God and are holy before Him, and they are ones that are a blessing to one's life.

The soul ties which are being addressed in this chapter have to do with soul ties that bring a connection, a hold, into your life spawned by evil strategists. Teenagers who are belligerent about wanting to hang around individuals who are "a bad influence" are an example. If the person in question seems to hold some kind of power over the teen, it may be possible that a wrong soul tie has been made.

Taking this instance as an example, a parent has legal right in the realm of the spirit to command any *evil* soul tie be severed in the Name and by the Blood of Jesus. In authoritative prayer, command *evil* association to cease and remove the teenager from the need for acceptance by evil relationships. (You would not want to take authority against soul ties that are good, so make sure you are speaking to demon personalities that have had *evil* influence or control.) Then speak into the life of the teenager, declaring to the spirit realm, all the good and valuable things they are before people and before God. When an opportunity to pray with the teenager arises, discuss the evil forces behind the relationship. If not, a parent can do this for their teenager without the child being present. It is a spiritual stand you take against spiritual entities. Pray in their room; pray over their bed; pray over their vehicle; break the hold of any evil objects in the room and remove them. Fill the room with spoken words declaring the presence and love of Jesus Christ. Continue doing so until breakthrough comes. Satan has no right to your child.

SEXUAL SOUL TIES

The most powerful soul tie occurs in the sexual encounter. Wherever soul ties have been established through immoral or adulterous relationships, demonic soul ties will seek to ensnare the persons involved into deeper nets of bondage.

SEVERING SOUL TIES

Severing soul ties may be a painful event for the persons involved. Call upon the Lord's healing grace and mercy for those persons involved in the prayer. The Lord loves the people involved. However, He does not desire injury and wrong influence to continue. Repentance and declaration are needed—repentance from involvement in evil soul ties, severing the tie by the Blood of Jesus, and declaration of scriptures from the Word of God against any further or future influence.

Father, I come to You in the Name of Jesus Christ. I ask You to give me strength to confront and deal with evil soul ties in my life. I ask for the Holy Spirit to reveal to my mind and understanding the effect the wrong soul tie has had in my life so I can have wisdom. I sever, right now, by the Blood of Jesus Christ, the evil soul tie in my life between _____ and me. By the Blood of Jesus Christ, I command my soul set free from any tie or connection that is not holy or acceptable to God. I command demonic influence in this relationship be cast out in the Name of Jesus. I proclaim that I belong to the Lord Jesus Christ and my life is under the protection of His shed Blood. I ask the Holy Spirit to fill me and saturate any empty place in me with the love of God and the counsel of the Holy Spirit. In Jesus' Name. Amen.

DEMONS DESIRE TO TORMENT

You must understand, demons will torment their host and as many people as may be affected by their presence. You and I are not to war against flesh and blood. Even though familiar spirit demons work through people toward those around them, we must not forget that the person who HAS the familiar spirit is under oppression and is miserable as well. When believers are free, they are capable of freeing others from familiar spirit demonic oppression. Discussion regarding what the Lord reveals about the people involved needs to be done by the guidance and leading of the Holy Spirit.

Believers must desire to be free, and gaining their freedom may mean they will suffer a soulish loss in order to obtain spiritual freedom. Again, the Word says, *"Be not deceived: evil communications corrupt good manners" (I Corinthians 15:33)*. Evil friendships breed evil actions. Many times we feel rejection in the midst of soul tie changes. Keep in mind that not wanting to feel rejection or cause others to feel rejection may prevent the bondage from being confronted and dealt with. Familiar spirits who are left to communicate their influence into someone's life will wither and ruin all the person *truly* desires and needs.

RELIGIOUS SPIRITS

Religious spirits are counterfeit influences to the Holy Spirit of God. They seek acceptance as holy and want to exercise control in the religious practices of church and private life. As the saying goes, you cannot recognize the counterfeit if you do not know what the genuine looks like. Religious spirits play on the ignorance of those who do not know the character of God or the inspired written Word of God.

Such spirits may represent God as a mean-fisted tyrant or as a god who does not regard sin as evil. Religious spirits run rampant in the segment of satan's kingdom ruled by spiritual wickedness because their focus is to instill and promote error and lies.

We are told in I Timothy 4:1,2, *"Now the Spirit speaketh expressly, that in the latter times some shall depart from the faith, giving heed to seducing spirits, and doctrines of devils; Speaking lies in hypocrisy; having their conscience seared with a hot iron."*

Religious spirits promote and draw attention to all the "good" they do but behind the scene they are ensnaring unknowing souls into religious practices that are void of gospel truth.

Religious demon spirits are the ones who speak lies of doctrinal error into people's ears. They follow the blue prints of satanic strategists in order to effect beliefs contrary to the Word of God. They speak the words that accuse and mock people who are seeking to follow purity in Jesus Christ.

CALLING EVIL GOOD

Much of what they do is speak religious alternatives to the gospel
to those who will listen. They also orchestrate religious practices.
Ritual, cultic, religious practices are the work of demonic influence carrying out a satanic strategy. Religious spirits try to portray
beliefs and ideals as sweet to the fleshly soul, when they are bitter and vile before God. Or they desire to make the truth of the
gospel and righteousness before God as bitterness in the soul. For
instance, religious spirits bring a doctrine to people who wish to
continue in sin but believe the love of God will ignore what they
are doing. They mislead people into believing that grace does not
call for repentance from sin.

Isaiah said, *"Woe unto them that call evil good, and good evil; that
put darkness for light, and light for darkness; that put bitter for sweet and
sweet for bitter"* (Isaiah 5:20).

DOCTRINE OF DEVILS

Religious-spirit demons take scripture verses and misquote them,
relaying a totally obscure and incorrect meaning. They may even
set forth statements, implying that they are biblical passages, when
in fact they are not found in scripture. Believers need not be afraid
to quote *correct scripture wording* to counter misuse or misquotation
of scripture. Demonic-religious spirits set forth satanic teachings
and beliefs that the Bible calls doctrines of devils. *"Now the Spirit
speaketh expressly, that in the latter times some shall depart from the
faith, giving heed to seducing spirits, and doctrines of devils"* (I Timothy 4:1).

Church leaders are targeted especially because the pure gospel
of the Lord Jesus Christ threatens the very presence and influence
of evil within the church. Religious spirits cause people to expect
the church to give worldly compassion in pampering their flesh
and making them comfortable holding onto their woundedness,
bitterness, unforgiveness and error. Religious spirits justify sin and
validate unbelief.

TRADITION OF MEN

The other end of the spectrum holds those who desire self-exalta-
tion and recognition within the religious setting. Jesus rebuked
the Pharisees because they had rejected the commandments of

God so that they might keep their own traditions. Religious spirits call for reverence and obedience to everything except the person of Jesus Christ. They present another "Jesus" which does not line up with biblical truth. We read, *"Howbeit in vain do they worship me, teaching for doctrines the commandments of men. For laying aside the commandment of God, ye hold the tradition of men, as the washing of pots and cups: and many other such like things ye do. And he said unto them, Full well ye reject the commandment of God, that ye may keep your own tradition"* (Mark 7:7-9).

Things done within the church setting or within our personal walk of faith that serve to replace the commandment and true character of God with religious acts of the flesh, are being influenced by religious spirits. Every person is vulnerable to the lies of religious spirits. Each of us has probably been raised with error of some sort regarding knowing, understanding and walking in spiritual things.

If we discern there are religious spirits working against us, we should consider it a possibility that we or someone we know (1) have error in our lives, (2) have a philosophy not of Christ, spoken about in Colossians 2:8, *"Beware lest any man spoil you through philosophy and vain deceit, after the tradition of men, after the rudiments of the world, and not after Christ;"* (3) have been taught the traditions of men as though they were the commandment of God (Mark 7:7-13).

Discernment by the Holy Spirit can be done through:

◆ Discerning with the senses (Hebrews 5:14).
◆ Discerning with the unction (I John 2:20-29).
◆ Discerning with the peace that guards the heart and mind in Christ Jesus (Philippians 4:7).
◆ Discerning between the righteous and the wicked (Malachi 3:18).

The Psalmist writes, *"Who can understand his errors? cleanse thou me from secret faults. Keep back thy servant also from presumptuous sins; let them not have dominion over me: then shall I be upright, and I shall be innocent from the great transgression. Let the words of my mouth, and the meditation of my heart, be acceptable in thy sight, O Lord, my strength, and my redeemer"* (Psalm 19:12-14).

We can listen to the inner man. The Holy Spirit will counsel us according to truth. In Christ, there is victory. Religious spirits are rooted out and evicted. Truth and mercy fill the soul and free the mind.

UNCLEAN SPIRITS

There are a number of different categories of unclean spirits. Viruses and diseases are actually unclean spirits attaching themselves to people in order to attack healthy tissues and cells. The human body is a wonderful work of divine art that satan wants to destroy. He seeks to defile God's wondrous creation with sickness and disease by unclean spirits. Whenever illness tries to attack me or my family, I come against the unclean spirit that is attempting to disrupt the divine order of the operations of the body *(Luke 6:18)*.

HOMOSEXUALITY AND LESBIANISM

Sexual perverseness, homosexuality and lesbianism are unclean spirits carrying out perversion to the holy purpose of God in the human relationship of love and marriage. Sexual perversion within a relationship is a manifestation of unclean spirits. Satan seeks to make people, relationships and actions unholy. He wants to defile that which God desires to remain holy.

The Lord loves everyone who has been overtaken by this satanic strategy. Even though they themselves have a gnawing knowledge that what they are involved in is unclean, the power that holds their lives seems impenetrable. The doctrine of error that accepts such sexual acts as normal, for some, has justified their feelings and actions. It negates any effort to seek freedom from unclean spirit control and domination. Many ensnared by this lifestyle are precious people who do not understand the strategy of death satan has set in place for them *(Romans 1:26-32)*.

UNCLEAN SPIRIT MANIFESTATION

It has been my experience (although I know of other believers who have had other manifestations) that when a demonic unclean spirit manifests, coldness is felt in the immediate atmosphere. On one occasion, I along with several other intercessors, were asked to pray at a residence where a suicide had occurred. A definite cold, clammy presence was there. I knew by the Holy Spirit that unholy sexual activities had taken place at the residence. Some weeks previous to this the Lord gave me counsel regarding how to deal with defiling spirits—spirits which want to take what is holy and make it unholy. When satan wants to make something defiled or unholy, the Lord said to declare the *Holy* Blood of Jesus against the defilement or against the defiling spirit. The very holiness of Jesus' Blood would war against all satan wanted to make impure. The Blood of Jesus cleanses from sin and all its effects. The Holy Blood of Jesus pronounces to the spirit realm the redeeming, cleansing power of Jesus' Blood.

According to the instructions given to me by the Holy Spirit, I began proclaiming the Holy Blood of Jesus against the uncleanness and asked for cleansing of what satan has attempted to profane and defile. Immediately, the atmosphere changed. The coldness and clamminess left. A brightness and warmth filled the room. It was a testimony to the power of the Blood, the Holy Blood, of Jesus. Unclean spirits had in some way influenced the suicide that occurred. Sadly, the person who was so tormented did not realize the danger such spirits presented.

PARROTING SPIRITS

Parroting spirits can sound tolerable if not trivial. They are not trivial. These spirits are called parroting spirits because of the nature of the repetitive words they spill into the mind of the person they are targeting. Parroting spirits have a strategic role of replacing your thought patterns with thought patterns concocted on satan's planning table. They repeat evil phrases over and over again into the ears and mind of the oppressed person. Expressions like "I can't take anymore;" "I hate myself; I hate everyone," "I NEVER do anything right;" "Can't I *ever* learn;" "I'll *never* get free;" "I'm a failure at anything I try;" "If I were *really* successful, I would have ____ and ____ by now;" "If God *really* loved me..." The list goes on and on.

Parroting spirits work closely with familiar spirits with the end motive of destroying the person's life. They are vexing spirits harassing the mind and emotions with hopelessness and thoughts that make the person feel they are trapped and have no avenue of escape. They try to navigate individuals in line with satanic plans for their lives. They often speak words like, "You'll fail if you try that," or "They don't like you, so stay away from them."

THE WAY THEY WORK

The way a parroting demon works is as follows: A demon is assigned a particular phrase or several phrases that speaks into the ears of a person. Let's take the phrase, "I can't take anymore" for example. In the course of daily trials and struggles, the demon will repeat the lie into the ear of its listener, "I can't take anymore." Then when a quarrel, a sickness, a death in the family, a chain of misfortune arises, again the lying demon speaks, "I can't take anymore." Sooner or later, the person who is ignorant to this type of spirit will begin to believe the lie. *"I"* can't take anymore. Every hurt, every disappointment, every rejection, every fearful situation then becomes a heavy weight of oppressive depression— all because of the presence of a lying parroting phrase which has no power in itself. Satan then brings his solution about how the person can escape. His answer will always involve sin, sickness or death. It may be the death of a marriage, an escape into alcoholism or drugs, a sinful relationship, and in many cases suicide, or whatever the weakness within the person will allow.

MIND TRAFFIC

Carefully examine the words that come into your mind and compare them to words of life and love. This will help you begin to discern when parroting spirits are at work. If a tormenting phrase or group of phrases bombards your soul (mind, will, emotions), listen with a spiritual ear and try to discern the motive behind it. What kind of feelings does it attempt to stir up? Who is getting the glory from the thoughts that are traveling the avenues of the mind? Are the words producing life or death? Examine the words that come out of your mouth. You may be repeating words of evil influence. It may be an indicator of demonic parroting voices with an agenda to hinder or harm. Are they thoughts of life and good things? Or of death and grief?

Demons work in conjunction with one another, and they may speak through a spouse, parent, co-worker, classmate or through evil lyrics in music, all the while reinforcing the phrases of the lie they perpetuate.

Demons, remember, are the peons of satan's army. They can only remain where they are permitted. Casting them out in the

Name of Jesus and resisting their return will accomplish the eviction of demon tormentors. Command them to shut up and leave, in Jesus' Name.

The Bible commands us, *"Casting down imaginations, and every high thing that exalteth itself against the knowledge of God, and bringing into captivity every thought to the obedience of Christ; And having a readiness to revenge all disobedience, when your obedience is fulfilled"* (II Corinthians 10:5,6).

Every thought demonic parroters put into the mind and every thought that has taken root that is contrary to the knowledge of God, can be brought into the submission of the Lordship of Jesus Christ. Every time the demon tries to pull the same phrase or one similar to it, be ready at all times to retaliate against its disobedience.

II Corinthians 10:4 says, *"For the weapons of our warfare are not carnal, but mighty through God to the pulling down of strong holds."* What has had a strong hold on your mind? If parroting spirits or familiar spirits have planted thought patterns that are laying claim to beliefs, strongholds need to be broken and replaced with the knowledge and truth of God's Word.

LEARNING MORE ABOUT DEMONS

Understanding the various aspects of demonic manifestations and characteristics is too wide a subject to adequately set forth here. There are volumes of good books and teachings by those who have ministered deliverance and exposed demonic operations. These include people like Lester Sumrall, Kenneth Hagin and Doris Wagner among others.

The Lord commands us not to be ignorant of the devil's devices and to not give place to the devil *(II Corinthians 2:11 and Ephesians 4:27)*. Fear is eliminated when we learn how demons manifest, and we gain information and counsel how to deal with them according to biblical truth. Essential to our boldness and foundation of faith is knowing the greatness of the One Who is in us Who wars against the evil one in the world *(I John 4:4)*. Wise believers continue to grow in knowing and walking in the power that is in the gospel of Christ. They believe God will guarantee and enforce the authority they have in the Name and Blood of Jesus Christ.

FIGHTING ON TWO FRONTS

Spiritual warfare means the believer will fight on two fronts—demonic and satanic. Believers will cast out demons, and they will resist the devil and his fallen-angel assignees. Casting out devils is part of becoming free (or getting people set free). Staying free requires knowledge and standing strong in the Lord and the power of His might. Standing strong in the Lord is necessary in order to resist the original satanic strategy contrived in satan's planning room which dispatched the specific demons. Thwarting the plan of the enemy at his blueprint will confuse any future plans he had in place. Demons can come and go, be cast out and others sent to replace them, but when you uproot the strategy behind demonic entrance and influence, you will be liberated to the uttermost.

We are promised in John 8:31,32, *"...If ye continue in my word, then are ye my disciples indeed; And ye shall know the truth, and the truth shall make you free."*

Demons must depart. Fallen-angel strategists must be resisted and displaced. Continuing in the Word of God and in the knowledge of who you are in Jesus Christ will set you free.

CHAPTER 11

POWERS OR AUTHORITIES

It wasn't the green grass that lured me from the road in rural Colorado where I lived. It was the asparagus growing wild along the ditch banks and fences that had my appetite watering. Between me and the asparagus were a fence, a herd of cows—and a bull.

Standing a safe distance away, I waved my arms and shouted. Both the herd of cows and the bull ran the opposite direction. I climbed over the fence, keeping a watchful eye on the bull while I picked tender, ripe asparagus. The bull watched, but showed no inclination to challenge me.

If that bull knew how powerful he was compared to my wimpy shouts, he would run me out of his pasture, I mused.

"My people are just like that bull," the Lord said. "They have the power and authority to protect their pasture, but they're scared and intimidated by the puny shouts of the enemy. They allow him to carry on his activity, never challenging his presence."

Without a doubt, if that bull had snorted and taken one step toward me, I would have scrambled over the fence as fast as my trembling legs could take me. I might have shouted again, but my intent would have been to put as much distance as possible between him and me.

Sometimes the Lord reminds me how the devil sees us. He sees a born-again believer as a creature who has power, ability and authority. He will jump and shout to do all he can to intimidate and bring fear to the believer hoping he will scare us enough to leave him alone while he crosses onto our property to kill, steal and destroy. Sadly, many of us do not know the power we have in Jesus while we watch the enemy carry on his activities.

GETTING BULLISH ABOUT JESUS

Jesus has given us authority in His Name, by His Blood, on His Word and by His Spirit to overcome all the strategies and activities of the enemy and his kingdom. We simply need to get "bullish," about walking in what Jesus has done.

In Acts we're told, *"How God anointed Jesus of Nazareth with the Holy Ghost and with power: who went about doing good, and healing all that were oppressed of the devil; for God was with him"* *(Acts 10:38)*. The Apostle John tells us why Jesus came, *"...For this purpose the Son of God was manifested, that he might destroy the works of the devil"* *(1 John 3:8)*. If Jesus' purpose was to destroy the works of the devil, then that should also be the purpose of those who are in Christ. *In Him* we have all power over the enemy, the power is not of ourselves. Satan will be bound and it will only take one of God's holy angels to bind him and throw him into the pit. But until that time, our Lord has commissioned and ordained us to enforce a victory He has already won.

Hebrews 11:6 tells us that it is impossible to please God without faith. Faith determines what we do. When we <u>truly</u> believe, actions follow. Presumption is when we *hope we are in faith and have to prove it to someone, even ourselves.* Faith IS and KNOWS and DOES.

What do you know so strongly within yourself that you will stand against the onslaught of the enemy? When you are challenged, what do you steadfastly believe so that you are not shaken?

Spiritual warfare means believers will challenge and also will be challenged. The purpose in the confrontation is we overcome and God is glorified. Defeat is not defeat if a failed challenge spurs us to greater strength to re-challenge. Sometimes our lack of "re-challenge" ability is because we just don't know what to do. Too often we don't know what or with whom we are fighting.

THE LORD SAID "AUTHORITY"

I understood fallen angels and demons were not the same after a devastating blow from satan's kingdom. A young girl received prayer for deliverance in my home. Demons were dealt with and afterwards everyone went home. However, later that night my family and I were bombarded by attacks from the enemy camp. I had participated in deliverance prayers many times previously, but for some reason, this time devastation settled upon me. "If we dealt with the crux of satan's authority when we cast out demons, then why are we under such assault?" I asked the Lord. I heard the Lord say one word, "Authority."

I was fully aware of satan's retaliatory nature, but I needed God to give me counsel regarding this onslaught from the enemy. For many months afterward, I studied the scriptures looking for answers and freedom from the heaviness that continued to weigh upon my soul. I studied everything I could find that related to "authority." Had I usurped my husband's authority? Had I misused authority? My husband bounced back to the normal activities of life, but the burden upon my spirit continued. If satan's power was dealt with in casting out demons, then why was I suffering from continuing evil oppression? What was the Lord trying to tell me about authority?

A year and a half passed. I continued to search for answers. One day I read a book about familiar spirits. The author listed the divisions of satan's kingdom in Ephesians 6. He wrote, "… principalities, powers or *authorities*…" All of a sudden the Holy Spirit lifted the veil from my spiritual understanding. The Spirit of God revealed I was being oppressed by a fallen-angel *authority*.

Immediately, the Lord spoke, "You overcome all the authority of satan's kingdom by *My* authority in you. It is authority verses authority." I was unaware up to that point that demons and angels were not the same. I knew within the very depth of my being that the Lord had revealed from the first day *who* was levying satanic blows at my soul. The authority He spoke about was not a demon but a fallen angel.

I realized I had neglected a battle about which I was totally ignorant. My rebuking demons was challenging only demons, but I had been under attack from a whole different segment of satan's kingdom.

I drew back from battle because I had become wounded and confused. Even though I knew that Jesus had overcome satan, and I knew many scriptures that proclaimed the triumphing power of God in Jesus Christ, I didn't know I needed to direct my faith in Christ's victory against fallen-angel forces. How exciting! I had authority over the authority set against me. I experienced victory. I learned to recognize authority attacks, and overcame them because of the authority of Jesus Christ in me.

PROGRESSION OF GROWTH

When we overcome the lies of wrong doctrine (set forth by spiritual wickedness in high places) and get grounded in the truth of the gospel, we stand against satan at the foundational level. We become people who are soul winners. We are witnesses who reflect love and give glory to Jesus Christ. We experience and acknowledge the power of the gospel. We are students of the Word of God and the Spirit of God guides our lives.

When we overcome the rulers of darkness by walking in light, truth and love, we become wise enough to outwit stumbling blocks of darkness. We do not let distractions, disputes or divisions keep us from flowing in the things of God. We increase in confidence and boldness concerning spiritual things. We persevere and continue to gain strength and maturity. With each level of growth, we become more of a threat to the kingdom of darkness. We become bold in the Lord even though we are gaining the attention of satanic strategists who see their kingdom being threatened.

AUTHORITY CHARACTERISTICS

Fallen angels in the authority realm use intimidation, accusations, threats of harm, instruments of terror, control and domination. They operate through position and places of power and influence. They like to give the impression they hold all power over our lives and want us to think freedom from their control is not possible. They manipulate people and situations to give the perception there is no way out of present problems. We can get God's viewpoint of our situation through reading the Word and talking to the Lord about what we need. In the Bible, we find examples of others who have traveled the path of affliction and have overcome.

RECOGNIZING AN AUTHORITY ATTACK

You can always tell when you are under attack by the division identified as spiritual powers, or authorities, because you feel hopeless. Hopelessness bombards your mind and pounds your emotions. No matter which way you turn there appears no solution, no letup, no glimmer of breakthrough.

Hope is basic to faith. Therefore, fallen angels are orchestrating a direct attack on your faith. Without hope, you are weakened and helpless. If authority strategists are able to set confusion and weakness against our faith, they know they can keep us from the strength we need to overcome their influence. In hopelessness, you lose the strength to fight.

In hopelessness, the enemy seems to have doubled his attack. During this time it is difficult to remember scripture. No matter the wealth of scriptures that may be within your memory bank, during an authority attack, they seem to have evaporated. It is then we must search deep within and draw out the Word written in our innermost being. <u>Even one scripture</u> can well up and flow out of our mouth to become the delivering salvation from the enemy's assault.

Spiritual warfare means there will be more than one encounter with fallen-angel authorities. Anytime we con-

Authority strategists direct their attack at your faith

front satan's kingdom, there will be entities who have positions that they do not give up easily. Therefore, learning their tactics and overcoming them is vital for victory.

OVERCOMING HOPELESSNESS

I learned this when an attack had been levied against me. I was at the hopeless stage, feeling the pressure of darkness and wondering if I would ever be released from a particular problem. I was at a point of despair. I felt the Lord say this was an authority attack. I knew I needed to inform satan of who I was in Christ and I knew he would have to release and retreat. But it was as though all the scriptures I lived by had disappeared. As I stood by my sink and realized the state of my soul, I sought one scripture, any scripture to recite out loud. From down within myself, I drew out of the well of salvation, one scripture. "I am the redeemed of the Lord, let the redeemed of the Lord say so" *(my paraphrase of Psalm 107:2)*.

By faith, I spoke rather weakly the scripture out loud. I felt a light "snap," like the cracking of a chain around my soul. I repeated the scripture again and again, each time with greater and greater strength and volume. The cloud of doom broke, scattered and then vanished. I knew I had broken through. I still had to address the people and circumstances that had contributed to my hopelessness, but I KNEW the backbone of the attack was broken. I would handle "flesh and blood" with a totally different approach and attitude. And indeed, the results brought God glory.

I learned an important lesson that day—not only <u>how</u> authorities (or powers) operate, but the power of the Word against them. In addition, I learned we don't prepare for war in wartime, we prepare for war during peacetime. I made myself a booklet, rewriting scripture with my position and standing in Christ inserted. A scripture which reads like, *"Are they not all ministering spirits, sent forth to minister for them who shall be heirs of salvation"* *(Hebrews 1:14)* I wrote as "I am an heir of salvation, my Father has sent forth ministering spirits to minister for me and in my behalf. I thank You, Father, for providing angels for me. I request angels to go forth and minister in this situation and to bring forth what I need and give me understanding." This eventually became my battleground field manual. Whenever I came under another "authority" attack, I would grab my field manual and start walking through the house reading the word I had placed there in peacetime—when I wasn't under attack.

The *Word of God is powerful,* whether quoted from the depths of your spirit or simply reading it aloud. It was the sword of the spirit spoken in faith, then authority, which commanded freedom from evil oppression.

AUTHORITIES RULE FROM POSITIONS OF POWER

Authorities have positions of influence and power. They are the strong arm of satan's kingdom who want to apply tormenting pressure and oppression. They want absolute control and are vicious against those who challenge their authority. If this were not so, why would Jesus say, *"the kingdom of heaven suffereth violence, and the violent take it by force"* *(Matthew 11:12)*?

When we declare the authority we have in Jesus Christ against the defeated position of fallen-angel authorities and declare the victory of Jesus Christ's triumphant stripping of satan's power, we cause violent things to happen in the spirit realm.

Authority verses authority means you must KNOW, be fully confident, scripturally based and unwavering in your place and position in Christ. Satan and his authority associates will challenge to see whether it is just hot air or if you are grounded on a solid foundation. When satan knows that *you know*, he will give retreat. Demons tremble, shake and must depart when you walk in your authority in Christ. Evil authorities will challenge and resist before they give up anything. The Bible admonishes us to stand, and having done all—stand! Be unmovable, unshakable, because evil authorities will lose their strength and depart.

Be aware, they will try to convince you that they have a right and authority to remain. They hope intimidation will make you become fearful and doubtful of your stand in Christ's authority. It is much like the bully who postures himself and makes threats until his defenses are stripped, then he begrudgingly turns and leaves.

Born-again believers have the authority of Jesus Christ in the earth *(Matthew 28:18-20)*. Jesus is physically sitting at the right hand of the Heavenly Father in the third heaven *(Ephesians 1:21)*. He gave us his "power of attorney" for everything He Himself did and would do in the earth *(John 14:12)*.

Jesus went about doing good and healing all who were oppressed by the devil. He went about healing people and casting out devils. He has given you that authority and responsibility. The authority of Jesus Christ was imparted to you at the moment of conversion. It need not be sought after, because it came with His presence as He came into your heart. It abides within you whether you know it or not. What a shame to leave such a valuable tool of victory unused when satan is haranguing your life.

> *Authority is what you are.*
> *Power is what you do.*

PRAYING FOR THOSE IN AUTHORITY

Since fallen-angel authorities operate through people who have positions of authority in our lives, they must have influence over people through whom they can exercise their domineering power. Therefore, any person who carries responsibility, position or power can be marked for evil authority strategies. This happens within the family unit. It happens within friendships, in areas of employment and business and within government—anywhere positions contain the capability for influence or control.

THE WAY THEY WORK

Authorities set their demons at work to find anyone in your life who can be used to bring accusations, degradation, harassment and threatening words. They play on the ignorance and weaknesses of their targets. Unbeliever and believer alike will say, "I don't know what came over me to say such a thing. I don't know what made me do such a thing." They are unaware that spiritual forces with a well-defined plan are manipulating them. Most of the time they dismiss such outbursts as unimportant, or somehow justify their words or actions.

The intent of evil authorities is to shipwreck your faith, weaken your spiritual boldness in Christ and discourage your endeavors. Don't think it unusual then when your faith is belittled and ridiculed by someone close to you. The words challenging your faith may be spoken through a human voice, but the words were supplied by authority-controlled demons. Because the person speaking hateful words holds a position of influence or value within your life, it can cause deep discouragement and hopelessness. That is, unless the believer understands that the family member, associate, superior or boss is also under attack by authority strategists who wish to use them for evil purposes.

When circumstances are trying to get you down, look for the source behind it

Whenever you are able to discern an authority attack is underway, you will begin to discern *who* is speaking. When you understand that the words being spewed at you are demons speaking and not really your spouse, parent, friend, or boss, you can go after the spiritual force behind the words. Knowing this, when hurtful words are discerned as demonic, you can choose not to take the words so personally that it throws you into devastation and depression. You must realize that the person was subjected to pressure inspired by an evil authority. Those most prone to fall into their trap are people who are not born again, those who are susceptible to weakness by past hurts, carnal believers and those who are ignorant to satan's tactics.

It isn't news to most believers that satan hates us, and it should not hurt our feelings that he does. We, as spiritual warfare warriors, must understand people close to us might come under attack in order to stop our aggression against satan's kingdom.

GOD'S PLAN OF PROTECTION

The Lord has devised His own strategy to thwart the enemy's plan. *"I exhort therefore, that, first of all, supplications, prayers, intercessions, and giving of thanks, be made for all men; For kings, and for all that are in authority..."* (I Timothy 2:1,2). Prayer provides protection. When we pray for those in authority, we exercise our spiritual authority on behalf of those in earthly authority.

Authority involves responsibility. The greater the responsibility, the greater the risks and pressures. People who have a heart to do what is honest and upright welcome prayer, because they realize they are vulnerable and weak in one way or another. They know prayer protects them and helps them in their areas of weakness.

Praying for those in authority runs the gambit from mom and dad to the president or prime minister. Wherever the Holy Spirit impresses you to pray for those in earthly authority, He is providing protection and provision for those who have influence over your life. In order of importance, this prayer is listed "first of all." Such prayer is necessary to hedge off opposition to success in spiritual matters.

Declaring protection by the Blood of Jesus, giving thanks for those who have important positions in our lives, as well as praying for their good—not only before trouble arises but also during the heat of battle—is purposed by the Lord to bring about a *"quiet and peaceable life in all godliness and honesty"* (I Timothy 2:2).

Verse one of I Timothy 2 gives a pathway of prayer for those in authority:

- ◆ Supplications—Calling on God on their behalf for impartation from God.
- ◆ Prayers—Earnest prayer for known and unknown needs and desires, lifting their names before the Lord as you worship the One who is able to meet every need.
- ◆ Intercessions—Standing in the gap for them, entreating God on their behalf and standing against satan's strategies.
- ◆ Giving of thanks—Trusting and believing that all those who are placed over your life were placed there by the Lord, and for the fulfillment of prayer petitions.

THE HOLY GHOST WILL GIVE DIRECTION

Since authority strategists will attempt (and many succeed) in using people against us, we must learn how to deal with the person who has come against us even if a fallen-angel force is behind it. When under "authority" attack, the response to those methods of assault must be lead by the Holy Spirit. Listen to His voice and promptings. He may direct you to confront them with truth. He may tell you not to open your mouth. He may remind you that a soft answer turns away wrath. The important thing to realize is that the person is under pressure and oppression from a spiritual force they do not see or consciously hear. By the Spirit of the Lord you can not only be set free, but also be a part of setting that person free.

Recognizing what is happening behind the scenes goes a long way in guarding yourself from receiving rejection, bitterness and pain. Anger turned inward or buried will eventually take an emotional and spiritual toll. It is possible to "Be angry and sin not" *(Ephesians 4:26-32)*. We can be angry at evil and yet not get outside the bounds of righteous anger.

There are also times when forgiveness is needed in order to stand strong. Forgiveness not only is healing for the spirit and soul, it also removes hindrances to powerful prayer. *"And when ye stand praying, forgive, if ye have ought against any: that your Father also which is in heaven may forgive you your trespasses" (Mark 11:25)*. Sometimes our deepest wounds come from those who hold a place of value and authority in our lives. Forgiveness is easier when we realize that we are dealing with more than human beings, that we are being dealt a blow from evil spirits.

There was a time in my life when I knew the principles of forgiveness and the requirement of the Lord to forgive. There was a particular instance, however, when I forgave, got hurt, forgave, got hurt and forgave again. My faith ebbed away at my seemingly inability to stay in forgiveness.

"You don't have to forgive satan for what *he* is doing to you," the Holy Spirit explained. Somehow that helped me deflect the arrows with which the enemy tried to wound me. I learned a valuable principle: Forgive the person and resist the enemy. It is part of the foundation of spiritual warfare. *"Submit yourselves therefore to God. Resist the devil, and he will flee from you" (James 4:7)*. Satan hates it when forgiveness nullifies his efforts to bring strife, division and injury.

MARRIAGES WILL BE FOCUSED

Many marriages would be together today if believing partners had understood who was behind those arguments with unwise words and responses. Whenever one partner gets on fire for the things of God, don't be foolish enough to think fallen angels haven't sought to devise schemes to use their partner as an instrument of discouragement and hurt. A marriage where both partners are on-fire believers is one of the most fearsome threats to satan's kingdom.

The Lord tried to save us from the pain of wrenching warfare that occurs when the household has one believing spouse and one unbelieving mate. The Bible clearly warns us not to marry unbelievers because the warfare between the kingdom of light and the kingdom of darkness inevitably occurs in the home.

In many homes only one spouse has come to know the Lord. The Lord's grace is mighty upon such a household. The protection God offers to the new babe in Christ embraces the home as well. The Lord promises us, *"For the unbelieving husband is sanctified by the wife, and the unbelieving wife is sanctified by the husband: else were your children unclean; but now are they holy"* (I Corinthians 7:14).

The word sanctify here is *hagiazo* which means to make "holy, purified, consecrated." The Lord has extended grace to the unbelieving mate granting them a place separated unto Him as holy. Blessings will flow to the unbelieving spouse because of God's intense love for His believing child. We can declare our home as a holy place before God and demand any evil intruders to leave.

WRESTLING AGAINST AUTHORITIES

Remember, you and I don't wrestle with flesh and blood but *do* wrestle AGAINST principalities and powers. We don't wrestle WITH them—we wrestle AGAINST them. Godly wrestling is done by exercising authority over all the power of the enemy. It is a fight of faith, and in that faith we *"live and move and have our being"* in Him *(Acts 17:28)*. What we believe is the springboard of our actions.

For instance, a tennis player picks up a tennis racket because he believes he can hit the ball over the net. He runs after the return volley because he thinks he has a chance of hitting it back. If he fails, he tries again, believing that next time he won't fail. The more he works at it the better he gets. The more he learns about tennis, the fewer mistakes he will make. His belief and his desire for success determine his actions and diligence.

When we enter into the realm of spiritual warfare, we are set for a series of wrestling matches. The extent of our desire to be set free and to set others free will determine the intensity of our quest to be strong in the Lord and in the power of His might. Being strong in the Lord means we must die to self and to fleshly attitudes, actions and responses. We aren't always ready to pay the price, but to the measure we desire God's best, God is prepared to do exceedingly above all we ask or think.

Wrestling involves pressure applied against pressure—until something gives. The stronger, the more enduring and the wiser tactics will displace the weaker opponent. Some people think, "The thought of sustained warfare makes me want to give up even before I start because I feel so weak." Our faith is not to be in <u>our</u> strength, but in His strength.

"For whatsoever is born of God overcometh the world: and this is the victory that overcometh the world, <u>even our faith</u>. Who is he that overcometh the world, but he <u>that believeth that Jesus is the Son of God</u>" (I John 5:4, 5, emphasis added).

THE BATTLE IS THE LORD'S

We can actually wrestle and rest at the same time. Hebrews 4:6 tells us that the Israelites did not enter the Promised Land because of unbelief. The verses that follow speak of entering into His rest and "laboring" to enter rest. Sometimes we have *to work at* entering the Lord's rest. We endeavor to become confident that the battle is not ours but the Lord's.

We can rest when we truly believe the power to overcome is supplied by the Lord and He is capable of insuring success

That rest can only come from faith in what Jesus has already accomplished, and faith that He has already given us authority to act using all that is in His Name. Remember, within every Name of Jesus is the endowment of power and authority to bring God's blessing and provision.

Our lives will continually grow in the knowledge of "who we are in Christ" and "who Christ is in us." Who you are in Christ is your standing before God in the righteousness of Jesus. He sees you as "in Christ" and everything Christ has is yours. You are hidden in Christ. You no longer live, but are alive in Him. You are standing in the spirit realm clothed in Jesus before angels (holy, as well as fallen angels) and demons. We are protected and can rest when we stand inside God's holy armor.

If you do not know who you are in Christ, you will hide from God when you sin. You will beg God for things He has already promised, or work to gain His favor and approval. You will think that you are separated from all that Christ has done and *all* the benefits of his salvation. You mistakenly believe your relationship and communication with the Father is based on you rather than Christ, and your life *in Him*.

Christ in you is the life, power and authority of Jesus revealed to those around us. You are also the vessel of manifesting the fullness of God in the spiritual operations of God in the earth.

When you don't know who Christ is in you, you believe satan when he tells you that you're not going to succeed. Satan knows if you fight in *your* strength, you will wear down, weaken and fall. The Israelites wouldn't go into the Promised Land because they decided they couldn't defeat the giants. They neglected to believe that God would do battle in their behalf.

AUTHORITIES WILL PROBABLY BE OUR "GIANTS"

Giants are "bigger than life" oppressors or obstacles—at least to the mind. Giant-fighting faith does not stem from the mind but grows out of the heart. Whether you are aware of it or not, the Holy Spirit uses seemingly insignificant occurrences in your life to lay giant-fighting faith foundations. Consider David, the shepherd boy who tended his father's sheep. Predators seeking a tasty meal of lamb threatened the flock daily. He was continually prepared to fight for the lives of his precious little lambs. He was not a passive protector who ran when the salivating, growling lions approached. He became skilled, confident and fierce about his responsibility.

A lion and a bear invaded David's flock and snatched a lamb. David recounted to King Saul how he went after the lion and the bear and wounded them. He rescued the lamb out of their mouth. He didn't rationalize, "better one lamb than my skin." He knew sooner or later the lion and the bear would be his foe if there were no resistance. When the lion and bear tried to rise again, he killed them.

How did he develop giant-fighting faith? David spent many hours alone speaking with the Lord. He knew his protection did not depend solely upon his own strength. *"David said moreover, The Lord that delivered me out of the paw of the lion, and out of the paw of the bear, he will deliver me out of the hand of this Philistine..."* (I Samuel 17:37).

During the day-to-day events of our lives, the Lord delivers us out of the paws of those who desire to snatch away and devour our lives. Experience in His sustaining grace, strength and protection gives us confidence and boldness. The Holy Spirit is working in us to develop giant-fighting faith so that when we face a "giant" it will not paralyze us with fear. Our confidence in the Lord's delivering and prevailing power will rise up strong.

DAVID FACED AUTHORITY OPPOSITION

David's father sent him to take food to his three older brothers and to check on them as they were serving in Israel's army. For many days, Goliath stood before the whole army, mocking, cursing and challenging them. David was not impressed. He asked his brothers why no one had done anything about *"this uncircumcised Philistine, that he should defy the armies of the living God"* (I Samuel 17:26). Why had they let the enemy berate them and defy their God?

The eldest son held some clout in the Jewish family. *"And Eliab his eldest brother heard when he spake unto the men; and Eliab's anger was kindled against David, and he said, Why camest thou down hither? and with whom hast thou left those few sheep in the wilderness? I know thy pride, and the naughtiness of thine heart; for thou art come down that thou might see the battle"* (I Samuel 17:28). He was angry at David's questions about their timidity. He recoiled with accusations. "What are you doing here? What makes *you* so important since you take care of a few sheep? You are a prideful wimp who just wants to see what is going on."

Eliab held a place of authority in David's family. He challenged the faith David showed, who demanded confrontation of the enemy who sought to defeat Israel and make them servants to the Philistines. Eliab rebuked David, undermined him and accused him. David's family turned on him in his effort to free Israel from harassment and domination. Without knowing it, Eliab actually opposed God's purposes. David was not dissuaded from the godly fire inside of him. He continued to declare his faith and his intent.

Another authority crossed David's path. King Saul was a great man of war with the impressive earthly armor to show for it. King Saul had once been a man of God, but he disobeyed the commands of the Lord. The Spirit of the Lord departed from him, so now Saul lived his life depending upon his own abilities and strength. His protection depended upon worldly things. Consequently, he cowered before the berating of Goliath.

King Saul offered David his armor—carnal, fleshly armor. David's battle was more spiritual than natural. Therefore, King Saul's armor was a distraction and burdensome. David would not

———◦◦◦———

Godly intercession and warfare is availing yourself to the Holy Spirit for His intervention in the methods and strategies of the enemy. Unguided attacks waste resources and energy. Holy Ghost led attacks hit the enemy's strongholds and hideouts.

———◦◦◦———

go to battle with earthly armor; he stepped forward in spiritual armor. *"...I come to thee in the name of the Lord of hosts, the God of the armies of Israel, whom thou hast defied. This day will the Lord deliver thee into mine hand; and I will smite thee, and take thine head from thee..."* (I Samuel 17:45, 46).

King Saul was the highest governmental authority in the land. His was an authority that could intimidate far beyond what family members could do. He was not only the king, but the most famous military leader in Israel. What, David? You won't do as the king suggested? You won't follow orders of the military expert?

Satanic authorities who cannot stop giant-fighting faith will attempt to offer worldly weapons for spiritual battles. Such armor will likewise be distracting and burdensome. Giants will fall when the Lord takes such things as small insignificant stones and turns them into Holy Spirit propelled missiles.

What do you know? What has the Lord brought you through which stamped His delivering power upon your heart? What lion has tried to steal the little lamb you love? The Lord is ready to deliver. Fallen angels fear those who stand confident and strong in Christ's authority. They know they will be defeated and undone.

Speak to your children, speak to your friends, and speak to loved ones and acquaintances of the victories the Lord has done in your life. It declares His glory and it fuels your faith.

WHERE IS THY GOD?

Fallen-angels authorities challenge the faithfulness of God. In their accusations and afflictions against you, they also accuse God. Some years later David wrote, *"My tears have been my meat day and night, while they continually say unto me, Where is thy God? ...As with a sword in my bones, mine enemies reproach me; while they say daily unto me, Where is thy God?" (Psalm 42:3,10)*. It isn't hard to see that David was in an emotional valley. His mind, will and emotions were going through the proverbial "wringer." He wept all the time and felt like he had been pierced with words like swords. We can learn from David as we observe how he handled his situation. What did he do? He gave himself a good talking to. Look closely at David's conversation. *"Why art thou cast down, O my soul? and why art thou disquieted in me? hope thou in God: for I shall yet praise him for the help of his countenance" (Psalm 42:5)*.

Again and again he bounced back by speaking of the faithfulness of God. *"Why art thou cast down, O my soul? and why art thou disquieted within me? hope thou in God: for I shall yet praise him, who is the health of my countenance, and my God" (Psalm 42:11)*.

We find the same thing in Psalm 43. David's *heart* spoke to his *head*. David's mind was troubled and tormented, but his heart (his spirit and innerman) knew God was always faithful. He decided to let his heart challenge the accusations which bombarded his mind. The victory may have seemed slow, which it often does, but victory is victory! As we read through the succeeding chapters of the Psalms we see manifestations of a triumphant servant of God, *"O clap your hands, all ye people; shout unto God with the voice of triumph ...Sing praises to God, sing praises: sing praises unto our King, sing praises"* *(Psalm 47:1,6)*.

King David was a believer under the old covenant. Jesus has given us a new covenant that is more glorious than the old. In the new covenant of Jesus' Blood and broken body, we have been given authority against all the works of the enemy. We are IN CHRIST. How much more should we be able to declare the faithfulness and overcoming power of our risen Savior and King? *"And they overcame him* (the accuser of the brethren) *by the blood of the Lamb, and by the word of their testimony; and they loved not their lives unto the death"* *(Revelation 12:11, explanation added)*.

When satan's authorities try to question the faithfulness of God in your life, you can accurately and boldly profess to the spirit realm, "My Lord is... 'seated on the right hand of God' *(Colossians 3:1)*, 'far above *all* principality, and power, and might, and dominion, and every name that is named. Not only in this world, but also in that which is to come' *(Ephesians 1:21)*. He has made me to be in Christ Jesus *(I Corinthians 1:30)*. Christ is in me *(Colossians 1:27)*, and greater is He that is in me than he that is in the world *(I John 4:4)*!"

You are equipped with what God says about you. Like David, you can "give yourself a talking to" when discouragement comes. You can make a heart decision rather than a head decision about your situation. You stand confident before the heavenly host, speaking words of faith that are grounded on solid truth. You are an overcomer in Jesus Christ!

CHAPTER 12

PRINCIPALITIES

Principalities are the chief and highest ranking strategists. They formulate plans, select targets and dispatch intricate schemes to subvert those who are a threat to them and to their place of power. They have information delivered to them on activities and histories of people, places and earthly activities. They send out fallen angelic and demonic spirits to accomplish their purpose. They are surprisingly organized, even though they are in a kingdom of confusion. Principalities are under the immediate control of their tyrant leader, satan.

Principalities have to do with laws, ordinances and places of power. They seek to make laws and implement ordinances to authenticate their plans and provide avenues to work their strategies. It is important to understand satan was part of the government of God before his fall. He was a chief angel and held a high position before God. He was the Anointed Cherub who carried great influence and position. As part of the government, he was well versed in spiritual law. This knowledge assisted him as he sought to defeat Adam. He looked for a law that would give him legal dominion and entrance into the earth again. When Adam disobeyed God's requirement by eating of the fruit of the Tree of the Knowledge of Good and Evil, he relinquished dominion of the earth into satan's hands.

Principalities rule best when they can institute laws and regulations to enforce their purposes. It is a tool to assist them in managing larger numbers of people within their areas. Governmental authorities on every level are vulnerable to oppression and manipulation. Satan and his principalities specialize in this area, for it enables them to bring about their deceitful plans in the earth. Prayer for people in authority is vital to counter their efforts.

TAKING THE 'PAL' OUT OF PRINCIPALITIES

When satan brought his followers onto the scene, he divided up areas of the earth and designated fallen-angel leaders, called princi-palities, to control them. Each of these leaders has a common goal.

They want to be like satan, and will operate by whatever means necessary to keep their position and place of power. As leaders, their influence and power depends on the numbers and the commitment of their followers. In order for principalities to remain in power, they must deceive people into allowing their influence. Therefore, they must convince ignorant people that there is some benefit to their influence and presence.

They represent themselves as the benefactor of some good—financial, economical, influential or social. They want to present themselves as a "pal" on behalf of deceived recipients. Many unsuspecting individuals have aspired to power, wealth, career, reputation, recognition or fame because their "pal" (principality of the region), offered them some earthy reward in exchange for their allegiance. What people do not realize is that the principality has set a trap of destruction for them, and their only use for such a person is to propagate error and promote satanic philosophies.

Principalities are limited. They may give orders and formulate strategies, but they are dependent on the subordinate activities of the powers (authorities), rulers of darkness and spiritual wicked doctrines of high places. Just as a general in any army may give orders, the success of any operation is dependent upon the devotion, ability and commitment of those under his command. It would be impossible for an Admiral to get an aircraft carrier to sea or back to harbor, if it weren't for the personnel who run the engines, weigh anchor and carry on the functions of the ship. Similarly, unless principalities can get cooperation, by force, intimidation or deception, they are limited.

There may be detailed operations planned by principalities and rulers, but they are vulnerable at anytime when souls come to know Jesus Christ. At the moment your soul was snatched out of the kingdom of darkness, satan's strategy was crippled. Like a cog taken out of a wheel which causes gears to grind to a halt, so is satan's use of the person who has been delivered out of the machinery of his operations. It causes him frustration, and regrouping is necessary. Consequently, satan's kingdom tries to lure the new believer back to their grasp.

God's holy angels rejoice when one believer is translated into the kingdom of light through faith in Jesus Christ *(Luke 15:10)*. They witness the spiritual impact of newness of everlasting life, the destiny of God's plan coming to pass in the person and they observe the ruin of satan's use of the person. They rejoice with believers in their victories, and join with believers in spiritual warfare as the Father gives them direction *(Acts 12:7-11)*.

KNOW YOUR RIGHTS

To wrestle against principalities, believers must know their rights. God has given His people power and authority. Believers are heirs of Abraham and joint heirs with Christ *(Galatians 3:13-14, 29)*. As heirs, we are entitled to our inheritance in Christ Jesus. When we know our rights and privileges, we can stand against the pressures that will inevitably arise when confronting principality opposition.

Satan is aware of the laws that govern the spiritual and the natural realms. He is obliged to submit to every spiritual law. He, therefore, will make every effort to keep God's spiritual laws away from anyone who will enforce them against him. For instance, the Bible tells us that the law of the Spirit of Life in Christ Jesus has set us free from the law of sin and of death *(Romans 8:2)*. Satan wants you to believe that walking in sin will not produce death. He wants to persuade you that he still holds the power of death. The law of the Spirit of Life sets free. Jesus, by His death, burial and resurrection has broken the

> *There are earthly laws and there are spiritual laws—both must be prayed for in line with the character and will of God*

power of sin and of death. Sin and death cannot imprison anyone who grasps the truth offered by the Spirit of Life. There are laws written in the Word of God that offer freedom for the children of God. Many people remain in bondage because they lack understanding and knowledge of their rights and privileges in the kingdom of light.

Laws govern both the spirit and physical realms. Laws were in place in eternity past. Lucifer was cast from heaven because iniquity was found in him, and the Godhead was just in doing so. The laws of nature set forth in Genesis 1 established boundaries by which the physical marvels of earth still remain in full force and effect such as seed time and harvest, the moon ruling by night and the sun by day.

IT IS WRITTEN

The Word of God sets forth ordinances and laws. When Jesus was standing against the chief principality—satan—He stated, *"It is written..." (Luke 4:4,8,10)*. When Jesus reproved satan, Jesus was demonstrating there are spiritual laws in place which determine and enforce a fact. Satan could not stand against the scripture spoken by Jesus. (Satan had taken scriptures and twisted them hoping to get Jesus to act in error). The law of life in Christ Jesus overrules the counterfeit plans and laws of the enemy. Satan is a liar and will twist words, laws and scripture. When you know the true wording and intent of laws and scripture, then you are able to discern and resist the lies of the adversary.

Chapters 6, 7 and 8 of Romans tell of laws that rule areas of our lives. We need to become equipped by knowing and obeying the laws of God. Many of the laws of God happen just because God is God—like the rain falling on the just and the unjust *(Matthew 5:45)*. However, walking in the laws of God concerning evil principalities involves knowing where the laws of the natural realm are subordinate to the law in the spirit realm. Several godly teachers have suggested believers look through the New Testament, underline and study all the instances where believer's rights are set forth. Jesus Christ establishes every believer's right. In studying the passages that refer—In Him, In Christ, In whom, In Jesus—you will gain knowledge into the rights and privileges obtained for you by Jesus. Seek out godly teaching on the laws of God. The Holy Spirit will help teach you how to appropriate those rights in your every day living and, in particular, spiritual warfare.

FORGIVENESS

Doris Wagner lays the groundwork for expelling hereditary demons in her book, *How to cast out demons*. She writes, "Forgiveness does not condone the action; it just removes the sting and the legal right for the hereditary spirit to hang in there for another generation. Forgiveness must be extended first so that the legal right is removed from the scene. The 'legal right' is defined as that which 'feeds' the demon and gives it permission to remain. Once the person forgives the perpetrator, the legal right for the demon to stay has been removed, and it must leave when commanded to do so."

When we understand that the thrust of principalities is to perpetrate and enforce legal right to carry on their evil workings, we can better understand the powerful role that forgiveness plays. Forgiveness has to do with legal rights within the spirit realm. Forgiveness brings godly freedom, unforgiveness opens rights of passage for evil.

As Jesus hung on the cross he spoke words that raised His heel to crush the head of the serpent. These words were, *"...Father, forgive them; for they know not what they do,"* He annulled the legal right satan had on humanity *(Luke 23:34)*.

We see the power of forgiveness when we look at the lives of Stephen and of the Apostle Paul. In Acts chapter 7, Stephen was stoned to death for his testimony of Jesus Christ. A young man named Saul stood nearby, guarding the coats of the stone throwers. He was well known for persecuting believers in the early church. Stephen, a devout man of God, spoke as he lay dying, *"...Lord, lay not this sin to their charge..."* *(verse 59)*. In forgiveness, he released powerful events to take place in heaven and in the earth.

THE POWER OF FORGIVENESS

Some time later, Saul traveled along the road to Damascus. Suddenly, a blazing light from heaven shone around him and he fell to the ground. The Lord spoke to him, *"Saul, Saul, why persecutest thou me?"* *(Acts 9:4)*. Saul, the church antagonist, had an encounter with Jesus that changed his life. Saul became a new man with a new name, the Apostle Paul. Was there a connection between Stephen's forgiveness and Saul conversion? I believe so.

The Apostle Paul walked out the rest of his life in Jesus Christ, writing most of the New Testament and leaving us record of words inspired by the Holy Spirit. As his impending death drew near, the Apostle Paul writes, *"...I pray God that it may not be laid to their charge,"* *(II Timothy 4:16)* —almost the same words spoken by Stephen. Yes, even as the young rebel stood by the tormentors' coats, a connection was made. The Apostle Paul experienced the impact of forgiveness firsthand. Even though many years passed and his own death was at hand, he knew forgiveness gave the Lord legal authority to work in the lives of those who had disappointed and hurt him in his years of ministry.

Does forgiveness carry powerful implications for us today? If we have problems and circumstances in our lives that loom as mountains of trouble for us, we have a guide to help us. In Mark 11:22-26, we are told that if we need a mountain to move we must forgive, if we don't, the spiritual law keeps the mountain in place, legally. Forgiveness puts the spiritual law on our side, and God can move in our behalf.

Many Christians repeat the Lord's prayer *(Matthew 6:9-13)*, which asks God to give us daily bread and keep us from evil. Yet we must not overlook the verses that follow which implore us to forgive, *"For if ye forgive men their trespasses, your heavenly Father will also forgive you: But if ye forgive not men their trespasses, neither will your Father forgive your trespasses" (verses 14, 15)*. Daily blessings and safety from the enemy requires forgiveness.

Principalities have their subordinates busy at work to produce wounds, injury and any misfortune that will bring offense and unforgiveness. Why? Because it gives them legal right to send demons on assignments against our lives.

Our Heavenly Father passionately wants to give us every good thing, to bless us far above all we can ask or think. As we read the passages that command us to forgive, we need to understand the heart of the Father. He *wants* to bless us. He is bound to the laws of the spirit realm. Even though Jesus is God, and He was with the Father and the Holy Spirit in eternity past, He still came as a man to earth to die on a cross—to fulfill spiritual law. A spiritual law that required a sacrifice for sin, one only He could pay.

As we learn spiritual law, we will mature in walking in our rights and privileges in the wars of the kingdoms. Forgiveness is warfare against *principalities*. Do you want to legally put your spiritual foot on the neck of the enemy? Forgive. Do you want mountains of pain and disappointment to move? Forgive. Do you want those who persecute and hurt you in despiteful ways to get a touch from the Lord *(Matthew 5:44)*? Do you want finances to be freed up *(Luke 6: 37, 38)*? Give the Lord the legal right to bless you with all of heaven's provision by understanding that forgiveness is a powerful spiritual force.

THE POWER OF WORDS

The words we speak produce life or death. It is a law. Words that come out of our mouths will produce fruit from what we have spoken. It will be fruit that will affect our lives, and we will live out the sweetness or bitterness of our words. *"But I say unto you, That every idle word that men shall speak, they shall give account thereof in the day of judgment. For by thy words thou shalt be justified, and by thy words thou shalt be condemned"* (Matthew 12:36-37).

Principalities use the words of your mouth to condemn you. Words also bring protection and can cause you to be justified from judgment. What do your words produce—life or death? Do your words give satan permission to bring destruction upon you and your family? Cursing at spouses and children does that very thing. Words of freedom and protection bring safety.

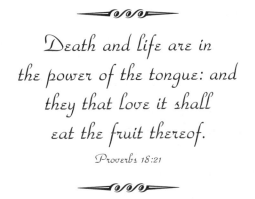

Death and life are in the power of the tongue: and they that love it shall eat the fruit thereof.

Proverbs 18:21

When God spoke, "Let there be light," light obeyed. Human beings are made in the image of God. Words, the power of words, are a characteristic of being a part of His image. Every idle word will be judged. Words are powerful gifts within us. God will judge us according to what we have done with them.

Satan and his underlings attempt to manipulate us into using our words to give him the legal right to steal, kill and destroy. When we speak, we need to be keenly aware to whom we are giving our permission and rights. Statements like, "Nothing ever goes right," will hinder solutions. Whereas, "There's a way this is going to work," gives life to the solution. Examine how your words have opened the door to the enemy. Are your present problems a product of your words? Are others suffering because your words gave place to the devil, and he had permission to bring trouble upon them?

ather God, I come to You in the Name and by the Blood of Jesus Christ. I acknowledge I have spoken words that were wrong. Forgive me for my words spoken in hurt, anger, hate and revenge. Your Word says if I confess my sins, You will forgive my sins and cleanse me from all unrighteousness (I John 1:9). I ask for the Blood of Jesus Christ to cleanse me and those I have spoken wrong words to or about. Cleanse me from sin and the effects of sin and make me new. Create a clean heart in me and give me understanding of the power of words so I do not continue to sin with the words of my mouth. Please give me strength by Your Holy Spirit to change the way I have used words in the past against others and myself. I choose words of Life and not death. I choose to honor You with the words of my mouth that You may bring honor to me. In Jesus' Name. Amen.

GODLY LEADERSHIP: THE ENEMY OF PRINCIPALITIES

Because they understand the power that accompanies places of position, principalities will be especially interested in a person who has leadership qualities in the kingdom of God. Satan knows informed, bold and anointed believers will wreck havoc to his plans. Believers who challenge and enforce the defeat of principalities will come under assault by them. The Lord admonishes His followers, *"To whom much is given, much is required"* (Luke 12:48). Walking in leadership brings with it the need for dependence on the wisdom, knowledge and revelation of the Lord in deep and powerful understanding.

You can have confidence knowing your power and authority because, *"... Jesus Christ: Who is gone into heaven, and is on the right hand of God; angels and authorities and powers being made subject unto him"* (I Peter 3:21-22).

The spirit realm is subject to Jesus Christ. who sits at the right hand of the Father. We gain knowledge and confidence in His glorious position and our place as seated with Him in heavenly places (Ephesians 2.6). All the principalities and powers of satan's fallen world are subject to the One who sits at the right hand of the Father.

POLITICAL OFFICE

The heart of the king is in the hand of the Lord *(Proverbs 21:1)*. Through our prayers, God is able to protect His people and fulfill His plan within the earth. His arm is not short that He cannot accomplish His ultimate plan. He seeks those who will pray in accordance with His strategic remedies. The Lord's admonition to pray for those in authority is to cooperate with God in directing the hearts of those who rule.

Many Christians shun all involvement in the trappings of politics. You must be obedient to the Lord if He is calling you to this area of service. You also must understand there will be spiritual warfare that accompanies it. You must be equipped with strong faith and assurance of your authority in the Lord as well as your position in earthly office. You must realize you are in an area where principalities do not want you to be, and you may come under opposition wherever you endeavor to effect godly change.

Intercessors who are burdened to pray for leaders and governmental officials must be aware of the importance of their call. Those whom the Lord has called to political office, as well as intercessors who pray for leadership on any level, are wise if they are knowledgeable in both natural and spiritual laws, rights and privileges.

We are told, *"Take away the wicked from before the king, and his throne shall be established in righteousness"* *(Proverbs 25:5).*

Many times people in positions of leadership depend on counselors and advisors around them. We should pray that evil counselors be removed from before the "king." We can, by the Holy Spirit, call forth godly counselors to be placed before the "king" (person in authority). Speaking the Word of God over leaders builds a spiritual hedge of protection around them and opens pathways of godly wisdom to come forth. If godly counselors surround those in leadership, God will impact their decisions.

We are also admonished, *"I exhort therefore, that, first of all, supplications, prayers, intercessions, and giving of thanks, be made for all men; For kings, and for all that are in authority; that we may lead a quiet and peaceable life in all godliness and honesty. For this is good and acceptable in the sight of God our Saviour; Who will have all men to be saved, and to come unto the knowledge of the truth"* *(I Timothy 2:1-4).*

It is our responsibility to pray supplications, prayers, intercessions and thanksgiving over all those in authority. Spouses, parents, employers, pastors, mayors, city officials, government officials—everyone in our lives who hold places of influence and leadership. Satanic strategists will focus on the one with authority, leadership responsibility and power in order to control or influence outcome. Complaints about what decisions are made do not find a sympathetic ear from the Lord when there has been an absence of prayer in behalf of those in authority.

God's will is perfectly clear: that all men will be saved. Praying for those in authority and leadership opens doors for the gospel. When the wicked rule, the gospel will be targeted. Therefore, the Bible encourages us to pray for every level of authority so the gospel may not be hindered and believers may lead a quiet and peaceable life. We all benefit when godly peace is present.

———✷✷✷———

The Blood speaks. It gives testimony.

———✷✷✷———

PRINCE OF THE POWER OF THE AIR

God's law warns us about wrestling with flesh and blood, but He commands us to carry the battle to the spirit realm. The Apostle Paul wrote, *"Wherein in time past ye walked according to the course of this world, according to the prince of the power of the air, the spirit that now worketh in the children of disobedience" (Ephesians 2:2)*. Obviously, some of the people Paul addressed had walked the course of the world, participating in the evil activities of the spirit who works in children of disobedience. But the prince of the power of the air was not able to keep them.

Since Ephesians 4:26 tells believers to be angry and sin not, then it must be possible to avoid being ensnared in hatred, bitterness and strife. We must discuss and confront issues without embroiling ourselves in vicious contention and arguments.

LAWS—IN CHRIST

There are laws in full force, ordained in heaven, that are available through faith in Jesus Christ and His gospel. The first and foremost is the law of love described in Galatians, chapter 5, *"For all the law is fulfilled in one word, even in this; Thou shalt love thy neighbour as thyself" (verse 14).*

God also promises to write His law on our heart and mind, *"For this is the covenant that I will make with the house of Israel after those days, saith the Lord; I will put my laws into their mind, and write them in their hearts: and I will be to them a God, and they shall be to me a people" (Ezekiel 36:26-28, and in Hebrews 8:10).* In Christ Jesus, and by the presence of the Holy Spirit within born-again believers, the laws and ordinances of God can be written within your heart and mind. Once you are born again, there is an awareness of sin and a deep sense of right and wrong. The conscience of a sincere believer will be pricked when evil arises. The law of the Spirit of Life in Christ Jesus wars against the law of sin and of death that wants to raise its head against you.

MOST IMPORTANT LAWS AND COMMANDMENTS

Jesus set the first two commandments in order in Mark, chapter 12, *"And Jesus answered him, The first of all the commandments is, Hear, O Israel; The Lord our God is one Lord: And thou shalt love the Lord thy God with all thy heart, and with all thy soul, and with all thy mind, and with all thy strength: and this is the first commandment. And the second is like, namely this, Thou shalt love thy neighbour as thyself. There is none other commandment greater than these" (verses 29-31).*

Throughout the New Testament we are told not to lose sight of the cross and the love of the Father for humankind. The Pharisees had instituted hundreds of laws, but were rebuked by Jesus for neglecting the people in their attempts to be spiritual. They observed their interpretation of the law to such an extent that they ridiculed Jesus for healing people on the Sabbath. They lost sight of the people in need and the loving expression of God performed by Jesus. Their law had alienated them from the heart of God.

THE FATHER'S HEART

In our efforts to war for the gospel of the Lord Jesus Christ, it is important to know the heart of the Heavenly Father for those He loves. At one time my own spiritual zeal caused me to judge certain people in authority. Their actions were definitely evil, and I reacted with self-righteous indignation. God required me to repent. As I wrestled with the rights and wrongs, the Lord showed me that I did not have His heart in the matter. This is the Lord's heart: He so loved the world that He gave his only begotten Son to die for *the world*. I condemned the wrong without praying in love for the wrongdoer. I was wrestling flesh and blood, and not addressing the evil-spiritual strategists behind the scenes.

Yes, of course, people involved in their sin will pay the price of sin, which is death in some form. However, it is the Lord's desire that such penalty be brought under the Blood of Jesus because He has already paid the price.

We can pray for sinners as if we were the ones caught in the sin, petitioning the Lord for the same mercy and deliverance we would desire. *That* is loving our neighbor as ourselves. The love which caused Jesus to endure the cross, and the love which prompted the Father to allow such brutality to His Son, applies to the vilest of sinners. It is easier to pray for them when we realize these people are targeted by fallen angels who seek to use them as instruments to bring about evil positions of rule in the earth, and eventually torment their souls in hell.

However, we are NOT required to love, nor give place to fallen angels. Ferocious aggressive battle is the order of the day when it comes to battling the enemy of the spiritual realm. Discerning what is behind people's actions is necessary in order to stand strong against satanic planners and yet not be frustrated and have bitter anger at the people themselves.

GOD'S LAWS ARE MORE POWERFUL

God always has laws that supersede the efforts of satan's kingdom. Jesus said, *"In the world ye shall have tribulation: but be of good cheer: I have overcome the world"* (John 16:33). Every place where satan seeks to bring his ruling control, God has ordained and provided avenues for his defeat. The truth is not bound (II Timothy 2:9, John 17:17). Truth frustrates the enemy because it unlooses; it frees. When truth goes forth, it prevails. Wherever the enemy has seemed to gain an advantage, seek the counsel of the Holy Spirit for the counter offensive plan of God. God has provided laws that guarantee success.

Galatians 5 reveals a marvelous secret. In the list of the Fruit of the Spirit, we find love, joy, peace, long-suffering, gentleness, goodness, faith, meekness and self-control. Without ending the sentence, a powerful phrase is added—AGAINST SUCH THERE IS NO LAW. When you and I walk in the Holy Spirit and display the Fruit of the Spirit, we transcend the power of the enemy because satan has no "law" to impede or hinder the work of the Spirit. There is a freedom that walking in the Fruit of the Spirit provides which paralyzes the enemy. He has no weapons against it.

Love is powerful. We know it is because God is Love and God is all-powerful. Walking in love is so powerful it undermines and sets the enemy to confusion. It is the same with the other segments of the Fruit of the Spirit. Faith, goodness, joy, peace, long-suffering, meekness, self-control have the power and strength to lawfully battle satanic maneuvers. Do not underestimate the powerful work of the Holy Spirit within the Fruit of the Spirit expressed in our lives. Satan is rendered powerless because such tools of the Holy Spirit are far beyond his capabilities.

PRINCIPALITY TACTICS

Principalities use propaganda. Propaganda is misinformation intended to allow a principality to gain ruling position and is designed to influence the broader spectrum of individuals.

Satan, as the prince of the power of the air, has elaborate schemes that draw attention to his objectives and promote his lies. Whatever medium of communication has been used throughout the generations, including television, radio and the World Wide Web, they have been used by satanic strategists to promote satan's agenda.

What changed the multitude of people who heralded Jesus' entry into Jerusalem (on what Christians call Palm Sunday) into the mob which a few days later cried, "Crucify him, crucify him?" We find the answer in Matthew 27:20, *"But the chief priests and elders persuaded the multitude that they should ask Barabbas, and destroy Jesus" (emphasis added)*.

Public opinion swayed Pontius Pilate to accommodate their demand to release Barabbas and crucify Jesus. Even though the crucifixion of Jesus was fulfillment of prophetic promises, those individuals who through envy and hate inspired the revolt against him were accountable for their actions.

THE LORD OF GLORY

Jesus is the Prince of Peace. He is the Prince of Life. He is the Prince of the Kings of the earth. He is the Lord of Glory. Jesus laid down His life so that He could overcome every strategy and tactic of the enemy. His princely sacrifice defeated all principality power. In His death and resurrection, victory was established.

Obviously, satan had no idea what Jesus' death would accomplish, *"But we speak the wisdom of God in a mystery, even the hidden wisdom, which God ordained before the world unto our glory: Which none of the princes of this world knew: for had they known it, they would not have crucified the Lord of glory"* (I Corinthians 2:7-8).

When Jesus died on the cross, He was a sinless sacrifice. Satan blew it. He instigated the crucifixion of One who had committed no sin. In doing so, he broke a spiritual law and forfeited all he had gained when Adam fell. If he had known the consequences, the *princes of this world* would never have crucified Jesus. Jesus, called the Last Adam, legally and eternally established the everlasting law of life for those who accept His sacrifice by faith. It also established a final end to satan and his followers.

The wisdom of God which was a mystery to satan (when he savagely crucified Christ) is yet a mystery to him. In God's divine wisdom, He continues to thwart the enemy's efforts through heavenly wisdom freely given to His beloved *(James 1:5)*.

Understanding the impact of the legal system of the spirit realm takes some time and study. We will be increasingly more effective in spiritual warfare as we become equipped in this very important area.

SECRET LAWS AND DECREES

Principalities also seek to put laws into place through secrecy. Evil entities maneuver people in authority to establish laws. Evil minds attempt to implement laws that affect the masses behind closed doors. We must become more knowledgeable and informed about the decisions made by those in leadership. Then we must pray about these matters that affect so many lives.

Daniel found great favor before King Darius and was placed highest of three presidents and a number of princes. Daniel was so highly favored that King Darius considered putting Daniel in charge of his whole realm. Jealousy and hatred by the other officials of the kingdom spawned a plan for Daniel's destruction. *"Then said these men, We shall not find any occasion against this Daniel, except we find it against him concerning the law of his God. Then these presidents and princes assembled together to the king, and said thus unto him, King Darius, live for ever. All the presidents of the kingdom, the governors, and the princes, the counsellors, and the captains, have consulted together* (in truth it was only the presidents and the princes) *to establish a royal statute, and to make a firm decree, that whosoever shall ask a petition of any God or man for thirty days, save of thee, O king, he shall be cast into the den of lions. Now, O king, establish the decree, and sign the writing, that it be not changed, according to the law of the Medes and Persians, which altereth not. Wherefore king Darius signed the writing and the decree"* (Daniel 6:5-9, notation added).

The presidents and princes devised a law and presented it to King Darius pretending that many more rulers were involved in the decree. They played on the king's ego and his ignorance of their motive. Some days later, they brought the decree before the king and accused Daniel of disobeying the decree because he prayed toward Jerusalem, giving thanks three times each day to his God.

King Darius was dismayed. He realized he had signed a decree that was intended to destroy his most trusted official. *"Then the king, when he heard these words, was sore displeased with himself, and set his heart on Daniel to deliver him: and he laboured till the going down of the sun to deliver him"* (Daniel 6:14). King Darius was bound to his own decree that required Daniel be thrown into a den of hungry lions. Anguish ravaged the soul of the king as he fasted, perhaps prayed through the day and throughout the night. Early the next morning he rushed to the den of lions. *"...O Daniel, servant of the living God, is thy God, whom thou servest continually, able to deliver thee from the lions? Then said Daniel unto the king, O king, live for ever."* Daniel took hold of a greater law. *"My God hath sent his angel, and hath shut the lions' mouths, that they have not hurt me: forasmuch as before him innocency was found in me; and also before thee, O king, have I done no hurt"* (Daniel 6:20-22).

King Darius issued a new decree throughout the land. It was one which proclaimed that the God of Daniel, the Living God, be revered and honored. The law of the spirit was greater than the law set forth by evil men. The men who sought to destroy Daniel were themselves thrust into the den of lions. Principalities work through people who regard evil in their hearts. These men paid with their lives for their cooperation with principalities. However, Daniel was established in God. His stand for righteousness overruled the decree of earthly enemies as well as the physical law of hungry lions.

FOR SUCH A TIME AS THIS

Haman used a sly decree as he plotted to kill Mordecai and all of the Jewish people under King Ahasuerus. Because of his hate for Mordecai he manipulated the king saying, *"...There is a certain people scattered abroad and dispersed among the people...their laws are diverse from all people; neither keep they the king's laws: therefore it is not for the king's profit to suffer them. If it please the king, let it be written that they may be destroyed..."* (Esther 3:8,9). Queen Esther, being a Jewess, would also be destroyed in the decree the king made. The king's lack of regard for the people who were spread throughout the 127 provinces of his kingdom did not have impact upon him until it became known that Haman's plan would require the life of the king's own wife.

Queen Esther, Mordecai and all the Jews throughout the provinces fasted and prayed. The night before Queen Esther planned to speak to the king, King Ahasuerus was so disturbed he could not sleep. *For some reason*, he called for the book of records and discovered that Mordecai had foiled a plot against the king's life. When Queen Esther explained that Haman was seeking to not only destroy her but all her people, including Mordecai, the king's heart was turned against Haman. Haman was hung on the gallows he constructed for Mordecai.

REPLACEMENT THEOLOGY

What would turn such hate for one man (Mordecai) against a whole people (the Jews), as was the case with Haman? Wicked Haman was in a position that carried great influence and authority. He was used by satan to seek to abolish the Jewish people under his rule. Satan has tried one plan after another seeking to destroy the lineage and people of the Messiah. Whether it was Pharaoh, Herod, Haman or Hitler, principalities have sought to bring those to power who have a bent toward destruction of God's chosen people.

Replacement theology has even infiltrated the church, seeking to displace the Jewish people as God's chosen people and replace them with the church. God will not deny His firstborn and He is serious about what is done concerning them. When Pharoah refused to release the enslaved firstborn of God, He responded by killing the firstborn of Egypt. *"And the Lord said unto Moses, When thou goest to return into Egypt, see that thou do all those wonders before Pharaoh, which I have put in thine hand: ...And thou shalt say unto Pharaoh, Thus saith the Lord, Israel is my son, even my firstborn: And I say unto thee, Let my son go, that he may serve me: and if thou refuse to let him go, behold, I will slay thy son, even thy firstborn"* (Exodus 4:21-23, emphasis added). The deaths of the firstborn of Egypt were the final blow that released the nation of Israel from the bondage of Egyptian dominance.

THE ONLY BEGOTTEN OF GOD

You might think that Jesus was the firstborn of God. Jesus is the only begotten Son of God. When the Holy Spirit came upon the Jewish maiden, Mary, and the power of the Highest overshadowed her, the holy child who came forth from her womb was the Son of God, Jesus. He was the Seed of the Highest and the seed of the woman. God had come to earth in human form. Jesus is the Holy One of Israel. The covenant with Abraham, Isaac and Jacob established the Jewish nation in which He promised that through Abraham the entire world would be blessed. In Abraham's lineage, the Messiah was to come as a Jew from the House of David. God's covenant with Abraham was like a spiritual umbilical cord for the Birth of His only begotten Son, Jesus Christ.

The Father remains in covenant with His people and continues to fulfill His promises to Israel. Jesus, the Messiah, will come again. His return will be to Israel where His feet will step onto the Mount of Olives *(Zechariah 14:4)*.

Many verses foretell the return of Jesus to His beloved Israel where He will be revealed as their Messiah. Satan's humiliation and open shame will be seen, this time by earthly observers.

Israel continues to play the key role in the events of end-time prophecy. Prayers for Israel and the Jewish people, including the return of the Jews to their homeland, are upon the heart of the Lord. Strong prayer for Israel will bring confrontations with principality entities.

REPUTATION

Another of the strongholds Christians encounter is the matter of reputation before men. Leaders who have a weak area in their lives concerning their reputation are vulnerable to manipulation by principalities. They may draw back from stands they feel are important because it is unpopular or under opposition. They court the approval of men and women while compromising core values and beliefs. In essence, the person begins to "chase" their reputation.

They may be targeted by seducing spirits and drawn into areas of error and sin. Once principalities manipulate someone into protecting their reputation, they begin their treachery of using them for evil purposes. This was the case in Jesus' day, *"Nevertheless among the chief rulers also many believed on him; but because of the Pharisees they did not confess him, lest they should be put out of the synagogue: For they loved the praise of men more than the praise of God"* (John 12:42,43).

Fear cripples anyone who attempts to protect their reputation by unholy means. Evil strategists play mind videos of your destruction to instigate fear. They also play out scenarios that could be implemented to save your reputation. Lying spirits offer plots of various ways to hide truth.

DAVID PROTECTS HIS REPUTATION

David, as king, tried a number of ways to cover his affair with Bathsheba which resulted in her pregnancy. Eventually he had Bathsheba's husband transferred to the front lines of battle to be killed. He murdered in order to conceal his sin and protect his reputation. When confronted by the prophet Nathan, David had a decision to make. Would he have Nathan also "disappear," or would he repent? His decision weighed in the balance whether he would go further into evil or would be drawn back into the presence of his Lord. David's love for the Lord settled his decision to repent. His kingdom would have been lost if he had chosen to justify his sin instead of repenting.

HERODIAS' PLOT

John the Baptist proclaimed the truth: That King Herod should not have his brother's wife, Herodias. Herodias was livid that the prophet challenged her marriage to the king. She had tried to have John the Baptist killed, but Herod refused. *"For John had said unto Herod, It is not lawful for thee to have thy brother's wife. Therefore Herodias had a quarrel against him, and would have killed him; but she could not: For Herod feared John, knowing that he was a just man and an holy, and observed him; and when he heard him, he did many things, and heard him gladly" (Mark 6:18-20).*

Herodias knew Herod's character, especially during his drunken feasts. At a feast in honor of Herod's birthday, she instructed her daughter to seductively dance before the king. Herod offered the damsel anything she would desire. Herodias instructed her daughter to ask for the head of John the Baptist. "It was for those who sat with him" that Herod was forced to grant her request. Herod, who didn't want John to die, was pressured into saving face before his colleagues. John the Baptist was beheaded and his head brought to Herodias' daughter, who brought it to her mother. What Herodias could not accomplish by personal pressure, she accomplished by attacking Herod's reputation before his peers.

REPUTATION MANIPULATORS

Evil accusers threaten to belie and destroy our place and position. Manipulation, as it pertains to reputation, can hold powerful strings. Religious spirits move us out of God's direction for our lives by whispering, "If you were a Christian you would..." They use self-seeking people to say, "If they were a Christian they would do this or that for me." The ploy of spiritual reputation requires discernment.

Maturity has learned to wait for the full completion of things. The Bible tells us that through patience we will possess our souls. Possess means to "keep a rein on, keep in check and in their proper boundaries." Possessing the soul involves keeping godly boundaries in the mind (with its thoughts); the will (in its choices); and the emotions, (even when they are taking roller coaster rides within).

——◦◦◦——

In your patience possess ye your souls. Luke 21:19

——◦◦◦——

REPUTATION REMEDY

What is the remedy for those who hold positions of power and leadership? We find a key in the second chapter of Philippians, *"Let this mind be in you, which was also in Christ Jesus: Who, being in the form of God, thought it not robbery to be equal with God: But made himself of no reputation...he humbled himself, and became obedient unto death, even the death of the cross"* (verses 5-8).

Jesus made Himself of no reputation. He left His throne in glory. You and I can trust our personal reputations, our political reputations, our professional and our spiritual reputations into the Lord's hands. We can commit the protecting of our reputations to the work of the Holy Spirit. He is a worthy keeper of our reputations when we are forced to "lay down" our reputations for godly purpose.

Do you want a good reputation? The Lord says, *"If you want favor with both God and man, and a reputation for good judgment and common sense, then trust the Lord completely, and don't ever trust yourself. In everything you do, put God first, and he will direct you and crown your efforts with success"* (Proverbs 3:4-5, TLB).

We can guard our reputations by not giving occasion to the enemy. The Bible tells us that, *"A good name is better than precious ointment..."* (Ecclesiastes 7:1). A good name is worth protecting from enemy invasion and opportunity. However, if you have fallen into satan's trap and failed, the Holy Spirit, who is the Spirit of Grace, can be called upon to bring forth a powerful solution. Remember, repentance releases grace *(I Peter 5:5, James 4:6)*.

FALSE PROTECTION

The deceiver would also have us protect our reputations with such tight-fistedness we miss the leading of the Lord. Jesus ate with publicans and sinners. He invited himself to eat at the home of a despised tax collector. He allowed a disdained woman of the city to wash his feet. He did not repel lepers, but healed them. He did not condemn the woman caught in sin, but told her to go and sin no more. He did not court the favor and acceptance of the religious leaders.

Jesus took a weapon out of His enemy's hand when He did not protect His reputation in order to gain man's acceptance. You and I are able to do the same.

The Bible tells us that if we will be willing to "lose" our reputations for the sake of the gospel, we will gain the promises of gospel blessings. *"Whosoever shall seek to save his life shall lose it; and whosoever shall lose his life shall preserve it"* (Luke 17:33).

HOLDING FAST THE VISION

A steadfast remedy against the manipulation of your reputation is to be sure of your purpose and calling. Many times Jesus stated and restated the purpose in His coming. His purpose was to draw sinners to Himself and unto His Father. Therefore, being among sinners was more important than His reputation. Knowing your purpose will strengthen your soul. It establishes your mind and settles your emotions. It sets the course of your steps and quiets the voices that attempt to change your course because of fear for your reputation. The counsel of the Bible tells us to, *"Commit thy works unto the Lord, and thy thoughts shall be established"* (Proverbs 16:3).

GRACE AND TRADITION

Legalistic religious practices fail to carry the grace of God as we see in Mark, chapter seven, *"And he said unto them, Full well ye reject the commandment of God, that ye may keep your own tradition"* (verse 9). The laws which were spoken against in this and other New Testament scriptures refer to the difference between "works" of man and salvation through grace. The Pharisees set up laws to make righteousness attainable through outward actions and rituals. Righteousness is a matter of faith, not of works.

Satan used the Pharisees in Jesus' day to establish numerous traditions that warred against the commandment of God. He uses the same tactics today. Many times our faith is attacked by traditions of men which hold no validity with God—although they are suggested to be from Him.

Understanding the law of the Spirit which includes righteousness, grace and God's ordinances and statutes, will keep you from religious bondage and is necessary to discern satanic lies.

KINGS AND PRIESTS

If you're like me, most days you don't wake up feeling like a king or a priest. However, kingship and priesthood were bestowed upon you when you were washed in the Blood of Jesus. *"...Unto him that loved us, and washed us from our sins in his own blood, And hath made us kings and priests unto God and his Father..." (Revelation 1:5,6).* Authority and royal position afford privilege and responsibility. We are seated with the One whose love purchased the authority we received. It is Jesus, by His Holy Spirit, who continually guides our pathway(s) to victory.

⎯⎯•❀❀⎯⎯

The legal side of redemption is the Blood Covenant

⎯⎯•❀❀⎯⎯

Principalities are far below the One who is seated at the right hand of the Father in the third heaven. Every effort they make is nothing but futile attempts to hold onto an existence that has an ordained end. They are going to endure eternal torment. The lake of fire is their fate.

Kings and priests hold positions that carry distinction as well as accountability. Such privilege has been bestowed upon you through the grace and purpose of Jesus Christ. You are a king and priest unto God, first and foremost. And in ministering to God as Supreme, Almighty, Sovereign and Magnificent, you will have the honor of imitating, honoring, trusting and loving Jesus Christ, as King of kings, Lord of lords, and as your Great High Priest. Jesus is the Servant King. You who are kings and priests in God's heavenly kingdom will be as your Lord, with the heart of a servant and a love for those whom He loves. You will be wise as serpents and gentle as doves. You will be wise to discern the tactics of serpent strategists, and be as gentle as a dove, as Jesus was to those who came to Him.

CHAPTER 13

FITTING IT ALL TOGETHER

How does all this information fit together? When we read the account of Paul and Silas in Acts 16, it reveals a progression that, in one story sequence, identifies the operations of the hierarchy of satan. Let us dissect this account and see what we can learn.

"And it came to pass, as we went to prayer, a certain damsel possessed with a spirit of divination met us, which brought her masters much gain by soothsaying: The same followed Paul and us, and cried, saying, These men are the servants of the most high God, which shew unto us the way of salvation. And this did she many days. But Paul, being grieved, turned and said to the spirit, I command thee in the name of Jesus Christ to come out of her. And he came out the same hour" (Acts 16:16-18).

Paul, Silas and others were on their way to prayer, doing God's work. A demon-possessed woman met them day in and day out, harassing and mocking the men of God. The demon spirit was a spirit of python which was associated with fortune-telling—a pressuring type of spirit that wears down, harasses and deceives.

Even though her words sounded accurate, *"These men are the servants of the most high God, which show unto us the way of salvation,"* they were said in such a way as to mock Paul and Silas, or to deceive people into thinking that Paul and Silas were soothsayers like herself, thus giving credence to herself and perverting the gospel. It was a false doctrine spoken through the woman by a demon spirit. Notice that the demon spirit is not referred to as a part of the woman's being but is referred to as "he" in verse 18. It was a personality separate from that of the woman.

A demon had possessed the woman and promoted false doctrine—sorcery and fortune-telling. Spiritual wickedness in high places sent a demon to control a human being to spread false doctrine. The demon was cast out and the woman freed. Satan's kingdom was upset at this deliverance.

FREE FROM BONDAGE

Paul, after enduring the mockery and perversion of this spirit for many days, finally had enough. He turned to the spirit and cast it out in the Name of Jesus. The demon had to obey the command spoken in the Name of Jesus, and he departed the same hour. The woman was freed from satan's bondage and released from his plan over her life.

However, notice the battle was not over for Paul and Silas. When the woman's masters saw what had happened, their greedy hearts sought revenge. They were used of satan to promote evil because of their love of money.

"And when her masters saw that the hope of their gains were gone, they caught Paul and Silas, and drew them into the marketplace unto the rulers, And brought them to the magistrates, saying, These men, being Jews, do exceedingly trouble our city, And teach customs, which are not lawful for us to receive, neither to observe, being Romans" (Acts 16:19-21).

COUNTERATTACK

These men were violently upset with Paul and Silas. They realized the demon had been cast out of the woman. Their wicked methods of financial gain were gone and they wanted vengeance. They grabbed Paul and Silas and brought them before the rulers of the city, covering the real reasons for their accusations. They spoke against them as Jews, and said they were teachers of doctrine against Rome. They attacked Paul and Silas for the gospel of Christ, which sets people free, suggesting that such teaching was contrary to Roman rule.

This was a coordinated effort of spiritual wickedness in high places and rulers of darkness. They reported what Paul and Silas was teaching was against Rome. Doctrine vs. doctrine. Rulers of darkness, as they always do, hid information and contorted true facts. In bringing Paul and Silas before the magistrates, we see satanic authorities also joined the attack. *"And the multitude rose up together against them: and the magistrates rent off their clothes, and commanded to beat them. And when they had laid many stripes upon them, they cast them into prison, charging the jailor to keep them safely: Who, having received such a charge, thrust them into the inner prison, and made their feet fast in the stocks"* (Acts 16:22-24).

The magistrates were used by satanic authorities to bring strong-arm tactics against Paul and Silas. The crowd was stirred up to join in the accusations. It seemed all of hell had been loosed against them. What we see are the segments of satan's hierarchy in operation, working a coordinated plan.

GLORIFYING GOD

Paul and Silas, on their way to prayer, took a stand against the harassing oppression of the enemy. Afterward, they were accused, sentenced, beaten and thrown into the darkest part of the city jail. Silas could have looked at Paul and said, "Look what you have gotten us into." But they were in unity about their call. They didn't whine and complain about their fate but continued their battle into the spiritual realm. *"And at midnight Paul and Silas prayed, and sang praises unto God: and the prisoners heard them. And suddenly there was a great earthquake, so that the foundations of the prison were shaken: and immediately all the doors were opened, and every one's bands were loosed"* (Acts 16:25, 26).

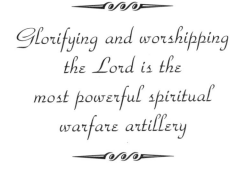

Glorifying and worshipping the Lord is the most powerful spiritual warfare artillery

Paul and Silas declared the glory to the Lord and worshipped—which is the most powerful spiritual warfare artillery.

LOUD AND STRONG

Prayers and praises unto God rose through the darkness, drifting along the passageways into the compartments that held other prisoners. They were not wimpy in their words, but spoke out strong and clear. They did not draw back from the deliverance of the demon-possessed damsel, nor did they make apologies for the God they served. They were not wrapped in defeat as their circumstance indicated, but they sang praises and announced their prayers for all to hear.

Heaven heard. At midnight, at the darkest hour, things changed. Paul and Silas' prayers and praises transformed the circumstances, and affected something more important—the people. The scripture said, *"every one's bands were loosed."* The doors opened and all the prisoners were loosed. It seems logical that all of them would run, but that was not the case. Those who were also imprisoned in the damp, dirty prison cells had encountered God and their lives changed. They not only heard, but they received something greater than freedom from bands upon their hands and feet. They received freedom in their innermost being.

"And the keeper of the prison awaking out of his sleep, and seeing the prison doors open, he drew out his sword, and would have killed himself, supposed that the prisoners had been fled. But Paul cried with a loud voice, saying, Do thyself no harm: <u>for we are all here</u>. Then he called for a light, and sprang in, and came trembling, and fell down before Paul and Silas, And brought them out, and said, Sirs, what must I do to be saved" (Acts 16:27-30, emphasis added).

The gospel of the Lord Jesus Christ was the power of God against doctrines and actions of error. And God's love set everyone free.

THE GUARD IS SAVED

The keeper of the prison expected every one to be gone when he saw the prison doors open. The guard drew his sword to take his own life rather than suffer the cruel Roman death for letting any prisoner escape. Paul called out to him to let him know they all were still there. His life was spared, and an amazing change took place within him. He, along with the prisoners, had heard the prayers and praises of Paul and Silas' songs. He had seen the power of the God who opened the prison doors and his plea was "What must I do to be saved?" Paul and Silas had a ready answer. *"And they said, Believe on the Lord Jesus Christ, and thou shalt be saved, and thy house. And they spake unto him the word of the Lord, and to all that were in his house"* (Acts 16:31, 32).

Paul and Silas were beaten and bloody. They were hungry and in miserable circumstances when they entered the prison, but notice what the jailor did.

"And he took them the same hour of the night, and washed their stripes; and was baptized, he and all his, straightway. And when he had brought them into his house, he set meat before them, and rejoiced, believing in God with all his house" (Acts 16:33, 34).

LET THEM GO!

The jailor took Paul and Silas to a place where their wounds could be washed. While they were there, Paul and Silas baptized the jailor and all those of his house. Keep in mind this took place in the wee hours of the morning. They then went to the jailor's home and were fed. Paul and Silas left in triumphant success. The jailor and his whole house had been snatched out of the hands of satan, saved, baptized and on fire for the Lord. And Paul and Silas were washed and fed—all before dawn.

"And when it was day, the magistrates sent the sergeants, saying, Let those men go. And the keeper of the prison told this saying to Paul, The magistrates have sent to let you go: now therefore depart, and go in peace. But Paul said unto them, They have beaten us openly uncondemned, being Romans, and have cast us into prison; and now do they thrust us out privily? nay verily; but let them come themselves and fetch us out. And the sergeants told these words unto the magistrates: and they feared, when they heard that they were Romans" (Acts 16:35-38).

We must know our rights in both the spiritual and natural realms

Paul knew who he was in Christ in the spiritual realm, and he knew his rights in the natural realm. The morning after, the magistrates sent word to the jailor to let Paul and Silas go. Maybe the earthquake shook their confidence; maybe they had second thoughts about their actions. In any case, they decided to let Paul and Silas go. Paul, however, was not going to steal away like a rabbit on the run. He knew his rights in the natural realm as a Roman citizen and proceeded to challenge the actions of those misguided magistrates.

THE TABLES ARE TURNED

The magistrates violated Roman law in condemning and beating Paul and Silas without due process. They had judged, beaten and thrown Paul and Silas into prison before marketplace spectators, and now the magistrates wanted to release them privately and have Paul and Silas leave town without their error being noticed. They themselves were vulnerable to being judged, condemned, possibly deposed or even executed for breaking Roman law.

A wise Paul understood the natural laws that protected him. We should be as wise, because satan will take advantage of any ignorance. We see this as Paul and Silas' accusers said they *"exceedingly trouble our city."* The woman's masters picked out only information that would play on the ignorance, weakness and perhaps the prejudice of the magistrates. But when all the information came to the light, the magistrates themselves could have become subjects of condemnation and judgment under Roman law if Paul and Silas pursued action against them.

"And they came and besought them, and brought them out, and desired them to depart out of the city. And they went out of the prison, and entered into the house of Lydia: and when they had seen the brethren, they comforted them, and departed" (Acts 16:39-40).

GOD HAD A PLAN

Remember, Paul knew he had authority in the spirit and in the natural realms. In this instance we see him exercise the authority given him in both realms. The magistrates of the city were humbled and meekly pleaded with Paul and Silas to leave town. They didn't want their error to bring trouble upon their own heads. The lie of Paul and Silas' accusers, turned out to be trouble upon the city magistrates. I doubt they forgot this whenever they had future dealings with those men.

Paul and Silas left the prison washed, fed, besieged with apologies from the city leaders, and leisurely made their way to Lydia's house where they comforted their brethren. Now *that* is being more than a conqueror.

Why didn't Paul object to the beating and accusations the day before? He could have protested to all the hearers that he and Silas were Romans and challenged the magistrates' legal right to condemn them or beat them without being heard under Roman law. But Paul and Silas were operating under a much higher law at the time. Their stint in the Philippian prison netted a far greater harvest. Lives were changed. The Bible doesn't record any details about what happened to the men who were in the prison cells within earshot of Paul and Silas. The fact they listened and cooperated with Paul's directions not to leave the prison when they had a chance to escape indicates that their lives were changed in some way. The jailor and his whole household were saved and baptized. The magistrates of the city were in their debt for not exposing their violation of Roman law. We cannot forget to mention freeing the woman who was demon possessed.

VICTORIES IN THE SPIRIT CARRY ETERNAL RESULTS

The Holy Spirit worked in the midst of every detail. He was available at every point of decision and His provision was sufficient in every need. The Christian walk does not free you from discomfort, pain or even abuse, but in the midst of every circumstance is an opportunity for victory. Just as it was powerful in the lives of those in the Philippian prison, prayer and praise will change lives—and people.

It would be nice if every victory had its manifestation within a day as we see in the account above. However, Paul was beaten, stoned, shipwrecked and put in prison at other times when victory was less evident *(II Corinthians 11:25-27)*. Victory was there, however. Each account reveals a plan and purpose of God that reaches to the generations to come. The letters Paul wrote while in prison declare freedom to Christians today as we read the biblical passages that he wrote. Victories in the spirit realm carry eternal results.

In the account that we have just reviewed, we also see how circumstances in your life may result from coordinated efforts of the hierarchy of satan. We also see the coordinated efforts of God and His angels in the lives of His children. Who sent the earthquake that shook the foundations of the prison? Who opened the prison doors? Who loosed the bands from the hands and feet of *all* the prisoners? Who loved the prisoners and the jailor enough to cause enemies to become friends? These were supernatural happenings that produced eternal commitments and changed lives.

The hand of God moved, and angels were dispatched to open prison doors and loosen prisoners' bands. The gospel was preached and lives were touched for eternity.

WOUNDED WARRIORS

Satan is behind the wounding and imprisoning of spiritual warriors. Wounded warriors can receive freedom and healing when we recognize the strategy of the enemy. The whole point of the injury was to stop us from pressing onto triumph. Wherever there is a wound, seek the Lord's revelation and counsel regarding the strategy satan may have used to cause it.

The Bible tells us that offenses will come, but woe to those by whom they come *(Matthew 18:7)*. Any person who has had experience in warfare realizes injuries can happen in battles, earthly or spiritual. In the case of spiritual battles, injury, insults and rejection will eventually result in anger. A valuable guard against becoming "a wounded warrior" is to know where and how to direct the anger to its proper place. It is possible to be angry and not to sin *(Ephesians 4:26)*. It's okay to be angry with satan for what he is doing, and to vent that anger against his abuse, lies, manipulation and harassment.

Anger turned inward results in hurt, pain, confusion and depression. Realizing there is a whole realm of strategists at work to inflict pain, torment, abuse and wounding upon humankind will help you not be ignorant regarding the fiery darts that have found entry into your life. One of the main purposes of this book is to help anyone who has been slam-dunked by *spiritual assailants*. We want to expose those who have been hiding behind cloaks of darkness and blaming others for the wounds they have inflicted.

The Holy Spirit, who is the Spirit of Truth, will bring what is needed for healing. Jesus will revive you with new life and strength for battle. Nothing is more frightening to satan than a resurrected believer who has been brought back to life in Christ with fearlessness and bulldogged determination to prevail in Him. Those of us who have had light and truth fill our lives, who are exhilarated by the freedom that we have found in Jesus Christ, carry a zeal that is uplifting to the Body of Christ and nerve-racking to the enemy.

We are overcomers who give glory and honor to the Lord Jesus Christ.

CHAPTER 14

ABRAHAM'S COVENANT

Even though I have been involved in spiritual warfare for many years, it wasn't until several years ago that I became aware of the impact anti-Semitism had in hindering spiritual warfare. Anti-Semitism is "prejudice against Jews; dislike or fear of Jews and Jewish things, discrimination against or persecution of Jews" *(Webster's New World Dictionary)*.

I had learned about renouncing any open door for satan permitted through cult activities such as palm reading, ouija boards, fortune-telling, tarot cards, transcendental meditation, hypnotism, new-age meditation, satanic videos, games and other mind control practices. Anti-Semitism was another matter. I had not considered the lasting impact hate and brutality to the Jews would bring. I didn't think it applied to me.

I heard many times about God's promise to Abraham: Those who bless the Jews will be blessed. The Bible makes it clear whenever a people or nation stands with them, they and their nation would be blessed and prosper. But whenever a nation turned its back on or persecuted the Jews, it would suffer in major ways. *"And I will bless them that bless thee, and curse him that curseth thee: and in thee shall all families of the earth be blessed"* (Genesis 12:3).

A number of years ago, I first heard some disturbing news about the teachings of the Protestant reformationist, Martin Luther. I was stunned to learn that the teachings of this man of God had a strong influence in Hitler's rise to power. In William L. Shirer's book, *The Rise and Fall of the Third Reich*, he wrote:

> It is difficult to understand the behavior of most German Protestants in the first Nazi years unless one is aware of two things: their history and the influence of Martin Luther. The great founder of Protestantism was both a passionate anti-Semite and a ferocious believer in absolute obedience to political authority. He wanted Germany rid of the Jews and when they were sent away he advised that they be deprived of "all their cash and jewels and silver and gold" and, furthermore, "that their synagogues or schools be set on fire, that their houses be broken up and destroyed…and they be put under a roof or stable, like the gypsies … in misery and captivity

as they incessantly lament and complain to God about us" —advice that was literally followed four centuries later by Hitler, Goering and Himmler."

In what was perhaps the only popular revolt in German history, the peasant uprising of 1525, Luther advised the princes to adopt the most ruthless measures against the "mad dogs," as he called the desperate down-trodden peasants. Here, as in his utterances about the Jews, Luther employed a courseness and brutality of language unequaled in German history until the Nazi time. The influence of this towering figure extended down the generations in Germany, especially among the Protestants. [1]

I was saddened by Luther's contribution to the holocaust, but that was as far as it went. It was information, I thought, which was past history and did not have any personal bearing on my life.

OUR FATHERS' OFFENSE

I attended a conference in June of 1999 where David Demian spoke. Dr. Demian's call is to draw the nations to wait in God's presence. He told us he had asked the Lord what was holding back the nations of North America from finding the favor of God and fulfilling their destiny. He asked why God is not feared and honored in this country. The Lord said to him, "The key, the root issue of this continent, of North America, is the anti-Semitism the European forefathers came with when they founded North America."

Immediately, the Spirit of the Lord reminded me of something He has told me nearly 26 years earlier. I had been praying for breakthrough for my husband. The Lord said, "He is carrying his fathers' offense." When I heard it, I thought the Lord said, "his father's offense." My husband's father was a wonderful, loving man, so I put the word on the shelf. However, as I sat in the conference many years later, the Holy Spirit took me back to that word. Only this time I understood that He said, "his fathers' offense." He was telling me that an offense, possibly going back several generations, was still on record. It had been hindering breakthrough prayer. The Spirit of the Lord continued to speak

---

[1]Reprinted with the permission of Simon & Schuster from *The Rise and Fall of the Third Reich* by William Shirer. Copyright © 1959, 1960 by William L. Shirer; copyright renewed © 1987, 1988 by William L. Shirer.

explaining that the offense was in the lives and backgrounds of many people. It gave satan legal right to hold back blessings and miracles from believers.

There are many denominations that stem out of the teachings of Martin Luther and others who, at some point, taught hatred of the Jews. My husband and I were raised in a denominational church that adhered closely to Martin Luther's teachings. It was difficult to reconcile the godly teachings that I had been taught with Luther's declarations about the Jews.

FATHER OF THE REFORMATION

In the heat of battle, Luther was fiery about what he believed. He stood against greed and indulgences within the Roman Catholic Church. He endeavored fiercely to bring the Bible into the hands of the common man. His influence and popularity among the populace of Germany gained momentum until his teachings became known as the Reformation. However, in 1543, he penned a manuscript that would change the course of history in another way. Having established a strong place of leadership and influence through his teachings of church doctrine throughout the years of his youth and middle age, in later years he wrote with bitter vengeance against those who did not accept his teachings. One of his last writings *On The Jews and Their Lies*, was received as a continuation of biblical doctrine that carried the weight and authenticity of the father of the Reformation.

I decided to investigate for myself what Luther wrote about the Jews. I found some information on the Internet in the Medieval Sourcebook: http:www.fordham.edu./halsall/source/luther-jews. html. I also found the writings of Luther expressing his fervent hate of the Jews and his instructions for their destruction at the local library in Luther's Works, *The Christian in Society*, Volume 47, pages 268-272, 292. It was disheartening to read the many hateful words and sense the intense rage he expressed. Among them were:

> First, to set fire to their synagogues and schools and to bury and cover with dirt whatever will not burn, so that no man will ever again see a stone or cinder of them. This is to be done in honor of our Lord and of Christendom, so that God might see that we are Christians, and do not condone or knowingly tolerate such public lying, cursing, and blaspheming of his Son and of his

Christians...Second, I advise that their houses also be razed and destroyed...
Third, I advise that all their prayer books and Talmudic writing, in which such
idolatry, lies, cursing, and blasphemy are taught, be taken from them. Fourth, I
advise that their rabbis be forbidden to teach henceforth on pain of loss
of life and limb...Fifth, I advise that safe-conduct on the highways be abolished
completely for the Jews...Sixth, I advise that usury be prohibited to them, and that
all cash and treasure of silver and gold be taken from them...Seventh, I
recommend putting a flail, an ax, a hoe, a spade, a distaff, or a spindle into the
hands of young, strong Jews and Jewesses and letting them earn their bread in the
sweat of their brow... I wish and I ask that our rulers who have Jewish subjects
exercise a sharp mercy toward these wretched people, as suggested above, to see
whether this might not help (though it is doubtful). They must act like a good
physician who, when gangrene has set in, proceeds without mercy to cut, saw, and
burn flesh, veins, bone and marrow. Such a procedure must also be followed in
this instance. Burn down their synagogues, forbid all that I enumerated earlier,
force them to work, and deal harshly with them...

He justified this by saying it would honor "our Lord and of
Christendom." Luther stated that he was exonerated, and that he
was furthering Christ by defending Christians from the "blind and
venomous Jews."

HITLER'S RESPONSE TO LUTHER'S WORDS

I always wondered how Hitler was able to brainwash millions
of people into such vehement hate for the Jews. But there had
been nearly 400 years of conditioning the minds and attitudes
of European and Scandinavian people. They had been led by the
Church to believe the extermination of the Jews was honorable
and necessary. Hitler lit the fuse and fueled the fire of another of
satan's strategies to destroy God's chosen people. The cooperation
of multitudes in the atrocities of the holocaust can only be explained when you understand that they believed they had moral, ethical
and religious rights to do so.

These teachings became woven into the lives of generation
after generation. Unknowing millions throughout Europe and
Scandinavia became party to satan's plan, including bringing this
evil doctrine to the Americas. Those who were deceived had been
duped by satan, causing them to grieve the heart of God. This has
separated them from the covenant blessings God made to Abraham.

CHRISTIANS AND LUTHER'S TEACHINGS

It was unusual to find people in the denomination in which my husband and I were raised who were aware of Luther's teachings concerning his hate for the Jews and his edict to destroy them. They have lived their lives in service to the Lord. Many of them have been to Israel and have a respect for the Jewish people. They were ignorant, as was I, about the teachings that inspired such hate.

Satan hid a generational curse that enabled him to hinder millions of people from success in spiritual and natural things.

The Lord continued to speak to me during the conference. The Holy Spirit reminded me of what Jesus said about his coming crucifixion, *"...the prince of this world cometh, and hath nothing in me" (John 14:30).* The Lord said, "If you have any anti-Semitism in you or in your background, satan can come and find place in you."

He went on to say, " If there is any anti-Semitic heritage, actions, beliefs within the person or his background, it provides a 'hook' into the life of the person for satan. Satan will come and 'find place' for the hook, giving him leverage to hold back the victory and blessings."

That hook has caused countless people to fall short of God's desired success. Noah was pure in his generation, having a pure bloodline, and his household was the only one to be saved from the judgment of God. Generational purity is very important. There are those who have not been stained by the blood of innocent Jews and were ones who sought to hide, protect and honor them.

Hate against the Jewish people has hindered the mighty hand of God from working miracles, signs and wonders within individual lives and within nations. The Lord told me, "If my people will root out and renounce the entry and occupancy of anti-Semitic beliefs, words and actions in their lives and in their backgrounds, the curse that has been hidden will be removed and the person will walk in signs, wonders and miracles."

"Furthermore," He said, "those who go forth in spiritual warfare will not greatly prevail if they have not repented of anti-Semitism, because it gives satan the right to withhold and resist. Satan can say, 'you can only go this far.' Anti-Semitism gives him that right."

ANTI-SEMITISM:
A HIGH PLACE OF DOCTRINAL ERROR

Anti-Semitism is a high-place doctrine. It is a belief system that carries cruel and horrific hatred, and seeks to ignite satanic plans against God's chosen people, the Jews.

The hierarchy of satan always works the same way. A false, evil belief system is introduced, promoted and implemented. It gains acceptance and brings unsuspecting people into cooperation with satanic schemes. Spiritual wickedness in high places work out their strategy and cleverly develop the seed of error.

The rulers of darkness hid the penalty for the curse that comes upon those who hate the Jews and Israel. Let's look closer at this. Genesis 12:3 says, *"And I will bless them that bless thee, and curse him that curseth thee: and in thee shall all families of the earth be blessed."*

God made a covenant with Abraham which promised, if Abraham were to obey Him, He would bless them that blessed him and curse those who cursed him throughout all generations. In Abraham, the Lord found a man who had the faith to receive the promise of the coming Messiah, the Seed promised in Genesis 3:15. God ordained that He would protect the bloodline and ancestry line of Abraham, so Jesus could come as the Savior of the world. First, there was Abraham, then Isaac—who was a form and type of Jesus. Abraham was asked to sacrifice his son, Isaac, like Father God was willing to do with His Son, Jesus. After Isaac, came Jacob, who was the patriarch of the sons who became the twelve tribes of Israel—the lineage of the Jews. It was the lineage by which the whole earth would be blessed, in the birth of the only begotten Son of God, Jesus the Christ.

KING OF THE JEWS

Jesus was born King of the Jews. He was acknowledged King of the Jews in His birth. *"Now when Jesus was born in Bethlehem of Judea in the days of Herod the king, behold, there came wise men from the east to Jerusalem, Saying, Where is he that is born King of the Jews? for we have seen his star in the east, and are come to worship him"* (Matthew 2:1,2). He was also acknowledged as King of the Jews in His death. We read, *"And Jesus stood before the governor: and the governor asked him, saying, Art thou the King of the Jews? And Jesus said unto him,*

Thou sayest" (Matthew 27:11). Even the cross acknowledged Him as King of the Jews. *"And they crucified him...And set up over his head his accusation written, THIS IS JESUS THE KING OF THE JEWS" (Matthew 27:35, 37)*.

Not understanding the purposes of God, spiritually blind people declared, *"He saved others; himself he cannot save. If he be the King of Israel, let him now come down from the cross, and we will believe him" (Matthew 27:42)*.

A HOUSE DIVIDED

Rejecting Israel and the Jews is rejecting Jesus and His people. Jesus said a house divided against itself cannot stand. Christians have a divided house if they love Jesus but disdain or disregard Israel and the Jewish people. How can believers revere the words of scripture when Jewish hands, under the inspiration of the Holy Spirit, penned nearly all of it? Such a "house" cannot stand.

Rulers of darkness have worked diligently for centuries to hide the curse that accompanies anti-Semitism. God himself is bound to His own word to Abraham that those who bless his ancestry will be blessed and those who curse it will be cursed. God has honored His covenant to Abraham throughout every generation. He honors His covenant today.

When God promised Eve that her seed would crush the serpent's head, Jesus was the Seed about whom He spoke. But God, following the government of heaven, needed a covenant by which that Seed could come. God found a man in Abraham who believed God by faith. The Bible says it was counted unto him as righteousness. In generation upon generation, the Israelites were set apart as the people of God, even in the midst of their wanderings and backslidings.

When Jesus was born, He was the physical Seed manifested in the earth. His death, burial and resurrection removed the separation between humankind and the Godhead.

Belief in Jesus Christ and His redemption is by faith. Believers are partakers of the covenant of Abraham. Galatians, Chapter three, tell us that believers in Jesus Christ are Abraham's seed—by faith.

WHY ME?

You might say, "But I had nothing to do with what my forefathers did, and I don't feel there is any anti-Semitism in my heart." The Ten Commandments have not been annulled. The penalty of breaking God's law is *"...for I the Lord thy God am a jealous God, visiting the iniquity of the fathers upon the children unto the third and fourth generation of them that hate me"* (*Exodus 20:5*). The generational curse, which was brought upon individuals must be renounced and broken. Not to do so permits its effect to continue.

Rulers of darkness continued their dastardly deeds by hiding such sin and its penalty. This allows satan to hinder the authority in our lives, holding back signs and wonders. We cannot walk in the miraculous, and stand against satan's stronghold, if satan has the legal right to oppose us.

Ignorance of the power of anti-Semitic roots keeps people in bondage.

CLEANSING OFFERED

God's mercy and goodness is upon those of us who have been ignorant of these generational curses, but further and complete cleansing honors and glorifies God. We may have seen God move in our lives, but if persecution and hate for the Jews goes unrenounced, we have never experienced God's best.

SPIRITUAL LAWS ARE IN EFFECT

We have learned that principalities work by laws and ordinances through which they attempt to gain rule over people's lives. They want to lay claim to our lives. These evil strategists seek to instill anti-Semitic attitudes, beliefs and actions, bringing people under the curse ordained thousands of years ago in the Abrahamic covenant. Satan's job of stealing covenant blessings is greatly simplified when he has anti-Semitic attitudes and belief systems in place.

The Lord first dealt with this when I was a young believer. Yet 26 years later He addressed it again because the curse still remained. At the time the Lord first spoke to me about the "forefathers' offense," I did not have a broad understanding what He was saying. But now, 26 years later, He revealed the sin so that my husband and I, our children, grandchildren, and following generations could walk in freedom.

JESUS—REDEEMER FROM THE CURSE OF THE LAW

Whatever has not been brought under the cleansing Blood of Jesus Christ remains under the law and the penalty of the law. Christ, the Anointed One, died on a tree, the cross, in order to redeem all humankind from the curse of the law. It is available to all who will receive the promise of the Spirit through faith. Jesus has provided the solution for the curse dilemma by His shed Blood and His sacrificial death on the cross. *"Christ hath redeemed us from the curse of the law, being made a curse for us: for it is written, Cursed is every one that hangeth on a tree: That the blessing of Abraham might come on the Gentiles, through Jesus Christ; that we might receive the promise of the Spirit through faith"* (Galatians 3:13-14).

Father God and Jesus desire to pour out upon us the abundance of heaven by the Holy Spirit. The Godhead is preparing us for a great outpouring. The Lord told me, "Those who will remove the anti-Semitic curse from their lives and repent for themselves and the sins of their forefathers, will see signs and wonders and miracles in their lives. Satan will have lost his right to hinder and withhold it from them."

When the offense of anti-Semitism is repented of and renounced, God is honored and is able to bestow the blessings of obedience and relationship promised. God's covenant with Abraham remains in full force and effect, and our lives will continue to be effected by the blessings and curse which He promised.

BELIEVERS BEING SET APART FOR MIRACLES

The Lord is dealing with individual people who are being set apart in the last days. You will not be able to be a part of the last move of the Holy Spirit if you retain any root in anti-Semitism, whether it is mentally, intellectually, financially, emotionally or generational. The Lord is working to expose this high place of offense against the God of Abraham, Isaac and Jacob.

Renouncing witchcraft, occult practices and mysticism in your life or background will free you from satanic and demonic influence. Repentance and renouncing anti-Semitism will free you from hindrances to covenant blessings.

REPENTANCE AND RENOUNCING

Repentance is prerequisite. Repentance cleanses from sin, severs satan's control and establishes your innocence by the cleansing Blood of Jesus Christ. The confession of repentance undergirds your soul when satan tries to claim he still has control. The Blood of Jesus cleanses you from all unrighteousness. The law of forgiveness annuls the curse of the law. Jesus hung on the cross in order to redeem all who believe from any and every curse.

For what do you repent? Of course, actual acts of hatred, persecution, mocking, gossip and harm. Repent for sins of the fathers, known and unknown, calling on God's mercy and asking for the Blood of Jesus to redeem you from the curse of the law. You can also repent for the high places of your heart where there are no outward actions, but inward opinions and attitudes that oppose the Jews and Israel.

What does "renouncing" mean? Renouncing makes a proclamation, spoken with authority, which kicks out the intrusion of satan's doctrine of anti-Semitism in your life. It cuts loose every tentacle of influence and control that has promoted hate and persecution to God's chosen people.

ENTERING SPIRITUAL WARFARE

When a group of intercessors embark on a prayer mission, they must examine their hearts for areas needing cleansing, forgiveness and repentance. They understand that sin makes them vulnerable before the enemy. Anti-Semitic attitudes should be included during preparation times of prayer and repentance. It is a requirement for prevailing prayer. In this age, anti-Semitism must be dealt with, individually and corporately. Then, believers who arm themselves for end-time warfare will have removed a place in their lives formerly open to the enemy. The Lord is revealing this hidden "hook" of the enemy because He desires prevailing prayer that will bring Him glory and honor.

ANTI-SEMITIC SPIRIT OF CONTROL

There is a spirit that dresses in Christian "lambskin" concerning the Jewish people. It is a religious spirit that stirs up rage within a person because the Jews will not believe Jesus is the Messiah.

There are many Jews who believe Jesus is the Messiah, but there are a great many who still are waiting for His appearance. The heart of God draws His people to Himself through divine revelation and through the love of Christian people.

Many Jews suffered concentration camps, torture and death under the pretense of misplaced Christian ethics, which were a perversion of true Christianity. It was the work of spiritual strategists who presented a religious doctrine, twisting truth into a web of lies.

The Crusades and the Spanish Inquisition are two manifestations of the spirit of control that, in the name of Christendom, attempted to coerce Jewish people by forcing them into becoming Christians. If not, they were tortured and often murdered.

The Lord is at work in the lives of the Jewish people. He is wooing them and revealing Himself to them in miraculous ways. The Lord is birthing love and commitment in Christian believers and is instructing them for His end-time plans. Christians have the responsibility and privilege of representing Jesus Christ, the Holy One of Israel, to those who have been blinded from knowledge of Him.

TAKING A STEP FURTHER

Repentance can take an additional step by rooting out hate against other denominations, people groups, color and ethnic backgrounds. Hatred against Catholics, Baptists, Afro-Americans, Democrats, Republicans, Protestants, other cultures or anyone else, will separate you from victory.

God hates such division—it is birthed in satan's kingdom.

LETTING GOD MAKE THE CHANGE

If there is a place where hate, strife, racial or ethnic prejudice and division has taken root in your heart, let the Holy Spirit change you. You must repent from your heart with correlating actions. Renounce the lies and hatred that satan ensnared you with. James admonishes us to, *"Submit yourselves therefore to God. Resist the devil, and he will flee from you. Draw nigh to God, and he will draw nigh to you. Cleanse your hands, ye sinners; and purify your hearts, ye double minded. Be afflicted, and mourn, and weep: let your laughter be turned to mourning, and your joy to heaviness. Humble yourselves in the sight of the Lord, and he shall lift you up"* (James 4:7-10).

PRINCIPALITY WARFARE

It is vitally important to understand the place repentance and renunciation have as warfare against principality power. *Repentance* is nullifying satan's right into your life, severing his tentacle of hold. The Blood of Jesus washes away the taint of his operation, his blueprint and his oppression against you. *Renunciation* is a vocal command that evicts satan's emissaries who have been involved in your life. In essence, you are saying, "Satan, you have lost your right to effect my life, now you and your associates—GET OUT AND DO NOT RETURN!"

Satan's plan has been revealed. His place of entry has been reversed. His influence has been annulled, and his future plans have been thwarted. Repentance and renunciation are powerful tools of the Holy Spirit. Wielding them strategically, freely and purposefully will dethrone principality strategies.

SEPARATE STREAMS

I am convinced that in this day spiritual warfare cannot be fully effective without the joining together of the Jew and the Gentile believers together in Christ. Even though the majority of Jews do not acknowledge Jesus Christ as the Messiah, there are many thousands who, through the love of Christians, have found Jesus to be their Messiah.

Sometime in 1992, the Lord showed me a vision of two streams flowing next to one another. I had been in continued prayer about the New Age Movement when the Lord showed me the two streams. At the bottom of the stream on the left were the words, "The Peace Movement." The stream on the right said, "The Charismatic Movement." (These movements were the ones going on when I dedicated my life to Jesus Christ in the early 70's.)

These two streams continued forward in time. He said the Peace Movement has grown up into the New Age Movement. He also said the next flow of the Holy Spirit would be much more powerful than the Charismatic movement. The Lord reminded me of the many people who were pulled out of the Peace Movement into the Charismatic Movement by the power of the Holy Spirit. He said the next move of God will pull people out of the New Age Movement <u>far greater</u> than what was done in the Peace Movement. The Lord did not tell me what the name of the new movement was.

GRAFTED BRANCHES

Many months later, I was in an extended time of prayer with three other people when, with our faces to the floor, the Lord showed me a vision of a flow joining the stream on the right, a powerful flowing into the new movement that had no name. The Lord said, "Unless you embrace Israel and the Jewish people, you will NOT be a part of My last move of the Spirit." When He spoke NOT—it was an emphatic—YOU WILL NOT! It was not a suggestion; it was a profound statement—an ultimatum. It offered two choices. Be a part of the last move of the Holy Spirit, or do not be a part of it.

As I pondered what I'd seen, the Lord reminded me of a scripture in Romans. *"And if some of the branches be broken off, and thou, being a wild olive tree, wert graffed in among them, and with them partakest of the root and fatness of the olive tree; Boast not against the branches. But if thou boast, thou bearest not the root, but the root thee. Thou wilt say then, The branches were broken off, that I might be graffed in. Well; because of unbelief they were broken off, and thou standest by faith. Be not highminded, but fear; For if God spared not the natural branches, take heed lest he also spare not thee. Behold therefore the goodness and severity of God: on them which fell severity, but toward thee, goodness, if thou continue in his goodness: otherwise thou also shall be cut off. And they also, if they abide not still in unbelief, shall be graffed in: for God is able to graff them in again. For if thou wert cut out of the olive tree which is wild by nature, and wert graffed contrary to nature into a good live tree: how much more shall these, which be the natural branches, be graffed into their own olive tree? For I would not, brethren, that ye should be ignorant of this mystery..."* (Romans 11:17-25).

The flow, which joined into the stream of the new movement, would have to do with the Jews being grafted again into the olive tree. The separation that has existed for the previous generations between Jew and Gentile will not be permitted in this last move. The Lord was emphatic, and I mean, *emphatic!*

ONE NEW MAN

The Holy Spirit did not give me a name for His move until the fall of 1998. I was at a retreat when the Holy Spirit dropped into my spirit, "The name of the last move of my Spirit is, the move of the One New Man." I knew the Holy Spirit was talking about the joining of the Jew and Gentile together in Christ.

The One New Man was mentioned by Paul, *"Having abolished in his flesh the enmity, even the law of commandments contained in ordinances; for to make in himself of twain <u>one new man</u>, so making peace; And that he might reconcile both unto God in one body by the cross, having slain the enmity thereby"* (Ephesians 2:15,16, *emphasis added*).

I finally understood why the Lord said that I, and others, would not be a part of the last move of the Spirit if we, individually and corporately, did not embrace Israel and the Jewish people. Because Jesus Christ, by His Spirit, is bringing to pass of the two—to make One New Man. It is the agenda of the Holy Spirit. We can be involved in His agenda if we want to be a part of mighty Holy Spirit maneuverings. We are involved in a heavenly peace process.

SPIRITUAL WARFARE REQUIREMENT

Consequently, spiritual warfare in this day will be different than what it has been previously. In order to cooperate with the Holy Spirit, we must have a heart for Israel and a love for His people, whether they are Messianic Jews or Jews who presently do not recognize Jesus Christ is the Messiah. The Holy Spirit is at work in their lives. Christians in this movement will not be manipulated by evil strategists who use ridiculing, controlling tactics to get the Jewish people to receive Jesus as the Messiah. The love of Jesus draws people, Jew and Gentile alike. Genuine love expressed to people is the greatest witness of Christ. It is the same for any person who does not know Jesus—but especially for the Jewish people who have suffered horrific cruelty and hatred through error within Christian teachings and motives.

Jesus states that He has abolished in His flesh the enmity—the hostility, opposition and separation—which was written in the natural and in the spiritual realms. For those who choose to enter the warfare of the kingdoms at this crucial time in eternal matters, this truth is powerful.

A MATTER OF THE HEART

The Holy Spirit will reveal to us the move of our Lord during this end time. It would be wise for us to consider what issues may arise as the move of the One New Man grows. I don't know about you, but I have been around the "movement mountain" enough times to realize there are wonderful manifestations of the Holy Spirit as well as actions which were not inspired by the Holy Spirit. Many of us have so desired to be a part of what the Lord was doing that we, either through immaturity, fleshly zeal or just plain peer pressure fell into the flow of emotions, teachings and expectations which were not led by the Holy Spirit. Consequently, what was not of God did not last or bring the life change which was necessary for enduring godly freedom and blessing.

Do you remember the faith message? How about the submission message? The prosperity message? The message of travailing to birth God's purposes in the earth? Laughter? Speaking in tongues? Healing? Every flow of the Holy Spirit has brought wonderful freedom when the heart was focused on Jesus. However, with each flow there were times when our eyes were riveted on what we could receive or experience for some selfishly motivated reason. However, we found that, *"When you ask, you do not receive, because you ask with wrong motives, that you may spend what you get on your pleasures"* (*James 4:3 NIV*). Only after disappointment raised its head did we begin to realize that perhaps we really weren't experiencing the "real" thing.

A HEART CHANGE

The way to tell whether or not you are experiencing the move of the Holy Spirit is if there is a *heart change*. Heart change does not have to perform to fit into what God is doing, the heart nature is *transformed* into what is upon the Heavenly Father's heart.

The move of the Holy Spirit is anointing designed to change us, to change our hearts, more and more into the image of Jesus Christ and to manifest the desire and purposes of the Father in the earth. Does God want us to realize we can walk in divine health? Does Jesus want us to learn faith? Does the Holy Spirit want to pray the will of God over our circumstances by speaking in tongues? Does He want us to laugh, or praise or dance because we are so full of His Spirit we overflow? Does He want us to obey because we *want* to or because we *have* to? The difference is at the heart of the matter.

Whenever the Holy Spirit was able to make a heart change in me, the enemy was not able to promote his error. I have laughed from my belly and felt the release of the Holy Spirit. I have

laughed in the flesh and afterwards felt foolish. It took some time
and experiences for me to discern where my heart was and at
times, needed to receive the Lord's counsel.

THE PENDULUM

Many of us have been on the pendulum swing (of what we thought
was the Holy Spirit) to an excess. If the Lord said healing was for
us, then going to the doctor was a faith crisis. If we were to submit,
then doormat mentalities arose. We rode the swing from nothing
to the extreme of too much, only to find that both were error.

However, I believe the wisdom and grace of God was in the
midst of it all. Many believers have been through the extremes
and found that the surest way to avoid them is to *fervently* seek
Jesus and have the Holy Spirit continually bear witness to what is
right and what is error. Our experience with having suffered the
disappointment and hurts we received by riding the pendulum
into error gives us an advantage, because we can approach
what the Holy Spirit is now saying with greater maturity and
watchfulness. In this last move of God, let's avoid those pitfalls and
wasted time.

We may make mistakes, but if our heart is genuinely pressing
hard after Him, those mistakes are only indicators for course
correction. There is no condemnation in that. We quickly return
to where we know we are in right standing. Our Heavenly Father
loves us. We are children growing up into the full stature of Jesus
Christ in faith. He has sent the Holy Spirit to help us grow, mature
and live fruitful lives.

WHERE IS YOUR HEART?

There is one verse that simply sums up what I believe the Lord
wants us to know concerning the moves of God and how they
impact our lives. The measure of their effect depends upon one
thing…where is your heart? Jesus said to the Pharisees, *"…this
people honoureth me with their lips, but their heart is far from me"* (Mark
7:6). We can say many admiring things to the Lord and about Him.
We can spend hours in worship services and yet have bitterness in
our hearts. We can say we have faith, but fear motivates us.

Will I embrace Israel and the Jewish people because what I
really want is to avoid missing out on the benefits of the next move
of God? Is my innermost desire to seek the benefits more than

expressing Jesus' love for His people? If so, then I am honoring Him with my lips, but my heart is far from Him. We can say and do all the right things, but sooner or later our words and our actions reveal what is in the heart. God is requiring one thing in the move of the One New Man: A pure heart. This is serious business to Him.

WE CAN'T CHANGE OURSELVES

Our thoughts and innermost motives are exposed before God, for we read that *"... all things are naked and open unto the eyes of him with whom we have to do" (Hebrews 4:13)*. The Lord says, "I see exactly what is in your heart, nothing is hidden from me." The good news is we can't change ourselves. We have One who is able to make that heart change in us. To create within us a clean heart, to renew a right spirit within us and to give us truth in our inward parts—in our inner being *(Psalm 51)*. We need the heart exchange, trading our evil hearts for His pure heart. We can be honest with Him. He is the mediator *(Hebrews 12:24)*. He is the One offering Himself. The power of the Holy Spirit makes the change within us. It is what He has promised us, *"A new heart also will I give you, and a new spirit will I put within you: and I will take away the stony heart out of your flesh, and I will give you an heart of flesh. And I will put my spirit within you and cause you to walk in my statures, and ye shall keep my judgments, and do them" (Ezekiel 36:26,27)*.

What is the Father's heart for Israel? Jesus is the Holy One of Israel *(Isaiah 37:23)*. Does God's love for Jesus embrace Israel? If our hearts are against Israel and the Jewish people, then we do not have God's heart on the matter. If we want to be in the move of God and use them for our own gain, then we are in error. We need a heart change.

EXTREMES BECOME ERROR

Teaching that the Church has replaced Israel and the Jewish people does not line up with scripture, and may have its roots in Martin Luther's writings and has become the doctrine of prominent church leaders. Teaching which implies that the Church is the "10 lost tribes of Israel" doesn't consider that the majority of believers are not of Jewish bloodlines. Gentile believers are adopted into the Jewish family—they don't replace it *(Ephesians 1:5)*. Nor are we to place Israel into such an exalted state that Israel or Jewish tradition becomes an extreme. Do not forget each move of the Holy Spirit has extremes that become error.

The Lord is looking forward to the day when all of Israel will be saved. The plan in the Father's heart for the salvation of Israel has yet to unfold in its fullness. However, I believe that the call of the Lord in this move of the One New Man is one that calls us to participate with Him in wonderful end-time happenings. We guard our hearts by fervently and continually seeking Jesus for truth, the Holy Spirit for counsel and our Heavenly Father for *His* heart. When the words of our lips and the convictions of our hearts are established through Jesus, we will release our own agendas and gain His powerful impartation. It is in *His power and might* that we will stand in boldness and truth as end-time events develop.

ENMITY ABOLISHED

Again, since principalities seek laws, ordinances and rights in order to carry out their mission, Ephesians 2 reveals that in His flesh, Jesus abolished such laws and ordinances which would permit enmity between the Jew and the Gentile. Satan doesn't have a leg to stand on, and *believers need to reinforce that fact.* Jesus has already won the victory if we choose to believe and walk in His victory. Jesus Christ, in His broken body, has abolished enmity in order to make of the two—One New Man.

PRAYER OF REPENTANCE AND RENUNCIATION

ather, God, the God of Abraham, Isaac and Jacob, I repent and ask for Your forgiveness for my sins and the sins of my forefathers against Your people, the Jews. I acknowledge I have been ignorant and negligent concerning my sin and the sin of my forefathers. I repent for any beliefs and actions that have come through teachings of those who have spoken and testified against Your chosen people. I repent for words, thoughts and actions of hate, bitterness, revenge, torture and murder. I ask for Your forgiveness and mercy, O God. I ask for the Blood of Jesus Christ to wash my hands and heart from any and all anti-Semitism against the Jewish people and the nation of Israel, and to cleanse me from sin. I ask for the precious

Blood of Yeshua to cleanse me from generational curses that have come upon my life and my household because of those who hated the ancestral line of Abraham. I call on the covenant of the broken body of Jesus Christ and His shed Blood, and through the cross of Calvary that cleanses me from sin and redeems me from the curse of the law. I ask for my heart to be transformed into Your heart for Israel and the Jewish people.

I shut every door of entry that has been open to the enemy. I renounce and expose every anti-Semitic religious spirit that has disguised and hidden itself in the belief systems, doctrine and practices in my life, my church. I proclaim the Light of the glorious gospel of Jesus Christ against every false doctrine and lie. I renounce any "hook" of control or bondage satan has had in my life, and in the lives of my household, because of anti-Semitism in my life or in my background.

I praise You that Your promise remains. I bless Israel and the Jewish people. I speak love, acceptance and provision to your people the Jews. Lord, according to your promise to Abraham, because I bless the Jews, I will be blessed. I call forth the covenant promises in my life and into the lives of my household and to my future generations.

I confess I am of the Seed of Abraham through Jesus Christ. I declare I am redeemed from the curse.

Thank you, Lord, for Your mercy and grace. In Jesus' Name. Amen.

I embrace Israel and the Jewish people in love and fellowship. I proclaim the work of the Holy Spirit who is bringing to pass—of the two—One New Man

PRAYER FOR THE NATION AND PROCLAMATION

ather God, the God of Abraham, Isaac and Jacob, I humbly call upon You to give Your counsel to those in leadership and authority. Search their hearts and give them grace to repent and ask for forgiveness for our corporate sin and the sins of our forefathers against Your people, the Jews. I pray that You would give our leaders understanding and that they would acknowledge where our forefathers or we have been ignorant and negligent concerning our sin of anti-Semitism. I pray for Your wisdom and grace for any leader whom Your Holy Spirit is wooing regarding repentance for beliefs and actions that have come through Martin Luther and others who have spoken of and testified against Your people. May corporate repentance arise on behalf of words and actions of hate, bitterness, revenge, torture or murder. We, as a nation, ask for your forgiveness and mercy, O God. May the Blood of Jesus Christ wash our hands and hearts from any and all anti-Semitism against the Jewish people and the nation of Israel. I ask for the precious Blood of Yeshua to cleanse us from generational curses which have come upon our lives and nation because of those who hated the ancestral line of Abraham. May we as a government and as a people, call on the covenant of the broken body of Jesus Christ and His shed Blood, through the cross of Calvary, which cleanses us from sin and redeems us from the curse of the law.

I ask for leaders who will repent for the sins of our land. I pray for and bless those in authority in our government. O God, have mercy upon our land and our people.

May those in houses of faith renounce any power or influence of the spirit of anti-Semitism in our lives and backgrounds. May they boldly shut every door of entry that had been open to the enemy. I pray that the revelation of God will quicken church leaders to renounce and expose anti-Semitic religious spirits that have disguised and hidden themselves in the belief systems, doctrines and practices of churches and in the Body of Christ. I proclaim the Light of the glorious gospel of Jesus Christ, who was born King of the Jews, against every doctrine and lie.

I renounce the control and bondage that is in our nation through the offense of our fathers against the Jewish people. Any law that is in the spirit realm that satan thinks he has against the Jewish people, I call into the light, I call his strategies to confusion and I speak release to the Jewish people in their hearts, souls, minds and bodies.

Reveal to our leaders that Your promise remains. Show them the blessings our nation will reap as we bless the Jewish people; as we bless Israel. May we as a nation show love, acceptance and provision to Your people.

Lord, according to Your promise to Abraham, because we bless the Jews, we will be blessed. May we as groups, churches, governmental positions and individuals call forth the covenant promises in our lives and the lives of those who cleanse their hearts and minds from the anti-Semitic curse that we may corporately speak FREEDOM AND CLEANSING TO OUR LAND. Amen.

CHAPTER 15

OVERCOMER BLESSINGS

The Lord rejoices in the overcomer. Jesus has provided every tool and weapon necessary for triumph. He rejoices when we put those provisions to use. He is exalted when we walk in the victory that He gained at the cross.

He promises mighty rewards for the overcomer, *"And he that overcometh, and keepeth my works unto the end, to him will I give power over the nations"* (Revelation 2:26). Not only power over nations, but He also promises, *"Him that overcometh will I make a pillar in the temple of my God..."* (Revelation 3:12).

Spiritual warfare is part of the training for ruling with Christ in the ages to come. Jesus is the Alpha and the Omega—the beginning and the end. In Him, the Heavenly Father has ordained that those who take their position on the wall will reign, *"And hast made us unto our God kings and priests: and we shall reign on the earth"* (Revelation 5:10).

Since Jesus is equipping and training us to rule and reign with Him in the age to come, the pressure, stress and confrontations of this age will be used as refiner's fire.

You will not be forged into a ruler by a bunch of formulas and methods. Christ is actively involved in our victories through the Holy Spirit. He is omni-present and able to pour Himself into each of our lives. We are not going to reign off by ourselves somewhere. Satan tried that. No, we will be *in Christ* in the fullest sense and manifestation. Our only success in spiritual matters will be accomplished by our being *in Christ*.

THE BATTLE IS THE LORD'S

By walking as children of light in this earth, we have the privilege of being a part of the manifestation of Jesus' penetrating light in the darkness of this world. When we pray the Lord's Prayer asking for "thy kingdom come, thy will be done, on earth as it is in heaven" —the magnificent light of Jesus is released.

When we get a grasp of the heavenly realities which exist in the third heaven and the presence of the Lord in our lives, we begin to comprehend how the battle is not ours but the Lord's. We must appropriate what God has in store for us in His presence when dealing in earthly matters.

God is long-suffering—there are instances when we, too, will need to be long-suffering. God is just and brings forth judgment when His wrath is full. We are told that the just shall live by faith *(Habakkuk 2:4, Romans 1:17, Galatians 3:11)*. We will execute judgment according to the direction of the Holy Spirit, but not out of our own fleshly desires.

JUDGING ANGELS

We will even judge angels. *"Know ye not that we shall judge angels? how much more things that pertain to this life" (I Corinthians 6:3)?* What angels? I don't know, this indicates there are responsibilities beyond our comprehension, matters beyond earthly reasoning that will take place when Jesus will reign over the whole earth. This passage also says *how much more things which pertain to this life*. The happenings of this life are not insignificant. Whatever is coming against the Church, whatever afflictions are buffeting humanity, whatever works and deeds are done, whatever successes are attained—are pertinent to eternal purposes. Jesus told the disciples even giving a cup of water in His Name would not be overlooked or without reward *(Mark 9:41)*.

SEEKING THE PRAYERS OF OTHERS

There is no wisdom in trying to fight your battles alone or in your own strength. The greater the call upon your life, the greater the need for those who will come alongside to encourage and pray. The Lord has divinely deposited a plan and purpose within every individual. Prayer unlocks the doors and establishes the pathway of the Lord's purposes and calling. There is powerful protection in being surrounded and undergirded by those who know God's heart and hear His voice.

THE LORD LIFTS HIS BELOVED

The challenges and afflictions we encounter in this life are not without value before a Holy God. He is passionately and actively concerned with the things that concern us and affect our lives.

"God is my strength and power: and he maketh my way perfect. He

maketh my feet like hinds feet: and setteth me upon my high places. He teacheth my hands to war; so that a bow of steel is broken by mine arms. Thou hast also given me the shield of thy salvation: and thy gentleness hath made me great. Thou hast enlarged my steps under me; so that my feet did not slip. I have pursued mine enemies, and destroyed them; and turned not again until I had consumed them. And I have consumed them, and wounded them, that they could not arise: yea, they are fallen under my feet" (II Samuel 22:33-39).

Jesus will enlarge our feet under us. He will make us stable and solidly plant our feet in faith so we do not slip. He will teach us how to war in such a way we will pursue our enemy, destroy his effect in our lives. He will, by the Holy Spirit, teach and help us to persevere until our enemy cannot rise again!

BE OF GOOD CHEER

What does the Lord call believers to have in the midst of tribulation? We are to be of good cheer, *"... In the world ye shall have tribulation: but be ye of good cheer: I have overcome the world" (John 16:33).* We are cheerful because we have confidence in the promise of overcoming.

The Lord does not intend for us to overcome spiritual or natural things in our own power and abilities. Independence from God is pride. The Pharisees found their own righteousness in the keeping of laws and rituals that ended up separating them from life in God—religious displays of spiritual things. God resists the proud but gives grace to the humble *(James 4:6).* Humility is a reverent reliance on the person and impartation of Jesus Christ. Many times the Lord will allow believers to "go it on their own." We find that apart from Him we can do nothing of eternal value.

We must measure all things with eternal computations. The well-known saying, "This life will soon be past, only what is done for Christ will last," simply sums it up. Whatever is done in the flesh for fleshly reward, whatever is done is the flesh for spiritual reward, will all burn in the consuming fire of God's judgment.

RICHES OF THE HEART

Christ spoke to the Laodicean church, *"Because you sayest, I am rich and increased with goods, and have need of nothing; and knowest not that thou art wretched, and miserable, and poor, and blind and naked"*

(Revelation 3:17). In the natural, we may be rich and have need of nothing, but yet in eternal matters be wretched, miserable, poor and naked. What benefit are riches to the one who is separated from life in God and is headed toward eternal damnation? There are riches of the heart and there is prosperity of earthly means. Both are the covenant blessings given believers in Jesus Christ. They are to be used for the furthering of the gospel of Jesus Christ so none are lost.

Jesus emptied Him*self*, became obedient unto death in order to overcome the world and bequeath His overcoming power to those who belong to Him.

———*◦/◦/◦*———

In Him, we overcome

———*◦/◦/◦*———

THE SEVEN CHURCHES OF REVELATION

The blessings of the overcomer are listed consistently in the Book of Revelation. Jesus spoke to John the Revelator and instructed him to write to the seven churches in Asia. With each church, He did several things: (1) He revealed and described an aspect of Himself; (2) He told them what He knew of the good and of the evil which existed in their midst; (3) He gave commands, counsel, warnings or comfort; and (4) Promised varying types of rewards for the overcomer.

Jesus, in each instance, first revealed Himself in His overcoming ability. He then described what needed attention and correction. He said what to do about it. Then He promised blessing for those who would obey and thereby overcome.

It sounds like a good way for us to bring our struggles to the Lord. First, we acknowledge the greatness of our Lord and tell Him what we know of Him that will deal with what we are facing or enduring. It will cause faith to rise within us because we will begin to see the Lord's ability and attitude concerning our plight. We can open our hearts and minds to hear what He has to say—to listen in quiet expectation. He will tell us what is going on in our midst. Listen further. He will tell us what *we* must do—repent, don't fear, hear My voice or maybe open the door. He will tell us what *He* will do. His promises flow freely to us because we are His beloved. And He will let us know a blessing will be ours as we persevere and overcome.

FRESH FELLOWSHIP

We can always be comforted with the fact Jesus is not ignorant to the force of the enemy which assaults the minds and emotions of men and women. His answer is the same throughout the generations—repent and turn from your wicked ways. We should not look at His counsel as a reprimand of condemnation but instead one of a deliverance from judgment. He has paid the penalty for our sin—why should we live under the penalty of our own sins when He has washed away our sins in His own Blood *(Revelation 1:5)?* He passionately desires us to live in the riches of his glory.

He offers blessings and rewards for those who are overcomers in Him. He does not reject but warns, counsels and offers Himself to come in to sup and abide. When Jesus spoke to the church at Laodicea, He was talking to believers, ones who were called by His Name, *(Revelation 3:14-22)*. He reminded them He is the faithful and true witness; He is the beginning of the creation of God. He has created every human being. In his goodness, He is causing believers to have the opportunity to overcome.

"As many as I love, I rebuke and chasten: be zealous therefore, and repent. Behold, I stand at the door, and knock: if any man hear my voice, and open the door, I will come in to him, and will sup with him, and he with me" (Revelation 3:19-20). Even though this scripture is often used to encourage unbelievers to ask Jesus into their hearts, which is beautifully applicable, the scripture is primarily spoken to believers who have need of fresh fellowship and intimate revelation of their Lord. Get the picture of who is doing the pursuing here. Jesus is wooing those whom he loves to repentance. His rebuke and chastening is coupled with supping one with another—not in harsh rebukes of rejection and condemnation but one of communion and counsel from a loving Lord.

INVITATION TO INTIMACY

He is also the One taking the initiative to invite Himself into our lives. He is the One standing at the door; He is the One knocking; He is the One speaking through the door's barrier asking for entrance in our muddles and messes. He is comfortable enough to sup with each us—a manifestation of covenant. He has covenanted with believers to bring each one to overcomer status.

There is nothing that can separate us from His love, and He is consistently interceding for us, desiring to make us more than conquerors. *"Nay, in all these things we are more than conquerors through him that loved us. For I am persuaded, that neither death, nor life, nor angels, nor principalities, nor powers, nor things present, nor things to come, Nor height, nor depth, nor any other creature, shall be able to separate us from the love of God, which is in Christ Jesus our Lord"* (Romans 8:37-39).

The love of God causes us to overcome all the power of satan, together with his principalities, authorities, rulers of darkness, spiritual wickedness in high places and his demons. Our Lord's love will not allow humankind to be comfortable in sin, in rebellion, in fornication, in idolatry and anything which separates them from His purposes and plans for their lives. Each of us rejoices when we overcome, a celebration that goes deep within and lasts. The person who has defeated alcoholism, self-pity, pornography, hatred, unforgiveness and other devastating bondages is the one who experiences the freedom only they can fully express.

THE PATHWAY OF PRAISE

It doesn't matter what place of despair we may feel, or the depth of the pit we may be in, praise is an appropriate starting place. King David faced many levels of oppression from many different directions—from enemies, from discouraged fellow warriors, from betrayal of friends and family, and from his own sin. Yet the Psalms are filled with page after page of praises to God in every stage of his struggles. Even in the midst of his complaints before God, he sandwiches in phrases of praises and exaltation of God. He declares the marvelous works of God. In whatever state of his soul, praise was not forgotten but heralded.

The Apostle Paul also understood this warfare of the soul. His praise included declaring the goodness, grace and faithfulness of the Lord. He also acknowledged that many times the praise and thanksgiving which needed to be lifted up to heaven would be a sacrifice offered in the midst of the soul's anguish and turmoil (Heb. 13:15). It would be a sacrifice of praise—something given as an offering to the Lord Who is worthy of praise. The Lord knows which praise comes to Him in the middle of emotional distress. He knows when praise is lifted up in desperation, maybe in confusion, and even by just plain obedience. He receives it as a precious offering.

Praising the Lord in the heat of the battle focuses our minds and emotions on spiritual truths and confuses the enemy. The enemy doesn't know how to counteract persistent and intentional praise.

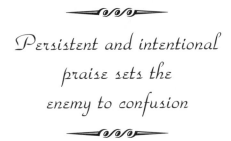

Persistent and intentional praise sets the enemy to confusion

YOU ARE HIS BELOVED

When we aim our praise to the Lord as a direct assault against enemy discouragement and harassing, our praise will be effective. Even hit and miss praises should not to be dismissed. In other words, praise the Lord in every season, situation and on every occasion.

Praises of adoration and gratitude, which spring forth out of an overflow of the heart, mind and soul, resound the heavens with glorious offerings. Strong words of worship lift up powerful expressions of glorious adoration to the One worthy. *"Thou art worthy, O Lord, to receive glory and honour and power: for thou hast created all things, and for thy pleasure they are and were created"* and *"And I heard as it were the voice of a great multitude, and as the voice of many waters, and as the voice of mighty thunderings, saying, Alleluia: for the Lord God omnipotent reigneth"* (Revelation 4:11, 19:6).

John, the Revelator, saw Jesus in his resurrected place as Lord of all. He saw Him in His glorified state—as He is today.

Entering the presence of God, we, too, begin to see Him as He is—high and lifted up, all-powerful yet gentle and compassionate. He is just yet merciful, all-knowing yet desiring to hear our words. Our Lord possesses all things, yet fervently yearns to receive our adoration and praise. Nothing is impossible to Him; yet He waits for the petitions of His beloved. Jesus abides as the resurrected Lord and offers resurrection power to believers.

SIMEON'S FAITH

I have a picture above my desk named "Simeon's Moment." It shows Simeon, a Jewish man, embracing a dark-haired baby in his arms. His bearded face radiates joy, which words cannot describe. His mouth is open with adoration and praise to a faithful God. Overlaid across the old man and the baby is the obscure outline of the continents of the earth.

The picture depicts the day Joseph and Mary brought baby Jesus to the temple to be circumcised *(Luke 2:25-33)*. Simeon was a devout man of God dedicated to prayer for the coming Messiah. The Holy Spirit had revealed to him that he would not die before seeing the Lord's Christ, his Messiah. The Lord had revealed aspects of Jesus' life and ministry to him, and Simeon interceded for the Son of promise. I believe there were many years of prayer and expectation, awaiting the precious Messiah.

The Holy Spirit drew him to the temple that day. He may not have known it was the day he would hold baby Jesus, the fulfillment of lifelong prayer in his arms. The Promise of the ages was born on earth to become the Lord of lords and King of kings.

Each of us will have our "Simeon Moment," our day of fulfillment for the faithfulness of our prayers. We, too, will say, "For mine eyes have seen thy Salvation..."

LOVE IS GOD'S IDEA

Effective spiritual warfare is grounded in love. The gospel of Christ is God loving the world so much He gave His only begotten Son. The gospel is telling people God loves them, has forgiven them and has provided His Son as the sacrifice for sin. The gospel without love propelling it makes it a doctrine without the person of Jesus giving it life. Love stands strong in the face of rejection and persecution. Jesus said His love is so great that it lays down its life for its brethren and it does not fail. When we refuse to take offense or to nurse our rejection, we are laying down our lives for others. Overcoming evil with good necessitates the God kind of love—love He supplies to His beloved children.

HEAVEN OR HELL

Each of us can love with God's purity and truth. We cannot obtain or maintain such an awesome capacity of love on our own, but it is readily available in Jesus. *"And I have declared unto them thy name, and will declare it: that the love wherewith thou hast loved me may be in them, and I in them"* *(John 17:26)*.

The whole Bible leaves us with one powerful foundation—love. Love must be at the base of every other activity. The love of God above all, love of others as God loves them, and love of ourselves as a precious being embraced and valued by Jesus.

Jesus is God. He is interceding for us so none are lost. He is aware of every person's needs. Jesus finished the work that the Father gave Him to do. However, the Bible says Jesus ever lives to make intercession *(Hebrews 7:25)*. Jesus is involved in lives with eternal purpose and focus.

Hence we come to the bottom line of what all the commotion is about. *Heaven or hell.* The kingdom of light with our Lord Jesus Christ or the kingdom of darkness with satan the tormentor. If we do not love, then going through all the buffeting, afflictions and wrestlings don't seem worth the price. The dying that is required (to self, self-pity, self-promotion, self-gratification, all the selfishness of the flesh) resists—until there is love.

LOVE LETTERS

God's kind of love can only be understood by reading His love letter to us—the Bible. The Holy Spirit is available to bring revelation and understanding into the fullness of its passages. The power of the Holy Spirit within us enables us to love with the God measure of love. He enables us to love beyond our own prejudice, insecurities and self-built walls of protection.

When we love, we will war in heavenly places. When we love, we will lay our lives down for people. When we are confident in the love of God for us, we will have boldness pursuing the enemy, God's defeated foe. When we are fully established in the love of God, we are strengthened and have the perseverance to overcome.

The Lord wraps His arms around His praying warriors. We are equipped with spiritual weapons of love, forgiveness, repentance, kindness, righteousness in Christ, words of truth, gentleness, self-control and with all the resources of the heavenly kingdom of God in Christ Jesus.

JESUS WON!

Jesus is the victor. He is the overcoming King, and He abides within each person who has asked Him to come into his or her heart. He will lead us to victory. Spiritual strategists are not able to pass off error as truth, but they are neutralized with the gospel of the Lord Jesus Christ. Rulers of darkness are exposed and their lies uncovered. Authorities of satan's evil kingdom must acknowledge they have no authority against Jesus Christ because their power was stripped from them at Calvary. Principalities are given notice of their loss of rule as the Resurrected Christ carries the government of justice and judgment upon His shoulder *(Isaiah 9:6)*. Jesus Christ has the government, the Sovereign rule and authority over heaven and earth, and under the earth. Devils know and tremble *(James 2:19)*. Believers cause demons to tremble when they walk as Christ on the earth. Satan has but a short time and his actions are desperate efforts to continue his parade of lies.

FIGHTING FOR LIVES

Lives weigh in the balance—heaven or hell. Every effort of the *third heaven* is focused on lives being ordained for eternal life in Jesus Christ. Every activity of the *second heaven* is geared toward steering lives from God's kingdom, which will result in eternal hell as punishment. Satan knows his doom is set, but his hate remains so intense he wants to hurt God by deceiving those whom God loves.

Spiritual warfare is fighting for lives. He asks us to lay our lives down so that He may fill us with His life for heavenly purposes. Jesus is a bold and compassionate leader of His followers. He has won all power and authority over His enemy satan. He is waiting for the word from the Heavenly Father to take the next step regarding our enemy.

Jesus is the Alpha and Omega, the beginning and the ending, the first and the last. All things begin in who Jesus is and what He was sent to do. All spiritual warfare revolves around the person, the power, the sovereignty of Jesus, the sacrifice of His death, the power of His resurrection, the Heavenly Father's love toward humankind and the power of the Holy Spirit working mightily in and through us.

BELIEVERS ARE OVERCOMERS

Jesus abides in born-again believers. He has equipped us to overcome and is continually interceding for us, bringing paths of deliverance and triumph. All of heaven is available for believers in the warfare of the kingdoms. We will utilize what we have learned through training. Each of us must press in and take hold of what Jesus has made available to us, because satan's evil kingdom will stand against any efforts they fear will undermine their place of power and control.

Wherever eyes are opened to the realm of the spirit that hinders growth and maturity in Christ, satan loses a foothold. Wherever foundational truths of the Word of God and the gospel of Jesus Christ are solid, the believer is able to stand firm and confident.

Be strong and of good (pleasurable) courage (alertness, steadfastly minded, established). You are overcomers in Jesus Christ. You are loved and equipped to overcome. Onward... Christian soldiers.

APPENDIX A

SPIRITUAL WICKEDNESS IN HIGH PLACES

The following is a list of <u>some</u> of the ways spiritual wickedness in high places seek to perpetrate their lies. *They deceive by*:

1. FALSE DOCTRINE AND FALSE TEACHERS: These will be a snare to a person's soul. Doctrines that deny God the Father, deny Jesus Christ as Lord and the work of the Holy Spirit, or attempt to replace them in any way is error and false teaching, *"But there were false prophets also among the people, even as there shall be false teachers among you, who privily shall bring in damnable heresies, even denying the Lord that bought them, and bring upon themselves swift destruction" (II Peter 2:1)*.

2. IDOLS: Idols are a doctrine of vanities. Idols are gods that are the work of man's hand or of nature. They are crafted *(Jeremiah 10:5, 6 and Psalm 106:34-39)*. *"The idols of the heathen are silver and gold, the work of men's hands. They have mouths, but they speak not; eyes have they, but they see not; They have ears, but they hear not; neither is there any breath in their mouths. They that make them are like unto them: so is every one that trusteth in them" (Psalm 135:15-18)*.

    We take on the likeness of whatever we worship. Those who worship violence will have violence manifest in their lives. Those that worship a god that has no life, will manifest deadness in their being.

    "And I will destroy your high places, and cut down your images, and cast your carcases upon the carcases of your idols, and my soul shall abhor you" (Lev. 26:30). Evil high places of worship are an abomination to God.

3. REFUTING THE DEITY OF JESUS CHRIST: *"He that believeth on the Son of God hath the witness in himself: he that believeth not God hath made him a liar; because he believeth not the record that God gave of his Son. And this is*

the record, that God hath given to us eternal life, and this life is in his Son. He that hath the Son hath life; and he that hath not the Son of God hath not life" *(I John 5:10-12)*. Also *I John 4:2-3*.

"In the beginning was the Word, and the Word was with God, and the Word was God" (John 1:1). Jesus is the Word. He is God come in the flesh. *"And every spirit that confesseth not that Jesus Christ is come in the flesh is not of God: and this is that spirit of antichrist, whereof ye have heard that it should come; and even now already is it in the world" (I John 4:3)*. Jesus is God. If there is any theology that questions or argues that fact, it is error.

4. ARGUING AGAINST THE RESURRECTION OF CHRIST FROM THE DEAD: Belief in the resurrection is a requirement for salvation, *"That if thou shalt confess with thy mouth the Lord Jesus, and shall believe in thine heart that God hath raised him from the dead, thou shalt be saved" (Romans 10:9)*. It is also needed to live one's life in Christ, *"Therefore we are buried with him by baptism into death: that like as Christ was raised up from the dead by the glory of the Father, even so we also should walk in newness of life" (Romans 6:4)*.

5. INTRODUCING ALTERNATIVES TO JESUS: Many religions try to convince their converts that their leader is sent of God, is a form of god, or are themselves god. Even some self-help groups or support groups that render counsel that does not point to the Lord Jesus Christ or in any way replaces the need for Jesus Christ are a seduction and a snare. *Galatians 1:8,9* (see section Storm Proof Foundation in Chapter 5).

6. MISINFORMATION: Gives misinformation about God, his attributes, purpose and provision. They misrepresent the conduct and character of the Father, of Jesus or the Holy Spirit. *"Ye have wearied the Lord with your words. Yet ye say, Wherein have we wearied him? When ye say, Every one that doeth evil is good in the sight of the Lord, and he delighteth in them; or, Where is the God of judgment?" (Malachi 2:17)*.

7. DENYING JESUS IS MESSIAH: Disregards Jesus Christ, the Messiah's role as the Holy One of Israel (blindness of Jewish people, as well as, blindness of church through believing the church has replaced Israel as God's holy people, known as replacement theology).

8. SEPARATION FROM OR BETWEEN BELIEVERS: Promotes doctrines that divide and isolate. Denominational strife, racial division and cultural difference strife. The Lord hates division and strife among the brethren, *"These...things doth the Lord hate...a false witness that speaketh lies, and he that soweth discord among brethren"* (Proverbs 6:16,19).

9. NO SIN CONSCIOUSNESS: Beliefs and attitudes that justify and give acceptance to sin. *"If we say that we have not sinned, we make him a liar, and his word is not in us"* (I John 1:10).

10. PROVIDING OTHER SOURCES FOR ENCOURAGEMENT AND PROTECTION AND DIRECTION: If you go to the wicked for counsel, you will be deceived, *"The thoughts of the righteous are right: but the counsels of the wicked are deceit"* (Proverbs 12:5). Following a vain people (those who are wise in their own eyes) lead people into a false wisdom that is a snare to their soul, *"He that tilleth his land shall be satisfied with bread: but he that followeth vain persons is void of understanding"* (Proverbs 12:11).

    The Word is the most trustworthy counselor. As people read the Word and the Holy Spirit bears witness to its truths, they will receive life for their souls, understanding and direction for their situation.

11. MURMURING: Isaiah recorded, *"They also that erred in spirit shall come to understanding, and they that murmured shall learn doctrine"* (Isaiah 29:24). Murmuring is complaint and accusation against God, his promises and provision, *"Yea, they despised the pleasant land, they believed not his word: But murmured in their tents, and hearkened not unto the voice of the Lord"* (Psalm 106:24,25). Murmuring rehearses wrongs done and questions the faithfulness of God. Murmuring doctrine exalts the wounded "self" and

infers that God is unmerciful, unsympathetic and forsakes the protection of His own.

12. MISTRUST OF GOD: It accuses God for injury, sorrow or misfortune. It suggests that God has let us down or been unfaithful to us. It instills fear of God's direction or provision. *"Ye have said, It is vain to serve God: and what profit is it that we have kept his ordinance, and that we have walked mournfully before the Lord of hosts? And now we call the proud happy: yea, they that work wickedness are set up; yea they that tempt God are even delivered"* (Malachi 3:14,15).

13. PUTTING FAITH INTO MANMADE OBJECTS, INTO NATURE AND INTO CHARMS AND SUPERSTITIONS: A fetish is an object believed to procure for its owner the services of a spirit lodged within it or something regarded with irrational reverence. Reliance on these things is a snare to the soul.

14. WRONG COVENANTS: These cause people to make covenants with those opposed to God. Making agreements not sanctioned by the Holy Spirit. *"And when the Lord thy God shall deliver them before thee; thou shalt smite them, and utterly destroy them; thou shalt make no covenant with them, nor shew mercy unto them"* (Deuteronomy 7:2). Israel disobeyed this command of God and had to deal with the oppression of their enemy for generations to come.

15. SPIRITUAL HARLOTRY: This introduces and promotes the doctrine of self. A doctrine that has many lovers. Loves every doctrine that feeds the flesh and depravity. Proverbs 7 tells of the harlot and her ways. Those that go in unto her are fools, an ox to the slaughter, as a bird to a snare. In Proverbs 8 we are told godly wisdom cries at the gates and at the high places warning of evil. James admonishes us, *"[Or] you do ask [God for them] and yet fail to receive, because you ask with wrong purpose and evil, selfish motives. Your intention is, [when you get what you desire] to spend it in sensual pleasures. You [are like] unfaithful wives [having illicit love affairs with the world] and breaking your marriage vow to God..."* (James 4:3, 4 AMP).

16. SELF-SUFFICIENCY: Promotes pride, self-reliance and doctrines that say that one does not need God. *"The wicked, through the pride of his countenance, will not seek after God: God is not in all his thoughts"* *(Psalm 10:4).* Jesus said, *"I am the vine, ye are the branches: He that abideth in me, and I in him, the same bringeth forth much fruit: for without me ye can do nothing"* *(John 15:5, emphasis added).*

17. TRADITION: Promotes the tradition of man as if it were the commandment of God. *(Mark 7:1-13).*

18. FALSE COMMUNICATION: False and evil (friends). Evil soul ties. *(I Corinthians 15:33 and II Corinthians 6:14-17).*

19. FALSE ANSWERS AND MISLEADINGS: Offers another answer to your need other than God's direction, provision or promise. *(Nehemiah 6:10-14).*

20. ENCOURAGING REBELLION AND LAWLESSNESS: *"For rebellion is as the sin of witchcraft, and stubbornness is as iniquity and idolatry. Because thou hast rejected the word of the Lord..."* *(I Samuel 15:23).*

21. PERVERTING PURITY: Calls sweet what is bitter and what is sweet to God, is portrayed as bitter. *"Woe unto them that call evil good, and good evil; that put darkness for light, and light for darkness; that put bitter for sweet, and sweet for bitter"* *(Isaiah 5:20).* This twists doctrine to make *evil* appear holy and righteous and seeks to make godly *truth* appear as unjust and unpopular.

22. PROMOTING SIN: Promotes beliefs that there are no consequences to sin. Makes acceptance of sin favorable and those who call sin "sin" as intolerant. *"For the wages of sin is death..."* *(Romans 6:23).* Sin requires a penalty.

23. RIGHTEOUSNESS THROUGH WORKS: The belief that promotes the idea that works will make one righteous before God is error. Our own righteousness is as "filthy rags" *(Isaiah 64:6).* Only the redeeming Blood of Jesus can make one righteous *(II Corinthians 5:17).*

24. ACCEPTANCE OF SIN, SICKNESS AND DISEASE AS GOD-GIVEN "CROSS TO BEAR": Jesus bore our sin, our sicknesses and our diseases upon His own body that we might have life and have it more abundantly. *(Isaiah 53:3-5; I Peter 2:24; John 10:10)* Jesus desires that believers in Him walk in freedom and health *(III John 2)*.

25. RACIAL AND ETHNIC HATRED AND DIVISION: *(Galatians 3:28, 29)*.

26. DISCOUNTING SPIRITUAL GIFTS AND CALLINGS OF THE HOLY SPIRIT: *(I Corinthians 2:14; I John 2: 20, 26-28)*.

SPIRITUAL WICKEDNESS IN HIGH PLACES WORK BY:

METHODS: A method is a mode or rule of accomplishing an end; it's an orderly procedure, an orderly arrangement or system. Method carries with it a strictness of procedure. Methods put a person into the law—the faith is in the procedure. Satan works by methods, and if he can get a person into a method, he can set up a trap. It gives him the luxury of predictability of a person's thoughts and actions. Believers are called to walk in the Spirit, be obedient to His leading, and they will frustrate the plans of the enemy. The mercies of God are fresh every morning. The Lord has a fresh plan for each person every day. Don't go by methods, but go by guidance on the daily mercies. *"This I recall to my mind, therefore have I hope. It is of the Lord's mercies that we are not consumed, because his compassions fail not. They are new every morning: great is thy faithfulness"* *(Lamentations 3:21-23)*.

SEDUCTION: Webster's dictionary states that seduction is "to draw aside from right conduct or belief, to entice, to corrupt, to lead astray; it is the act of enticing from virtue by promises, allurement, or attraction." Take heed to what you hear, what you learn, what comes into your understanding *(I Timothy 4:1)*. Discern, by the Holy Spirit and by the Word of God, that which is good and that which is evil *(Hebrews 5:14)*.

OATHS: Spiritual wickedness in high places endeavor to draw people into oaths. An oath is a solemn promise and statement that binds the person to what is said. That is why almost every organization—good and bad (cults, gangs, clubs and organizations)—has a statement or oath that they desire their members to agree with, support and quote. The quoting of any oath is a powerful binding to the statements presented. It writes in the person's mind, as well as establishes in the spirit realm, that they are bound to it, thereby calling unto itself all that the person is and has. An oath is a statement of doctrine with a commitment to action.

Churches have creeds, like the Apostles Creed, or a reading that the congregation repeats. Likewise, the quoting of the statement of belief establishes in the spirit realm a foundation of belief. Worship songs are proclamations to the spirit realm of binding oaths of honor, reverence and servitude to the Lord. Likewise, evil inspired oaths as well as songs carry a binding force to its hearers and singers.

Cult practices require oaths for allegiance and sacrifice by its leaders and followers, knowing such oaths are binding to their souls.

IGNORANCE: Lack of understanding in the things of God produces forms of death in one's life. *"The man that wandereth out of the way of understanding shall remain in the congregation of the dead"* (Proverbs 21:16).

ENTICEMENT BY DECEPTION: Luring unsuspecting people into what they think are good, honorable deeds and beliefs, but behind the scene is an evil doctrine promoting evil purpose.

ENTICEMENT BY FLATTERY: Raving about attributes and accomplishments that are insincere. Telling someone they are "needed" only to entice him or her into commitments that will ensnare them into false beliefs and actions.

FEAR: Plays on insecurity, ignorance, and rejection in order to control, *"There is no fear in love; but perfect love casteth out fear: because fear hath torment. He that feareth is not made perfect in love"* (I John 4:18).

PREYING ON THE IMMATURE: *"Whom shall he teach knowledge? and whom shall he make to understand doctrine? them that are weaned from the milk, and drawn from the breasts"* *(Isaiah 28:9)*. We are not to stay as babies in spiritual things.

Those who refuse to grow up in spiritual matters will be susceptible to error. Refusing to read the Word of God or mature in spiritual things will leave doors of opportunity to the enemy. *"For to be carnally minded is death; but to be spiritually minded is life and peace"* *(Romans 8:6)*.

PHARISAISM: Doctrines of religion that sound spiritually good but have the effect of doing the spiritual thing in the flesh. They are not God breathed or God sustained. Vain repetitions are of the soulish nature as well as much praying in order to be seen of man. Pharisaic doctrine vehemently defends spiritual doctrines of man.

SPIRITUAL MANIPULATION: Misrepresentation and misquotation of scripture, twisting words. The Bible commands believers to take heed <u>what</u> one hears *(Mark 4:24)*, as well as to take heed <u>how</u> one hears *(Luke 8:18)*. Spirits of error will speak. One must learn how to hear (to perceive and discern and cast down every thought unto the obedience of Christ). Compare what is said to the counsel of the Word of God.

SPIRITUAL CONTROL: Demand for allegiance and obedience outside the boundaries of the Spirit of God. No freedom to seek God as an individual and hear from God personally.

WITCHCRAFT: Using spiritual force to overpower the mind. Dulling the mind through drugs and mind-control practices. *"There shall not be found among you any one that maketh his son or his daughter to pass through the fire, or that useth divination, or an observer of times, or an enchanter, or a witch, Or a charmer, or a consulter of familiar spirits, or a wizard, or a necromancer. For all that do these things are an abomination unto the Lord..."* *(Deuteronomy 18:10-12)*.

STUPOR: Dullness of the senses and mind—feeling of "drugged" mind even though no medication or drugs have been taken. Lack of focus and purpose. Lethargy in learning about and walking in spiritual truths.

APPEALS TO BASIC NEEDS: Every person has three basic needs—love, acceptance and forgiveness. In the need for love, each person seeks to feel special, valued and emotionally secure. In acceptance, they desire fellowship, a sense of belonging and security. In forgiveness, they seek to fill the need to worship and find significance by a god-like being, even if they think themselves to be it.

CONFUSION: Mixture of truth and lies *(I Corinthians 14:33)*.

REASONING: Webster's dictionary describes reasoning as "allowing oneself to be convinced or talked around." Reasoning puts one into considering the facts presented in the natural realm rather than the actualities of the spirit realm. It causes people to lean upon their own understanding which is limited in knowledge or experience *(Proverbs 3:5-8)*.

PRAYERS

Praying these prayers of Paul is a wonderful weapon of warfare.

"That the God of our Lord Jesus Christ, the Father of glory, may give unto you the spirit of wisdom and revelation of the knowledge of him: The eyes of your understanding being enlightened; that ye may know what is the hope of his calling, and what the riches of the glory of his inheritance in the saints, And what is the exceeding greatness of his power to usward who believe, according to the working of his mighty power" *(Ephesians 1:17-19).*

"For this cause we also, since the day we heard it, do not cease to pray for you, and to desire that ye might be filled with the knowledge of his will in all wisdom and spiritual understanding; That ye might walk worthy of the Lord unto all pleasing, being fruitful in every good work, and increasing in the knowledge of God; Strengthened with all might, according to his glorious power, unto all patience and long-suffering with joyfulness; Giving thanks unto the Father, which hath made us meet to be partakers of the inheritance of the saints in light: Who hath delivered us from the power of darkness, and hath translated us into the kingdom of his dear Son" *(Colossians 1:9-13).*

The Lord honors His Word. Holy angels wait upon the Word of the Lord spoken over our lives.

The Holy Spirit has been sent to live within born-again believers. We can invite Him to help us discern, mature and press on to victory. Jesus said that the Holy Spirit would guide us to truth, *"Howbeit when he, the Spirit of truth, is come, he will guide you into all truth: for he shall not speak of himself; but whatsoever he shall hear, that shall he speak: and he will shew you things to come. He shall glorify me: for he shall receive of mine, and shall shew it unto you. All things that the Father hath are mine: therefore said I, that he shall take of mine, and shall shew it unto you"* (John 16:13-15). Ask the Holy Spirit to help you discern that which is truth and that which is error. He is our Helper and He is the Spirit of Truth.

APPENDIX B

WHY IS THE BAPTISM IN THE HOLY GHOST IMPORTANT?

Jesus is the Baptizer into the Holy Spirit. He is the One who is drenching us in the Spirit of Himself. John the Baptist understood that a wonderful promise was going to be imparted by the promised Messiah *"...There cometh one mightier than I after me, the latchet of whose shoes I am not worthy to stoop down and unloose. I indeed have baptized you with water: but he shall baptize you with the Holy Ghost"* (Mark 1: 7,8).

Jesus told his followers before He ascended to heaven, *"And behold, I send the promise of my Father upon you: but tarry ye in the city of Jerusalem, until ye be endued with power from on high"* (Luke 24:49).

They expected to receive power from on high, *"And, being assembled together with them, commanded them that they should not depart from Jerusalem, but wait for the promise of the Father, which, saith he, ye have heard of me. For John truly baptized with water; but ye shall be baptized with the Holy Ghost not many days hence...But ye shall receive power, after that the Holy Ghost is come upon you: and ye shall be witnesses unto me both in Jerusalem, and in all Judea, and in Samaria, and unto the uttermost part of the earth... And they were all filled with the Holy Ghost, and began to speak with other tongues, as the Spirit gave them utterance"* (Acts 1, 4,5,8; and Acts 2:4, emphasis added).

1. **That we may receive power to be His witnesses.**
   Jesus imparts godly power so believers will be able to be His witnesses in every corner of the earth. Why do we need such power? He is giving supernatural power against a supernatural foe, satan. We are able to do as Jesus did in the earth. He is equipping us to fulfill His commission.

2. **To speak with other tongues.** We are able to speak in a language with words given by the Holy Spirit in order to communicate unhindered by satanic influence or eavesdropping.

3. **The Holy Spirit helps our infirmities.** Our infirmities are our weaknesses and shortcomings in godly matters, as well as, the areas of our lives that are vulnerable to

the enemy. *"Likewise the Spirit also helpeth our infirmities: for we know not what we should pray for as we ought: but the* (Holy) *Spirit itself* (Himself) *maketh intercession for us with groanings which cannot be uttered. And he that searcheth the hearts knoweth what is the mind of the Spirit, because he maketh intercession for the saints according to the will of God. And we know that all things work together for good to them that love God, to them who are the called according to his purpose"* (Romans 8:26-28, explanation added).

4. **The Holy Spirit helps us to pray the way we ought to pray.** Because the communication of the Spirit is not tainted by our own prejudices, ignorance or fears, we are praying bold, confident and effective prayers in heavenly matters. Such prayers help us not to lean upon our own understanding *(Proverbs 3:5,6)*, and help us let go of our own reasoning.

5. **The Holy Spirit speaks what is too deep within to utter.** There are times in our lives when hurts are too deep to explain and confusion too perplexing to describe. It is then the Holy Spirit touches the innermost needs and desires of our hearts and lifts them to our Holy Intercessor, Jesus Christ. *"...It is Christ that died, yea rather, that is risen again, who is even at the right hand of God, who also maketh intercession for us"* (Romans 8:34). Jesus loves us. Nothing can separate us from His love. Jesus continues to make intercession for us. We have the God of Heaven involved in our problems.

6. **The Holy Spirit searches the heart and lines our heart up with the Word of God.** There can be areas in our lives that are wicked, ignorant and prideful. All too often we are unmindful to the state of our innermost motives, thoughts and intents. Many of us don't know the areas of our hearts or minds that are in error. We have areas of our lives where we are manipulating and controlling and feel justified in being so. We have areas where we are filled with unbelief and selfishness and

don't know what to do about it. The Holy Spirit sees where we are and because He is God, He is attuned to where we need to go. The Holy Spirit prays for us in line with the Word of God. In doing so, it gives the Lord legal right to become involved in our situation. Even though the Holy Spirit is speaking in the language of "Spirit," He is speaking forth rights and privileges that must be obeyed by spiritual beings—both good angels and evil angels. Good angels are released with godly provision and evil angels and agents are resisted in their efforts.

7. **The Holy Spirit will pray in line with the purposes of God.** The Holy Spirit is not going to coddle the flesh or carnality, but gives power to overcome them. The Godhead is busy with plans and purposes and is looking for those who want to please and honor God. The Holy Spirit is praying about avenues of opportunity and protection, as well as, for all things that are needed for life and godliness. Whenever someone prays in the Holy Ghost, they are aware they are praying beyond their own ability to speak in an unknown tongue. They are dependent upon the Holy Spirit to speak the words and the needed meaning behind the words. Whenever one speaks in an unknown tongue, they are releasing themselves to the will of the Father. It is conversation to God saying, "Not my will, but thine be done."

8. **If your heart is set on the purposes of God, then all things will work together for your good when you pray in the Holy Ghost.** When you pray in the Holy Ghost, the Lord is going to pray the purposes of God. Therefore, those who pray in the Holy Ghost can have confidence that every aspect of their lives is being formed into a wonderful tapestry of heavenly threads. Every dark and light event in your life will be woven into an epistle "known and read of all men" *(II Corinthians 3:2)*. God has the ability to not waste anything. He can take even the thread shreds and make them fashionable. He can take anything in our lives and turn it into a work

for His glory. By praying in the Holy Ghost, all things past, present and future can work together for your good, according to the calling He has for your life.

9. **The Holy Spirit speaks to God in mysteries.** When you speak in an unknown tongue of the Holy Spirit, what you speak is not a mystery between the Godhead, but it is a mystery to you. *"But he that speaketh in an unknown tongue speaketh not unto men, but unto God; for no man understandeth him; howbeit in the spirit he speaketh mysteries... He that speaketh in an unknown tongue edifieth himself..."* (I Corinthians 14:2, 4). There are times, however, when you do receive knowledge into your prayers. Sometimes the Lord will do so through personal revelation, by praying with understanding (translation by the Spirit) or through the interpretation (paraphrase of the one speaking) of tongues.

Most definitely, praying the Holy Ghost is a mystery to satan and his cohorts. That is why satan is so intent on hindering people from praying in tongues. The only way he is going to find out what has been said is through hearing what we say about what the Lord has revealed. Satan cannot detect what plans are being set in place by the Father and it causes him great apprehension about where he is going to be assaulted. He has no clue as to what is going to happen.

Holy Spirit prayers can be orchestrating divine appointments and opportunities or healing deep wounds. In addition, I have had the awesome privilege of asking the Holy Spirit to lift the praise and worship of my heart that I did not have words to express but knew *He* did. How wonderful it is to have confidence that your prayers are touching the heart of Jesus and of the Heavenly Father because the Holy Spirit is being your Communicator expressing words beyond human explanation or description.

10. **The Holy Spirit's prayers cause us to be strengthened and edified.** When we lift up prayers in the Holy Spirit, He is setting everything in order in the spirit realm because He is talking about spiritual matters (spirit

reveals spirit). It establishes strength in the inner man and in the soul (mind, will, emotions). You become not only strengthened to endure, but also are built up with strength to overcome *(Ephesians 3:16)*.

11. **The Holy Spirit causes you to be built up on your most holy faith.** We are encouraged to pray in the Holy Ghost to help us be built up in faith that is not shaken by circumstances or people. *"But ye, beloved, building up yourselves on your most holy faith, praying in the Holy Ghost"* *(Jude 20)*. The just shall live by faith *(Romans 1:17)*. We cannot please God without faith *(Hebrews 11:6)*. Mark 11:22 instructs us to have the God kind of faith. Now if faith is that important to God, and the Holy Spirit has been sent to be our Helper, doesn't it stand to reason that an important job of the Holy Spirit is going to involve getting our faith built up and in line with God. Wherever we are on the growth chart of faith, the Holy Spirit is involved in taking us to the next level of spiritual growth and faith in Christ. Praying in the Holy Ghost gives Him the opportunity to add muscle and elevation to our faith. There are scriptures that speak of weak faith, faith as a grain of mustard seed, great faith, but this verse says "building up yourselves on your most holy faith." What could *most holy* faith mean? Perhaps it would be faith that it is an impartation of the Holy Spirit—an enabling that is given by the person of the Holy Spirit to fulfill the desire of the Heavenly Father. How can we not avail ourselves of such a powerful and precious offering?

There have been times when I have said to the Holy Spirit, "I am praying in tongues with the purpose of having You build me up on my most holy faith" —faith that is available when praying in the Holy Ghost. I am taking the Bible's truths and receiving what it says. I am expecting a most holy faith to be built up in me that will cause me to overcome in Christ Jesus.

12. **God's strategies come out of praying beyond our own intellect and understanding.** We need answers beyond our own knowledge and abilities. Praying in the Holy Ghost links us to wisdom that surpasses human wisdom—it connects us to the fullness of God. In His wisdom, knowledge and understanding we are able to receive strategies for God's purposes and for our needs.

13. **We become bold by the power of the Holy Ghost in us.** We find examples of boldness welling up in people after the baptism in the Holy Spirit. *"Now when they saw the boldness of Peter and John..."* (Acts 4:13). Also, *"And when they had prayed, the place was shaken where they were assembled together; and they were all filled with the Holy Ghost, and they spake the word of God with boldness"* (Acts 4:31). The Holy Spirit will take our individual personalities and graciously fashion boldness within us that glorifies our Lord.

14. **We are empowered for service and ministry.** When Paul came to Corinth, he found twelve men who were John the Baptist's disciples. Paul questioned them saying, *"Have ye received the Holy Ghost since ye believed? And they said unto him, We have not so much as heard whether there be any Holy Ghost. And he said unto them, Unto what then were ye baptized? And they said, Unto John's baptism. Then said Paul, John verily baptized with the baptism of repentance, saying unto the people, that they should believe on him which should come after him, that is, on Christ Jesus. When they heard this, they were baptized in the name of the Lord Jesus. And when Paul, had laid his hands upon them, the Holy Ghost came on them; and they spake with tongues, and prophesied"* (Acts 19:2-6).

These men experienced three baptisms, one time with the baptism of repentance under John the Baptist's ministry, baptism in water signifying their baptism into Jesus Christ, and then the baptism in the Holy Ghost (Spirit) with the evidence of speaking in tongues. Paul, being the apostle that he was, made sure these men would be well equipped to serve the Lord and to walk in all the Lord had made available to them for service with boldness and strength *(Acts 19:10)*. Jesus baptizes believers into the Holy Spirit empowering them for service.

PRAYER TO RECEIVE
THE BAPTISM IN THE HOLY SPIRIT:

ather, I come to You in the Name and Blood of Jesus Christ. I acknowledge that I have asked Jesus Christ into my heart to be my Lord and Savior. Lord, I desire to become strong in the things of God. I need help with the weaknesses and infirmities within my heart and life. I need the Holy Spirit to cleanse the areas of my life that are hidden deep within, to heal me and strengthen me. I acknowledge that the Holy Spirit will pray according to the will of God. I believe that He is making all things work together for good according to Your purpose. I yield my tongue, the unruly member (James 3:8), to the control and use of the Holy Spirit. I desire to receive the promise of the Father. I submit my tongue and my voice to Jesus, who is the Baptizer, to baptize me now in the Holy Spirit with the evidence of speaking with other tongues. I choose to speak words that are the language of the Holy Spirit to speak in mysteries to God. Holy Spirit I welcome You to speak for me, for I need You. In Jesus' Name. Amen.

Now, <u>release sounds with your voice</u> and allow the Holy Spirit to shape those sounds into words that you have never spoken before. The Holy Spirit is gentle and will not "overpower" you in order to make you speak. Yield your tongue and the sound of your voice to the gentle nudging of the Holy Spirit. As you begin to speak with other tongues, don't be surprised if you sound like a baby with baby-like utterances. After all, you are taking baby steps in a new language. Maybe, new words will come along with a melody, as it did with me. Within minutes, you will realize that a language is forming as more and more words take shape in your mouth. You are able to stop and start your heavenly language just as you do your known language. It is your decision when to speak or not speak.

There are times when the Holy Spirit will bear witness with you the gist of what you are praying about. Many times the Holy Spirit is able to bring revelation about things because of the obedience of your heart to pray spiritual mysteries. Pray daily. Be aware that your enemy is intimidated by his ignorance of the significant and strategic things being prayed. *Resist his lie* that you are making up such words or that there is nothing powerful or significant happening. You are being built up on your most holy faith. Faith that moves mountains and walks the pathways of the overcomer!

"For the Lord your God is he that goeth with you, to fight for you against your enemies, to save you" (Deuteronomy 20:4).

"And the very God of peace sanctify you wholly; and I pray God your whole spirit and soul and body be preserved blameless unto the coming of our Lord Jesus Christ. Faithful is he that calleth you, who also will do it" (I Thessalonians 5:23-24).

HALLELUJAH!

To order additional copies of

IDENTIFYING THE
HIERARCHY
OF SATAN

A HANDBOOK FOR WRESTLING TO WIN!

WATER OF LIFE UNLIMITED
P.O. BOX 348
FORT COLLINS, COLORADO 80522-0348

ORDER ONLINE:
E-mail: joy.wolu@gmail.com
Web: www.wateroflifeunlimited.com

ORDER BY PHONE:
970-482-8699

ORDER BY MAIL:
Please make your check or money order payable to:
WATER OF LIFE UNLIMITED and mail to the above address.